AMERICANS
ANONYMOUS

AMERICANS ANONYMOUS

RESTORING POWER TO THE PEOPLE ONE CITIZEN AT A TIME

MEL K

POST HILL
PRESS

A POST HILL PRESS BOOK
ISBN: 979-8-88845-696-5
ISBN (eBook): 979-8-88845-697-2

Americans Anonymous:
Restoring Power to the People One Citizen at a Time

Cover design by Cody Corcoran

This is a work of nonfiction. All people, locations, events, and situations are portrayed to the best of the author's memory.

Post Hill Press
New York • Nashville
posthillpress.com

Published in the United States of America
2 3 4 5 6 7 8 9 10

*For my soul mate and fearless protector Robert Kaufman,
who encourages me every day to be brave, bold and resolute
in my passionate desire to empower people with information
to empower themselves towards freedom and liberty.*

"No government should be given too much power, or the people comprising that government will use the power in the worst ways possible; individual freedom, when used within the boundaries of morality, is the highest good. The Constitution was written as a living testimony to this view."

—Andrew Breitbart

CONTENTS

PART 3: CONCLUSION AND ADDITIONAL CONTEXT

PREFACE

i. My name is Mel K, and I'm an American. I am grateful to be afforded the opportunity to share my thoughts and ideas with you today thanks to God's gifts of free will, critical thinking, and grace.

The above statement is a variation of what you might expect to hear from someone at a traditional 12-step meeting as they begin to share their story in a group setting. No matter the type of group (AA, NA, OA, etc.), a person attending one of these meetings always opens with some statement of fact like this. The first sentence is designed just to let people know who you are and that you are willing to acknowledge *what* you are. A second sentence, if used, is often simply a way to express gratitude for having the opportunity to offer the first, publicly and safely.

Like many of you and the incredible people I've met traveling all over this country during the last several years, I'm deeply concerned about America and the state of our great nation. Many of us feel that something is terribly wrong—that the constitutional republic promised by our founders is slipping away. Our government and institutions no longer seem to serve We the People nor care about gaining the requisite consent of the governed, let alone seem to respect each other or themselves. Many people are demoralized and exhausted, sick and tired of being sick and tired of it all.

But I'm not interested in lamenting the state we find ourselves in, as I believe there is tremendous hope in this time. Just as an addict can hit rock bottom and then surrender to a higher power to begin a journey of recovery and transformation, so too can We the People rise up from wherever we find ourselves today and come together to heal our nation. By following a simple path of common solutions, achievable goals, and shared purpose, we can restore sanity to our country and protect the freedom and liberty that define the American spirit.

In my travels across this incredible country, I've witnessed the amazing strength, resilience, and goodness of everyday Americans, from big cities to small towns, from rural farms to thriving suburbs. Every state I've driven through on my great American road trip since 2020 has had its own flavor and vibe so unique yet so American that it has been a revelation to me how breathtaking and beautiful our country actually is. Unfortunately, I've also seen how well-orchestrated, coordinated forces of division have infiltrated and infested this nation from within—forces that seek to undermine our unity and strip away our God-given rights in any number of ways. The events of recent years have made it clear that there are those who want to fundamentally change America, replacing our freedoms with top-down control and replacing auto-determination by the people and for the people with surveillance, coercion, and infringement against our rights and our private lives on an increasingly disturbing and unconstitutional scale.

However, I firmly believe that we are on the precipice of greatness, not defeat. The power to save our nation lies within each of us as individuals. Many people are well aware that there are any number of dangers facing our country but say that they are just one person or too busy just getting by to do anything that would make a difference. Not only is that not true, but it is the individual citizen taking what is happening to this country—locally and globally—personally and deciding to get intimately and actively involved in a course correction that will make all the difference. By humbly uniting, identifying the root issues, seeking truth, and working to rebuild America around our shared values, we can rise above any and all of the challenges we face.

That's why I wrote *Americans Anonymous*—to provide a roadmap for national renewal based on timeless principles of recovery and transformation, using our founding principles and God's gifts to guide us. I'm calling on you to be part of this peaceful and proud movement to restore our nation to its highest potential. Together, we can work through this shared program to break free from the ideas that divide us. We can each reclaim our individual spirit to form an unstoppable coalition for freedom and justice.

The light of hope still shines brightly, even in dark times. If we act now with courage, conviction, and a commitment to the ties that bind us, we can save the United States of America, and reignite the spirit of brotherly love and community fellowship for a common cause. We can all be part of securing the blessings of liberty for ourselves and for generations to come.

To do this, we need honesty, open-mindedness, and willingness. We must be introspective and, above all, humble. Saving our country will require facing hard truths, but the reward—a renewed America—is worth it.

I invite you to join me on this journey of national recovery and revival. Together, we can reaffirm the principles that make America great, and work together to build a more perfect union. If we stand united, nothing can stop us.

PART 1

AN INTRODUCTION TO AMERICANS ANONYMOUS

CHAPTER 1

AN AMERICAN INTERVENTION

WE THE PEOPLE OF THE UNITED STATES HAVE BECOME DANGEROUSLY ADDICTED TO PERPETUAL CONFLICT AND CHAOS.

n November 2016, just days after the election, a friend and I were discussing the upcoming Thanksgiving holiday. My friend said that his large family that had celebrated Thanksgiving together for decades, a tradition passed down through generations, had just canceled their family turkey-day dinner for the first time ever. Why? Because the family was so conflicted and divided over the election of Donald Trump that they felt they could not possibly break bread together.

That cancelation might have happened overnight, but the feelings of animosity that led to it surely had a longer history. While people might suddenly snap over a red wine spill on a new white carpet, the decision to cancel a long-held family tradition has a much longer fuse that's been smoldering, possibly unseen, for a long time. In this case, that fuse can be found in what has become a recent and virulent American disease, and that disease is an addiction to conflict and chaos.

Today's America presents as a fractured society, with a culture of excess, endless distractions, and manufactured division. This environment can lead many of us to negative feelings, reactions, and behaviors, not the least of which is addiction. Many of us have either had personal experience with addiction of one kind or another, or have been a witness to a loved one or close friend's battle with addiction. We humans have a propensity to get addicted to many things. It might be alcohol, drugs, gambling, food, codependency, sex, social media, or any other destructive habit. Even if we never hit the proverbial rock bottom that leads many to seek treatment and recovery, we still may have gotten to a place where our lives had become unmanageable, and a serious change needs to be made in order to reverse our downward trajectory.

From my own experience and having known dozens of people who have sought treatment or recovery in their lives, I have discovered that as Americans we have become dangerously addicted to the conflict and chaos that is destroying our communities and our country. I have observed that as individual citizens, we have allowed ourselves, knowingly or unknowingly, to be tempted to succumb to a steady campaign of manipulation from a myriad of different suppliers and dealers that in a lot of ways has caused our lives and ultimately our nation to become totally unmanageable. As difficult a time as we find ourselves in, we all still want to live our lives as we see fit, find someone to love, maybe have a family, find purposeful work, and be left alone to enjoy the fruits of our labor. How can we do this in such troubled times?

It is important to understand the nature of the suppliers, dealers, and triggers of conflict and ensuing chaos. We will explore many elements including the impact of technology, entertainment, stress, and financial pressures, as well as many other influences both benign and nefarious in nature that have brought on this surge of addiction over our nation. We have been led to fractured social connections and disrupted interpersonal communication, and have been corralled into silos of tribal identities leading to groupthink and a loss of discernment. All this leads to learned helplessness, which is a debilitating side effect of our current societal disease. You will come to understand that political polarization along with mainstream and social media influence have created a mass delusion of division. We are living in a society where groups are being contrived then pitted against each other, where people feel superior because they perceive they are right and the other is wrong. This dynamic leads to total polarization, a breakdown of communication and the loss of the ability to be empathetic and to compromise. In this state we will not regain the fundamental ingredients for a healthy, happy, productive life towards establishing and living in a more perfect Union. This fundamental breakdown of civil discourse must be fixed in order for us to get back on track towards continuously striving to build a more perfect union.

If the word addiction is hard to swallow, then let's start with habit. The word "habit" here is key. Habits—sometimes good, sometimes bad—form within our brain from a very simple cycle: cue, reward, response. Cues, in the world of addiction, are commonly referred to as "triggers." These are things that happen in our everyday lives that lead us toward engaging in behavior that is self-destructive. As an example, for many problem drinkers, being around people they have habitually partied with or walking into a beloved local bar can lead them to crave a drink even though they shouldn't have one. In our country today, our cue, or trigger, can simply be found in encountering anything or anyone with which or with whom we do not fully agree.

From a psychological and biological perspective, a response to a cue or trigger is what we do repeatedly, habitually, often reflexively whenever it presents. It is a form of behavioral and emotional programming from repetition that over time becomes default behavior. Consider, for some, the social norm of instinctively stopping at their regular happy hour spot after a long day, surrounded by coworkers. Someone suggests shots to celebrate whatever it may be, drinks are poured, someone gives a toast, and down it goes before even pausing to consider the consequences of it or the next few that might follow.

Americans are increasingly responding to disagreement, no matter how mild, by ordering a double shot of hostility with a social media chaser. We are being programmed through a barrage of rapid-fire news, contentious social media, and constant pressure to take sides on any number of issues being propagated everywhere we turn. We have habituated to reflexively react to anything we don't agree with or that triggers us with anger and frustration before even considering the content of the trigger or the consequences or our reaction. When we do that, one thing can lead to another, and in that state of anger or agitation our critical-thinking skills are severely diminished and our rational, logical ability to react is replaced by confusion and negative emotions that can lead to unintended consequences.

Generally a reward is some sort of positive thing we can get by responding to a cue. It is a form of satiation. What are Americans getting through their intolerant, often emotionally driven responses these days? It varies by person, but in general there is a cathartic, albeit momentary, release and satisfaction that comes from shouting down the other guy. That momentary high from lashing out at someone who did not agree with your side or was not aligned with your thinking can be a thrill driven by the emotional jolt of a dopamine hit. We feel so justified in our correctness and validated by our being on the intellectually or morally superior side or team that our ego and arrogance becomes temporarily emboldened. This is not a good formula for a healthy society.

While strong responses have their place in interactions from time to time, for the person addicted to conflict and chaos, one is too many and a thousand is never enough. We are challenging and debating almost everything, so much so that we don't even need much of a cue to set us off on another binge. Many of us seem to be actively seeking out cues and triggers instead of doing what recovering addicts do, which is to try to avoid engaging in these triggering situations whenever possible.

Americans Anonymous is a part of my body of work to help We the People recover ourselves and our country. I'm asking you to join me in this journey to a more productive way forward. We will explore many tools and tactics but importantly you should substantially reduce your intake of mainstream media, consider your social media habits and usage, and learn how to replace both with your own research and exploration to find the truth for yourself without outside influence. As you become more confident in your own thoughts through your well-researched opinions and facts you will be less likely to be triggered or emotional during interactions or when consuming content. When engaging with others in dialogue you'll be okay with the other person disagreeing or even being completely out of their minds wrong as you will be centered and self-aware and not impacted by a win or a loss. Remember the old Dale Carnegie book *How to Win Friends and Influence People*? Being confident, strong, and centered in your beliefs is a much more productive and positive way to interact with others than the

"I'm right, you're wrong, and that's the end of it" world we are living in today.

Over the past decade there have been numerous polls showing how Americans have become increasingly partisan and divided. While true, my work has proven to me that much of the social division has been planned, orchestrated, and stoked by those who use this tactic to control the masses. What is interesting is that there are also polls showing that Americans are deeply concerned over the intense polarization and division in the country. We are, as a society, waking up to this madness, and like in the old movie *Network*, the character says, "I'm mad as hell, and I'm not going to take this anymore!"

For those who are familiar with addiction, it is not inconsistent to know you have a problem and know you need to stop. Have you, or someone you know, ever uttered the phrase, "I know I should stop but I just can't"? Being an addict and being an idiot are not necessarily the same thing. While there are many people suffering from addiction who won't admit there is a problem, there are just as many who know deep down that their behavior is self-destructive, but they just don't have the will or means within themselves to actually quit. That is until they hit rock bottom, and my contention is that America has hit rock bottom.

That is what these seemingly conflicting poll results demonstrate about everyday Americans. We know this is bad, but we are conditioned from a very young age to pick a side, or to accept the illusion of two distinct sides to choose from, and we continue to play along despite knowing it is bad for us and for society. This is why we need a national intervention, and this is why I developed *Americans Anonymous*. We must recognize that We the People have hit rock bottom, and that we need to change our own behavior. We are the solution, but we do need help, guidance, and fellowship.

When we as individual citizens begin to detox our heads and hearts and meet with humility, empathy, and compassion to unify under our founding principles towards a more perfect Union, we will be well on our way to breaking our addiction to conflict and chaos. What lies ahead can be a wonderful future if we take responsibility and understand that we are the answer, and that we must do the work to accomplish our collective mission to save our great nation.

HOW DID TRUMP GO FROM BELOVED CELEBRITY TO VILIFIED TYRANT?

There has been much talk about how divisive the country has become since the election of Donald Trump in 2016. The anecdote that led off this chapter has been repeated in homes all across the country with many variations on the theme. That said, polling showing concerns among Americans over the increasingly divisive nature of our engagement actually predates the Trump presidency. The myth that this is new to the psyche of the nation could not be more false, but it was Donald Trump himself who turned the lights on brightly for all to see regardless of the elitists' desire for the narrative to remain in the dark.

Remember all Trump's talk about "the fake news"? Many of us didn't quite understand the scope and scale of the controlled narrative, but we felt the emotional triggers and now more and more Americans are seeing just how much propaganda and programming we are being bombarded with nonstop from all mediums. The simple truth is that while who is president matters, who is president isn't all that matters. It is also true that Trump was a revered celebrity and businessman until he began his run for the presidency. The question could be asked as to why he was so vilified by the media when he began to challenge the establishment political bodies.

As for Donald Trump, there is no question that his celebrity, demeanor, and decades-long, larger-than-life style might rub some the wrong way. The media and much of Hollywood who used to seek his favor abruptly turned and leveraged his celebrity and brand to vilify him as a character unworthy of respect or consideration, totally disregarding his past successes and substance as a businessman and leader. As it turned out, many Americans and people worldwide felt it was his confident swagger, unwavering fight, and fierce belief in our country's greatness and traditional values that made him a great leader. His passion for greatness ignited in hundreds of millions of people a renewed pride in being a citizen along with a newfound purpose in the idea he espoused of making America great again.

Trump, who the media dismissed as a billionaire playboy of some sort, awakened the masses as he seemed to speak for the hardworking, tax-paying, middle-class people that the overtly arrogant elitists in DC and Wall Street and academia had dismissed as irrelevant to the important conversations of the business of this nation. While Hillary and her ilk demeaned the working class and middle America "deplorables" with her globalist partners and uniparty moneyed friends laughing and clapping along, the masses felt a spark of "wait a minute, this is my country too." That said, the false description of Trump being the catalyst of the divide totally neglects to admit that his predecessor Barack Obama, who was presented as a uniter in chief ended up being the great divider in retrospect. When Obama was elected he was put up as a symbol of how far we had come since MLK's "I Have a Dream" speech, but ultimately he left We the People divided by immutable characteristics, perpetually angry, constantly berated and shamed for being proud of our nation. His administration left the country demoralized and more separated than arguably any president in history.

President Trump came into a long-simmering stew of conflict, and by the media creating a caricature of "orange man bad" as diametrically opposite to Obama as the hope, change, and unity statesman, the cauldron of division was quickly and purposefully taken to the boiling point. Yes, we Americans were manipulated into a divisive state where only those who lurked in the shadows plotting and planning the controlled demolition of the United States of America for years could be happy. The division was toxic, unsustainable, and dangerous to this nation and our way of life way before Trump won the 2016 election, but understanding why this was done and who was behind it will help us better understand where we find ourselves today.

The primary difference in public perception between Trump and Obama, aside from their obvious philosophical and ideological differences, was the way that each was portrayed by the mainstream media. Trump's style was constantly hammered by reporters and pundits as being hostile and angry. He was rarely if ever given any positive press, nor was he portrayed as the man I met years ago or saw for decades who was witty, engaging, compassionate, and genuinely concerned for America's future.

Whatever one thinks of that portrayal, what is not debatable is that Obama's style, which was openly hostile to his political adversaries and often towards America itself, did not receive the same sort of negative amplification from the legacy media or Hollywood. In fact, it was completely ignored. Also totally avoided when it came to Obama were the mountains of evidence from his earlier life, meticulously laid out by both Joel Gilbert and Jack Cashill, among others, that showed inconsistencies in his own history as well as a preference towards Marxism and communist ideologies.

This was greatly influenced by his close friendship with sixties radical domestic terrorist group the Weather Underground's Bill Ayers and Bernadine Dohrn, as well as his self-described mentor Frank Marshall Davis. Information that was crucial for the American people to know about Obama's past and that we should know about any candidate was completely hidden or ignored as the country was introduced to the one-term senator and community organizer from Chicago in the run-up to his first term. His harsh statements inflaming racial division after Ferguson, Missouri did not garner even a drop of attention or get the same negative spin as Trump's misconstrued comments after Charlottesville, Virginia.

While it is not my contention at all that somehow either of these men "started this," the point is made here to try to get the reader to understand that the problem is much bigger than any one man. The problem is "yuge," and, if we are to change the current trajectory of our society and culture, we have to be fearlessly honest that the problem is, in fact, ours and our perception of reality.

While the polarizing personalities of anointed and amplified leaders of our commingled DC uniparty have contributed to our division, they have done so more by giving an excuse to the masses to be exceedingly hostile in situations or circumstances that only a decade ago would have been unimaginable. Addicts always need to first look in the mirror. Nobody forces us to take a shot, do a line, or place a bet. We are not victims, we are volunteers. We can't blame the suppliers or the dealers of our vices if we continue to buy what they are selling. We will look more closely at how we got to this point in the next chapter but for now let's just look at where "here" is.

A HISTORY OF DIVISION

America has been divided before. Given the fact that we actually fought a full-fledged violent Civil War makes that statement axiomatic. Anyone denying this simply does not know our country's true history, and that is where a lot of the false expectations that lead to disappointment and anger begin. Our Founders were bitterly divided on many things, but, unlike where we find ourselves at the moment, they knew if they did not compromise they would fail and likely die. They were forced to debate with the shared goal of establishing a new nation free from the ties to a tyrannical king. They had to be firm yet diplomatic and willing to find unity to survive literally and figuratively. Other periods of time have found us seriously at odds with one another. Consider the examples of the civil rights movement or the Vietnam War to name a couple of very prominent examples. Why then, if the country has been divided and yet not only survived but thrived after, do we need to be worried about where we are today? Won't this, too, pass?

THIS IS NOT BUSINESS AS USUAL

It is clear by the facts that what we are dealing with now is not business as usual. Outside forces not as fully developed, implemented, or weaponized in the past have created an acute, unprecedented crisis of societal division on both a macro and micro level. This division has manifested in the people as a level of addiction to conflict and chaos that requires intervention. We cannot go along to get along until the next time, as there may not be a next time if we lose our country. The distinction lies in the fact that we are now being manipulated by the suppliers and dealers of chaos and conflict as they incessantly fabricate and amplify disagreements in an attempt to deliberately create and express conflict. It is clear that, based on my last four years traveling this nation in all circles—conservative, libertarian, independent, unaffiliated, democrat, even anarchist groups—there is a deeper problem that transcends the old paradigm. Our current crisis is manufactured, acute, and systemic, and it leans heavily into faith and spirituality and therefore requires more of an individual awakening or intervention rather than a sands-through-the-hourglass passing of time. This will not go away. It must be fixed for us to survive as a nation.

The Civil War, which erupted in 1861, was triggered over a sort of geographical dispute between Southern states—which were mainly agrarian and slave-owning—and Northern states—which were more industrial-based and slave-free—as well as attendant issues over states' rights, taxation, and federal authority. It was the North against the South, or blue versus gray. They wore different uniforms and had fairly clear boundaries. The North prevailed and the South, albeit slowly and reluctantly, assimilated. There was profound residual bitterness to be sure, but eventually there was healing.

Other great societal divisions, including the civil rights movement and the Vietnam War, did not have geographical divisions but rather ideological divisions and were somewhat binary in nature, as in for or against certain ideals. Some of those divisions had some demographic features to them, such as with Vietnam, when you were more likely to find younger Americans protesting while older Americans were wanting to "stem the red tide." With the civil rights movement, you were more likely to find supporters among White Americans in the North where slavery had long been not just forgotten but rejected. Today, however, as noted above, the differences are more thinly sliced.

Let's take the issue of abortion and people who declare themselves "pro-choice." While sitting together, they quickly learn that they are in agreement that a woman has a right to choose what happens to her unborn child. Upon further discussion, one learns that the other does have a problem with what is referred to as partial-birth abortion, and believes a fully formed fetus, especially in the very late term, is considered off-limits. The person who has no such inhibition will quickly turn to saying things like, "You're not really committed. You're a plant for the other side trying to undermine our work. You can't call yourself pro-choice." This can quickly lead to the other person saying, "You just want to kill babies. You and I are nothing alike. I don't want to have anything to do with you." And so it goes that two people who are predominantly in agreement, but with different ideas on limits, end up attacking one another and becoming enemies rather than respecting the other and recognizing that they simply disagree on elements of their commonality.

The "cue" in this case is the disagreement over limits or degrees. The response is to attack and generate conflict. The reward is in the sense of pleasure derived from being able to tell someone else they just aren't as righteous or committed on the issue as you are, or that the other is an absolutist and therefore somehow superior to and declaring the other individual now not worthy of any discussion at all. Nearly all issues of disagreement have degrees and boundaries, and finding acceptable compromises is key to any functioning relationship or society.

Addictions involve a craving for the reward. Americans are craving the reward of expressing outrage, winning some battle, and the associated adrenaline that accompanies it, driven by anger, perceived oppression, or feelings of being right. What is interesting is that most Americans, if you ask them, will tell you they don't want to have conflict, and they will condemn those who do. Yet, they engage in the behavior anyway at almost any opportunity.

They will deny it if confronted, just like an alcoholic will deny their drinking problem, but they will do it just the same. What could possibly be happening inside of our hearts that leads us to behavior that we despise in others when we see it, but that we turn to ourselves almost reflexively?

The answer lies not in our hearts, but in our minds—quite literally in our minds. Americans seemed to have been programmed in their neural pathing towards the direction of chaos and ensuing conflict for a reward that really is not something that has any true benefit and that proves time and again to be destructive.

MIND WARS AND ADDICTION

Much has been learned about the human brain over the past half-century with still so much to be understood. One of the great discoveries has been that of how neural pathing works and its feature called neural plasticity. Neural pathways are a series of neurons that send signals from one part of the brain to another. At one time, it was thought that these pathways were developed only in our youth and then sort of "set" for the remainder of our lives. Advancements in technology over the last few decades, though, have allowed for the study of brains and the mapping of activity that clearly shows that neural pathways can be altered or reprogrammed throughout our lives. This kind of research has led to positive results for both behavioral disorders and in assisting stroke victims to regain some otherwise lost capability by training the brain to do a "work-around" of a damaged area. Literally remapping the way information is processed and transmitted.

The ability to alter how our neurons connect has led to the concept of neural plasticity, which is just what it sounds like. It reflects the sort of "bendable" nature of the brain and how it works. Basically, the more you do something or think about something, like athletes do when they visualize their action in a sport, the stronger the brain or neural pathways become. Neural plasticity is what helps us to both make and break habits by rechanneling how we respond to cues or triggers. It takes work, but the brain can be trained to blaze new trails. With this now proven, let's embrace it and use science to change behaviors and emotions in us that we once accepted as ingrained and unchangeable. Said simply, repetition of anything, such as feelings, thoughts, or actions, creates and strengthens the neural pathway thereby enforcing or enhancing a new behavior or habit.

Addiction is a behavior that can happen through neglect of the brain's ability to form new pathways or through repetition of thoughts or behavior, enhancing that pathway negatively or in ways that harm us. In reality, that is likely the typical case since most people don't wake up one day and say, "Gosh, I think I am really going to commence working on becoming addicted to something starting now!" What can happen is that through our behavior we start to alter our pathways almost involuntarily. Our brains are a bit like water; they follow the path of least resistance. Once we start to engage in chaotic behavior it becomes easier for our brain to follow that path, so much so that it begins to follow it naturally. This seems to be the case in America today. Whether programmed through media by toxic manipulation or organically arising from unproductive behavior, Americans have enhanced their neural pathways in the brain that satisfies a craving. That craving, that addiction, is conflict and ensuing chaos.

Why would we do this? Why would we start to channel a behavior that if you asked anyone they would tell you they wanted to avoid? One answer to that relates to our nature as humans, something that will be discussed later when we focus on how we developed this national addiction. A very simple general answer is that we have become negligent in our vigilance over protecting and developing more positive neural pathways. At the same time, the suppliers and dealers of division are bombarding us with cues to act out, reinforcing and enhancing that behavior, even rewarding it in some ways. Another answer can be found in the state in which many of us have found ourselves to be living over recent years. That is the state of fight or flight.

FIGHT OR FLIGHT

From the time we are young, we learn in school about the "fight or flight response." This is an evolutionary biological mechanism built into us in order to protect us from sudden danger. When we are confronted with a threatening situation, a whole series of chemical and electrical impulses are sent through our brain that trigger us either to fight or to run. It is instinctive and it is designed to be a momentary burst of action, a biological response designed to save us from a threat. We are not meant to stay in this state. We are supposed to use it to avoid annihilation and live to fight or flee to survive another day. Unfortunately, in America today many people seem to have gotten stuck in or driven toward a seemingly constant state of fight or flight mode.

This has been building for a while, and key contributors to it have been mainstream and social media. While that causative element has been around for a while, it has been supercharged by recent traumatic events that have sent many Americans into a sort of fight or flight "bender." Those traumatic events include: the COVID, the George Floyd incident and subsequent riots, the 2020 election, the J6 event and its aftermath, constant escalation of wars or threats of violence, and other physical or psychological mass casualty occurrences. Let's touch on a few of these traumatic events.

THE ADVENT OF COVID

The COVID bomb and media narrative that made its way onto American shores in early 2020 created a level of fear in people that has perhaps never been experienced in our nation. The tragic wars of the last century that cost hundreds of thousands of lives were generally seen through a narrow media machine articulating a sense that something terrible was happening "over there." It was not on our soil or in our communities. During the COVID times, the unseen and unseeable villain was everywhere and endlessly reported with added drama. We can never forget the continuously updated death tolls, hospital reports, celebrity warnings, politician pleadings, and corporate cajoling piped into our communities through twenty-four-seven media for months on end.

Fear and panic messaging was continuous and all-encompassing, paralyzing society unlike anything our country had experienced before. To add to the assault physically and psychologically, anyone questioning the narrative, treatment, spending, or science was now the enemy of the people, the state, and the media and branded as such publicly and loudly. Division upon division arose quite literally out of thin air stoked by the deafening narrative that overshadowed our every waking moment. The masked vs. unmasked, the vaxed vs. unvaxed, treatment protocol disagreements and fact finders and fact checkers all arose quite quickly, separating the masses who were susceptible to any number of triggers. Who can forget the videos of dancing nurses, grannies waving through windows, and endless famous faces regularly telling us to comply, conform, and line up for the next set of protocols? It was a continued coercion campaign telling us that good people will follow orders and comply, and those who do not are to be shunned and dehumanized if not expelled from society. The fight or flight, divide and enrage battle was in full swing on a global and local scale, and it became more and more heated and pervasive as the months rolled on.

THE GEORGE FLOYD KRISTALLNACHT TRAUMA

When George Floyd died ultimately from a drug overdose after an incident involving Minneapolis police, the nation once again seemed to erupt in well-organized uprisings overnight. We will not get into the facts or merits of this case as there is plenty of great work out there to better understand this event, but it's safe to say that all was not as it seemed. But it is clear that this was used as another "trigger" event to launch into an already well-paved narrative path towards conflict and chaos. The Trayvon case and "hands up don't shoot" marches had quieted into a lull, but here we were once again in full-blown national upheaval. Of course there is racism. The world can be unfair and justice is critical to a healthy society, but this trigger was used as skillfully as a surgeon uses a scalpel to sow hatred and division. Some became so outraged and consumed with anger that they joined the mostly peaceful yet violent protesters taking to the streets in unbridled rage, burning buildings, smashing stores, looting en masse, and terrorizing the populace. The seeds of the disaffected mob were sown, the fuse was lit, and the accelerant was poured on the fire.

At the same time those causing unrest were given a pass as they were deemed oppressed in some way. Their outrage was deemed by the media as justified and largely went unpunished, and in fact was sometimes rewarded. Then there were those who, watching the violence, became terrified that their home, town, or business would be targeted next. Lots of fights, lots of flights. Again the media, the multinational corporations, the NGOs, and the politicians told people what to believe, destroyed and slandered anyone who asked questions, and connected the incident to a largely false and divisive narrative long in the making that America was systematically racist and the cops were hunting Black men in large numbers. The narrative that George Floyd was murdered in cold blood proved the defund-the-police, racist America narrative. As promised by Obama, the fundamental transformation of America was continuing as his plan of reimagining policing got a huge push forward, and law and order became a vague term that would evolve into not just defunding but dismantling and in some cases all together forgoing policing all over the country.

If you questioned any of this narrative you were deemed to be "other," labeled a racist and a bigot, then dismissed, silenced, or destroyed. You were not allowed to know that George Floyd was a career criminal, resisting arrest, and high on a potentially fatal concoction of drugs. It was never even considered that there was actual medical evidence that he had advanced heart disease that was considered a ticking time bomb. The othering of skeptics to create deeper divide with no open, honest, fact-based conversation mixed with the accusation of racism for even asking questions was accepted and adopted by the masses either overtly or covertly.

THE 2020 ELECTION: AN EXISTENTIAL THREAT TO OUR DEMOCRACY

Many Americans went to bed on November 3 believing Trump would win the election, only to wake up to a miraculous Biden victory. The controversies surrounding the many anomalies on election night and the weeks that followed angered many. There were legitimate questions that deserved answers, but almost immediately, for the first time in history, questioning an election or wanting to get details of clear suspicious activity that night became off-limits and unacceptable. Many Americans, after decades of uneasy outcomes, finally fully lost their faith in free and fair elections that night, and found little support in terms of answers or getting to the truth at all. When the aggrieved showed up in their nation's capital to peacefully protest what they felt needed investigation, it devolved into a narrative of epic proportions. The weaponization and continued lack of transparency surrounding the incident on January 6th at the nation's capital only served to further inflame and terrorize Americans heavily manipulated and divided from nonstop trauma events prior. Many were angry that their fundamental right to a fair and honest election had been stolen from them. They were not allowed to redress their government about their grievances and were arrested, and are still being hunted down and incarcerated to this day for doing so.

The highly charged and partisan portrayal by the media, leading politicians and a Hollywood-produced, one-sided, televised committee hearing along with a coordinated media campaign served to heighten anger and fuel fear in the populace. This trigger was especially impactful to those (on both sides of the political divide) who were already preprogrammed and traumatized beyond their ability to comprehend as they were led to consider that the fundamental structure of their country was about to be overthrown. Again, the masses were driven to choose sides, declare the other the enemy, and hold tight to their belief in order to save their reality.

When we say that "people can only take so much" what we are really saying is that the human brain can only take so much. Americans found themselves facing threat overload. They became stuck in fight or flight. They were manipulated by media, global entities, media-hungry politicos, and fellow citizens to pick a side, and once one chose there was a heightened sense that dissent or skepticism were tantamount to betrayal. None of which is healthy, rational, or productive, yet under the repeated multiple psychological and spiritual attacks of just a few years, most people did not realize their hearts and minds had been subconsciously and unknowingly altered by rhetoric, societal discord, and unseen malevolent forces.

If the tendencies toward addiction to conflict and chaos were already present within Americans prior to 2020, we certainly got a double dose of triggering since. For those who had previously been able to engage in conflict and chaos "responsibly," 2020 drove them into an abusive phase towards others and sadly themselves. It changed our behavior and identity in many ways on a grand scale. It seems we as a society have been nudged, cajoled, and led to a revised reality, new neural programming, and a new normal, if you will, as the globalists droned on about reimagining everything and "Building Back Better" for our much-needed Great Reset.

One lingering question might be: Were we even aware of these structural shifts in society, and as with drug dealers did we willingly partake or were we manipulated while suggestible and vulnerable into unconsciously feeding an addiction we hadn't even been aware of? While it is necessary for the addict to take personal responsibility for their actions, the tendency or potential to become addicted makes it easier for people to exploit and take advantage of the opening when presented. If we were taken advantage of by suppliers and dealers of chaos and divisive conflict, we need to be asking ourselves who are the suppliers, who are the dealers, and to what end are they tempting us towards.

THE SUPPLIERS AND DEALERS OF CONFLICT AND CHAOS

Any good drug supplier knows they need a reliable dealer network to get their product to market. And good dealers know that if they want to sell product, they need reliable supply and preferably many hooked users. That means they have to make a reasonable quality product affordable enough to make sales and gain market share, and that sometimes they might even have to give a little bit away to make sure the user has to keep coming back. That is exactly what the power structure in our country today has done. They have learned that anger and conflict keep us voting, buying, consuming, and using their stuff. When we need a fix, they provide it. This isn't new in the last few years, but it has accelerated via social media and its unholy relationship with our intel community. Powerful people, like suppliers and dealers, are learning creatures. They have watched as Americans have become more and more addicted to conflict and they realized they could benefit from the addiction. Our addiction has helped them acquire more power, profit, privilege, prestige, and ultimately control.

Those control elements have been around since the dawn of man. There is nothing new about people in positions of authority and influence using them to benefit themselves at the expense of the masses. While the objectives haven't changed, the tools available and capabilities are undergoing rapid advancement due to the massive consolidation of global power and the ways we interact with media and technology in today's society. Today, the influence of multinational corporations, Big Tech's power and pervasiveness, the internet's reach and its anonymity, and the vulnerability of continuously shaken-up human beings have given these people of ill intent lots of room in which to play.

Throughout the course of this book, we will look at various ways that Americans have been strung along by the suppliers and dealers of division. What is important to note is that it goes back much further than 2020. These folks have been at it for a while. There are numerous obvious examples, especially from politicians and media, but let's take just a quick look at one so subtle that the typical addict might miss it when trying to identify their triggers (a key part of recovery). That hidden-in-plain-sight example is primetime television programming and its recent companions, reality TV and binge-watchable streaming content.

Scroll through your channel listing on the major networks and you are likely going to find a disproportionate number of "reality" TV shows. These shows are anything but "real," and as someone who worked in that industry for decades, I know that nearly every aspect of script, casting, setting, set, music, score, and product placement is used solely for the purpose of manipulating the audience. The media and television industries are experts at programming you to get you emotionally and psychologically invested in a false reality, addicted to the show, characters, plotlines, and intended outcomes. That said, if you travel back in time you would find that primetime television was filled with fictional stories, comedy or tragedy, that continued the tradition dating back to centuries of theater aimed at letting people escape into a clearly fictional world of idealized or fatally flawed characters. Laughs could be had, lessons could be drawn, tears might be shed, all of which are a clear function of the arts. Unfortunately, today it is clear that much of the artistic and creative industries have been infiltrated and taken over to drive very specific agendas, narratives, and societal outcomes.

I am convinced that reality TV was initially created as a special kind of manipulative psychological operation perpetrated on the masses. The networks and studios realized that this low-cost, high-profit programming served to let people substitute their own real life for watching in voyeuristic fashion the lives of others. We could take pleasure in watching the dysfunctions and conflicts being had by someone else. Shows like *Survivor* or *Big Brother* created fake competitions, typically between people of very suspect moral character, to see who could out-cheat who best to not get "voted off the island." Every night, millions of us sat at home being drawn into the dreadful, self-serving behavior of others. However, unlike fictional stories that were written to compelling conclusions, these stories were just simply about conflict, winning, hubris, and narcissism. Reality TV ended up continually glorifying the seven deadly sins. We had shows celebrating morbid obesity or gluttony, dating or lust, the sorrows of hoarders, lifestyles of the rich and famous, or greed and vanity as in *The Kardashians* and *Real Housewives*. The emotional hook for the audience was that these were presented as real people with whom they could have a superficial connection—voyeurs who felt like virtual friends. Whether they were flawed, propped up, struggling, or thriving, the idea that you knew them and felt connected in a personal way to the characters allowed for greater manipulation either to emulate behavior, consume as they were, or to create false idols to follow beyond the show to the marketplace of goods and ideas.

Either way, reality television was known to be programming by those who ushered it in to replace actual scripted entertainment. With this powerful new tool's success and business model, the powers that be amped up societal conflict, vanity, conspicuous consumption, sexual exploitation, rampant infidelity, toxic relationship drama, and the worship of ridiculous wealth. Adopting the seven deadly sins as a new moral code did nothing positive for society and culture, and in fact, did a lot of damage. Many good people got lost in the illusion, and its consequences have been quite devastating.

This sort of programming has created more than a numbing effect on society. Much of the conflict programming was without any redeemable lessons, and it has made our minds fertile for neural pathing and developing self-destructive habits and false expectations. A different version of this can be seen in programming for young people, either cartoons or *iCarly*-type shows where adults are made to appear as idiots who can be, should be, disrespected. Of course we can say the same about other modern Hollywood creations in the same realm like gangster rap, satanic-symbolism-drenched pop singers, and endless nods to a dark cult with satanic rituals in fashion shoots and live performances. The entertainment industry is just one element of our mass cognitive programming, and these are just a couple of examples of how the suppliers and dealers of conflict and chaos have entered our psyche and gotten a large swath of the younger population hooked.

America wasn't always like this. How did we get here and who or what made us so prone to develop our addiction to conflict and chaos? While social media has played a major role, it is much bigger than you might think. And while there certainly are many malevolent outside forces driving us down this path, the bourbon can't pour itself. The addict has to participate. In the next chapter, we will further explore how we became addicts and start the process of taking responsibility for our own actions.

CHAPTER 2

AS SICK AS OUR SECRETS: HOW WE BECAME ADDICTS

n a speech delivered on April 27, 1961, before the American Newspaper Publishers Association, then president John F. Kennedy said, in part, the following:

> The very word "secrecy" is repugnant in a free and open society; and we are as a people inherently and historically opposed to secret societies, to secret oaths and to secret proceedings. We decided long ago that the dangers of excessive and unwarranted concealment of pertinent facts far outweighed the dangers which are cited to justify it. Even today, there is little value in opposing the threat of a closed society by imitating its arbitrary restrictions. Even today, there is little value in ensuring the survival of our nation if

our traditions do not survive with it. And there is very grave danger that an announced need for increased security will be seized upon by those anxious to expand its meaning to the very limits of official censorship and concealment. That I do not intend to permit to the extent that it is in my control. And no official of my Administration, whether his rank is high or low, civilian or military, should interpret my words here tonight as an excuse to censor the news, to stifle dissent, to cover up our mistakes or to withhold from the press and the public the facts they deserve to know....

Today no war has been declared—and however fierce the struggle may be, it may never be declared in the traditional fashion. Our way of life is under attack. Those who make themselves our enemy are advancing around the globe. The survival of our friends is in danger. And yet no war has been declared, no borders have been crossed by marching troops, no missiles have been fired....

...If you are awaiting a finding of "clear and present danger," then I can only say that the danger has never been more clear and its presence has never been more imminent. It requires a change in outlook, a change in tactics, a change in missions—by the government, by the people, by every businessman or labor leader, and by every newspaper. For we are opposed around the world by a monolithic and ruthless conspiracy that relies primarily on covert means for expanding its sphere of influence–on infiltration instead of invasion, on subversion instead of elections, on intimidation instead of free choice, on guerrillas by night instead of armies by day. It is a system which has conscripted vast human and material resources into the building of a tightly knit, highly efficient machine that combines military, diplomatic, intelligence, economic, scientific and political operations.

Its preparations are concealed, not published. Its mistakes are buried, not headlined. Its dissenters are silenced, not praised. No expenditure is questioned, no rumor is printed, no secret is revealed. It conducts the Cold War, in short, with a wartime discipline no democracy would ever hope or wish to match.

On November 22, 1963, President Kennedy was assassinated while riding in his motorcade through the streets of Dallas on live television for all the world to see and replay. This caused great distress for a massive number of human beings simultaneously, and the shock was followed by immense collective sadness and pain. There has been endless mystery and controversy over that assassination as to whether arrested shooter Lee Harvey Oswald acted alone, or if, as I lean towards, the assassination was part of a much greater conspiracy and power play behind the scenes. While the details have been hidden from the American public for over a half century, and powerful forces seem to want to keep it hidden forever, there are many, myself included, who believe that Kennedy was assassinated by enemies within and their globalist cohorts who saw him and his agenda as an obstacle to their long-term plans. One can speculate, but there is evidence that he was taken out for many reasons including what he articulated in this speech to the press he had given two-plus years earlier, as well as the actions he had both taken and intended to implement after that speech to address the repugnancy of the many secrets in our free society. He was seeking to turn a chapter towards transparency, empowering the people, and putting the military-industrial complex and the intel agencies back into the service of We the People and not to a small group of unelected elitist masters uninterested in the self-determination of individuals as intended by our Founders and our God. This clearly proved a dangerous and ultimately deadly direction for this great man and our nation.

Most of you who watch my show know I am quite confident that the coup or capture of our nation actually kicked into high gear on November 22, 1963, the day the globalist oligarchy and those aligned within our government likely murdered JFK. My research has taught me that this history-changing event was done for many reasons, including a desire to continue endless wars and the profits they generate, to thwart JFK's decision not to go into Vietnam, and his desire to end the proliferation of weapons, but also to psychologically traumatize the population to begin a slow and methodical march, without us being aware of it, towards the ultimate long-term goal of worldwide top-down global governance. I often tell people to look at Prof. Caroll Quigley's book *Tragedy and Hope* as an inside look at the obvious agenda written by the Georgetown professor who Bill Clinton considered his mentor. He laid out the belief shared by his contemporaries and one of the main architects and biggest funders of the top-down one-world governance model, David Rockefeller, that a supranational intellectual elite and world-aligned bankers should and would run the world above governments, allowing the people to live in an illusion of freedom and sovereignty somewhere below them until that façade was no longer necessary at all. When in doubt, go look at their own words if this concept of elitist, top-down, global governance control seems too conspiratorial for you. In fact, with those involved now, unlike when the plans were put into action decades ago, their own organizational websites and think tank white papers do not even hide this agenda.

The globalist oligarchy have messaged endlessly for decades their goals of a top-down global governance plan, and a desire for a totalitarian technocratic centralized world where nation-states no longer exist and all central control is in the hands of a tiny group of world "stakeholders" that rule over this planet as if they are the parent company and the nearly eight billion other human beings should be grateful that they even allow us to live here. They dress it up today as *Agenda 2030*/The Great Reset/Sustainable Development Goals and other linguistic deceptions. The globalists use neuro-linguistic programming and a form of coded doublespeak to mask their true intentions and drive people to willingly accept top-down, totalitarian, technocratic slavery in a fully tracked and traceable digital prison they have been building around us on a global scale. Those implementing this plan and their protégés are of the same ilk that would not allow JFK to empower the people to resist their agenda, clean up corruption, cooperate towards peace and shared prosperity, or maintain strong national sovereignty. That is why it is crucial to read and understand that speech JFK gave only a few months into his presidency, and understand that it could easily be given today without altering one word. There is no clearer sign of a fifth column—or, as the CFR calls it themselves, a super-class of unelected officials above our selected/elected officials all the way up to the president—than that administrations have come and gone, on both illusionary sides, yet so much of the corruption, disillusionment, and lack of accountability or transparency by the government continues unabated year after year without end or adjudication.

The realization of this agenda, and how long it has been going on, can be jarring but also empowering. To think you personally have been kept in the dark, deceived about multiple well-timed coups along with decades of cover-ups while continued manufactured trauma events designed to keep you, yes you specifically, controlled and in line for decades without your consent or even knowledge can be extremely shocking and unsettling. But I encourage you to see it as motivating in terms of breaking out of the programming now and freeing yourself from the installed tendency towards the addiction that has kept so many unconsciously marching towards Bush Senior's bold proclamation from the floor of the UN of a coming new world order lead by the globalist entities.

If you step back and gain perspective, based on facts and actions, you can see that the new world order vision wasn't just a platitude, but in fact a plan. JFK did not want our nation, our people, or free people anywhere to suffer the dystopian fate of a captured nation. It is past time we awaken to the fact that we are today still fighting the battle of JFK, MLK, RFK, and so many others who warned about forces above our nations subverting our auto-determination, by the people for the people, as laid out by our Founders and in our founding documents. This, to me, is more of a call to action, and a unique opportunity we all have to redefine our sense of purpose and passion towards freeing ourselves and our nation in this specific time in which we live right now. Some say we are in biblical times; others say an existential battle between light and dark or good and evil, which to me makes the challenge of these times and the possibilities for each one of us to play a part even more exciting.

There have been numerous secretive and underground movements over history that have placed the great American "experiment" at risk. These movements have often led to creating conflict and chaos because they involve the restriction of individual liberty, something that is built into the American foundation and ethos. Whenever you attack something foundational, be it in society or in a building, you get a form of upheaval. With buildings you get quaking and collapse, with society you get anger, chaos, and conflict between people that too often leads to violence and destruction.

Not everything that has happened has been completely secretive. Much of what has taken place, and is taking place presently, is hidden in plain sight. The World Economic Forum sets its visions quite clearly on its own website for all to see. Similarly, the United Nations publishes its 2030 Agenda and 17 Sustainable Development Goals on their website, and on all of their many sister agency sites all over the world including UNESCO, WHO, IPCC, UNICEF, and others. The international financial institutions that work directly with these organizations also have their 2030 Agenda on their sites including the IMF, World Bank, and the BIS. Every one of these globalist institutions have the exact same goals and use identical language. The problem is that what they show, the tip of the globalist iceberg, typically does not reveal the true nefarious intentions of its members. They only show the typical American the bright, shiny object, not the dark, dystopian, destructive intentions of authoritarianism and totalitarianism that it shrouds. The messaging, and hence feelings of division, today in America that has led us into conflict and chaos addiction is largely the byproduct of an unholy union, a peculiar one in a sense, among three different elements:

THE BUSINESS OF CONFLICT AND CHAOS

1. The "drug" *suppliers* of conflict and chaos
       Are the powerful elitists and institutions pursuing global control.
2. The "drug" *dealers* of conflict and chaos
       The Marxist-leaning infiltrated and controlled institutions of academia, media, and nonprofits seeking a more collectivist/communistic model of organizing society.
3. The useful idiots and uninformed citizens *consumers* of the "drug" of conflict and chaos are all the indoctrinated activists on the "manufacturing floor" deliberately or unknowingly disrupting the machinery of American society to break down our systems in America and globally to build back better their Marxist utopian dream of socialism and collectivism.

       This also includes the well-meaning citizen that just doesn't understand they are being propagandized by false narratives but goes along with those seeking to upend the system. These people are usually lifelong followers or joiners who want to be led and are more comfortable being part of a group or collective where they are told what to do or believe for a sense of belonging or worth.

We say this is a peculiar union because the exact goals of the three groups are not necessarily fully aligned.

The first group, the global oligarchy of elitists trying to gain control over the population of the globe is not one that has any real ties to communism. They might be saying that they are heading toward a utopian future, but it is not a utopian future filled with everyone self-governing and realizing their full potential. Their utopia is one in which they, the masters of the universe, are managing our every move. They seek dominion over the planet, its resources, and its people that survive their societal transformation. They will, in their own words, replace God.

Consider the following from Yuval Noah Harari, right-hand man to Klaus Schwab who heads the World Economic Forum. It is from a 2018 interview, but he has said variations of it on numerous occasions:

> We are about to create the first inorganic life forms after four billion years of evolution. In the process, *Homo sapiens* are likely to disappear. Not because we will destroy ourselves, but because we will change and upgrade ourselves into something very different. The combination of AI and bioengineering will create completely new bodily and physical and mental traits. Consciousness itself might be disconnected from any organic structure; or alternatively, we might see the decoupling of intelligence from consciousness. And earth will be dominated by entities that are super intelligent but completely non-conscious: computer programs that have no minds, no feelings, and no emotions. So, we are in the process of becoming gods and the big question that faces us is what to do with our new god-like powers. We need ethical guidelines and goals, and nationalism cannot provide us with the necessary guidelines and goals. Nationalism thinks on the level of territorial conflicts.

Becoming gods? Harari and his ilk espouse a kind of narcissistic, sociopathic intellectualism and seem to exhibit someone so in love and attracted to their own perceived brilliance that it is almost self-seducing.

The critique of nationalism is a common theme among the globalist leaders of the oligarchy. They are clever in their use of terms because "nationalism" still has an association (perpetuated by the oligarchy) with the likes of Adolf Hitler and Mussolini and their fascist movements of the 20th century. While the oligarchists know that condemning nationalism resonates instinctively with many people, what they really want to do is eliminate the nation-state. They want a world without borders. Do you think that there may be a reason that George Soros calls his NGO (non-governmental organization) the Open Society? The most important and difficult nation-state to destroy in achievement of their globalist goals is the United States. The US is a faith-based country built on Judeo-Christian values and individualistic, freedom-loving people. Under communism or totalitarian rule there is no God; the ruler or the party is God or the father. When you have faith, you have hope, and when you have hope, you have the will to fight. Our national identity based on our Constitution, Bill of Rights, and the Bible is foundational to the American ethos, and that kind of populace is uncontrollable and antithetical to the new world order gang. Because of our foundation and culture, if we remember and preserve it, the USA and its people could be considered the most powerful in the world and a direct threat to those who seek global control and dominion.

There was a number of prominent players in the present-day global oligarchical movement including one of its founders, the late David Rockefeller (1915–2017). He was the grandson of the famous Standard Oil founder John D. Rockefeller. David was one of the most visible players in forming virtually every secret, near-secret, international globalist organization present today. He has his fingerprints on the United Nations, the Club of Rome, the Council on Foreign Relations, the International Monetary Fund, the Trilateral Commission, the pharmaceutical-, educational-, and medical-industrial complexes, the federal reserve, and more. All of these groups share the common goal of establishing something called "global governance." This is the simple idea that a handful of self-selected rich and powerful people can become even more rich and powerful if they can oversee the activities of the global populace now approaching eight-billion-plus people.

The globalists and their plans have been thrust into overdrive and brought out in the open over the past few years. They have made a good deal of progress lately, but read this quote from David Rockefeller's *Memoirs* back in 1991:

> We are grateful to the *Washington Post*, the *New York Times*, *Time* magazine and other great publications whose directors have attended our meetings and respected the promises of discretion for almost 40 years, it would have been impossible for us to develop our plan for the world if we had been subjected to the lights of publicity during those years. But the world is much more sophisticated and prepared to march towards a one world government. The supranational sovereignty of an intellectual elite and world bankers is surely preferable to the national auto determination practice in past centuries.

They have been at this for a while. If you think that David Rockefeller has done all this alone, consider this series of statements from a list of names you are very likely to recognize.

QUOTES SOURCED FROM HC PRESS:

BROCK ADAMS, DIRECTOR, UN HEALTH ORGANIZATION

> "To achieve world government, it is necessary to remove from the minds of men their individualism, loyalty to family traditions, national patriotism, and religious dogmas."

HENRY KISSINGER

> "Today, America would be outraged if U.N. troops entered Los Angeles to restore order. Tomorrow they will be grateful! This is especially true if they were told that there were an outside threat from beyond, whether real or promulgated, that threatened our very existence. It is then that all peoples of the world will plead to deliver them from this evil. The one thing every man fears is the unknown. When presented with this scenario, individual rights will be willingly relinquished for the guarantee of their well-being granted to them by the World Government."

WILLIAM CASEY, CIA DIRECTOR

"We'll know our disinformation program is complete when everything the American public believes is false."

STROBE TALBOTT, PRESIDENT CLINTON'S DEPUTY SECRETARY OF STATE

"In the next century, nations as we know it will be obsolete; all states will recognize a single, global authority. National sovereignty wasn't such a great idea after all."

GEORGE H. W. BUSH

"If the American people knew what we have done, they would string us up from the lamp posts."

WILLIAM COLBY, FORMER CIA DIRECTOR

"The CIA owns everyone of any significance in the major media."

DAVID ROCKEFELLER

"Some even believe we, the Rockefeller family, are part of a secret cabal working against the best interests of the United States, characterizing my family and me as 'internationalists' and of conspiring with others around the world to build a more integrated global political and economic structure, one world, if you will. If that's the charge, I stand guilty, and I am proud of it."

"We are on the verge of a global transformation. All we need is the right major crisis and the nations will accept the New World Order."

Anyone having the recent COVID-19 operation come to mind?

There have been many volumes written, especially in the past dozen or so years, that have been pointing out these orchestrated global conspiracies. Indeed, the very fact that a site exists that has assembled such quotations is evidence that the plot is being uncovered and revealed to citizens. Unfortunately, the vast majority of people are unaware as to the full extent of what has been taking place. Their ignorance is either intentional (I don't want to know) or inadvertent (I'm too busy to look at such things). Either way, they are experiencing the effects of an ever-controlling global authority of elitists and that is making them angry. They just don't know why.

Our own government is equally controlled and complicit in running secret programs and keeping truths from the American people. Harry Truman once said that he never would have formed the CIA if he knew it would turn into the American Gestapo. That is, of course, exactly what it has become. Despite its repeated failures as an international intelligence agency (it's supposed day job), it has found the time in-between to promote various forms of international mischief and regime meddling to conduct such programs as:

OPERATION MOCKINGBIRD

The control and manipulation of journalists to support CIA preferred narratives.

MK-ULTRA

A top-secret government run cognitive manipulation program for "covert use of biological and chemical materials" along with other mind control operations.

MK-Ultra was especially despicable. It centered around behavior modification via electroshock therapy, hypnosis, polygraphs, radiation, and a variety of drugs, toxins, and chemicals, including LSD. The experiments relied on a range of test subjects: some who freely volunteered, some who volunteered under coercion, and some who had absolutely no idea they were involved in a research program.

The CIA covertly and despicably drew from mentally impaired boys at a state school, American soldiers, "sexual psychopaths" at a state hospital, as well as many others to advance their program and capabilities. MK-Ultra experimenters often took advantage of the most vulnerable members of society who they found were most easily manipulated. The CIA considered prisoners especially good subjects, as they were willing to give consent in exchange for extra recreation time or commuted sentences.

The program eventually devolved into using prostitutes to lure men into lairs equipped with audio-visual recording equipment, drugging them, and then using the information for leverage. I wonder if Hugh Hefner or Jeffrey Epstein had ever heard of these programs. Much of that part of the program likely was done simply for the lurid, voyeuristic pleasure of the agents watching. MK-Ultra has long since been exposed and ordered to be ended, but has it? Consider the use of predictive programming in film, TV, music, and the arts. Consider the US educational system and its Common Core. How about the infiltration and control of nearly all science, medical, and education journals used by professionals as their science-based, authoritative sources. Or the governments funding and globalists controlling of nearly all the leading social media juggernauts that curate your stories, news, and information and censor or hide nonconforming narratives. It is clear to me that they have gone electronic and global with their mass manipulation and propaganda tactics to continue and accelerate their dominion over the masses.

Whether it is a modern-day global cabal of elitists flying around in private jets and being chauffeured in black tinted-glass SUVs, or people working in our own government inside of laboratories or offices conducting "experiments" on We the People, everywhere we turn we are being used by others to promote their own agendas. While this is being done secretively for the most part, we are feeling the effects. The secrets take the form of an almost silent killer, like a carbon monoxide leak in your home. We the People are choking but we often don't know why. We are frightened and we are angry. These secrets being kept by powerful people have made us all sick.

These oligarchs can't take over the world on their own. They need help. As we mentioned at the outset, they are receiving it from a few not necessarily unlikely, but certainly a bit coincidental, sources: academia and activists.

Larry McDonald, a United States congressman killed on Korean Airlines flight 007 shot down in 1983 by the Soviets once said this:

> The drive of the Rockefellers and their allies is to create a one-world government combining super capitalism and Communism under the same tent, all under their control…. Do I mean conspiracy? Yes I do. I am convinced there is such

a plot, international in scope, generations old in planning, and incredibly evil in intent.

It is the strange bedfellows of capitalism and communism that have come together in the early part of this century but with seeds planted long before in the last century.

Let's look at the academic piece to this puzzle that has been producing secrets, again, some in plain sight and some harder to spot, that have led to our addiction to conflict and chaos in America.

AMERICAN COMMUNISM AND THE FRANKFURT SCHOOL

In 1923, the American educational system was about to be changed forever by an event that wasn't even taking place within our country. A wealthy patron by the name of Felix Weil used his money, and Carl Grunberg used his mind, to start a new school in Frankfurt, Germany, for the purpose of accelerating the move toward communism. Marx had predicted that the movement was inevitable but that it would be driven by the forces of production—a sort of materialistic and economic approach. Weil, Grunberg, and others felt as though Marx might have been partially right, but maybe not right enough. Something needed to be done to move things along faster.

The Frankfurt School was born. It was inhabited by academics who have since become giant names in the historical field, such as Herbert Marcuse, who became the most famous member of the group when he emerged as the thought leader of the sexual and cultural revolution of the 60s. Other members included Max Horkheimer, the group's director and a philosopher and social theorist; Theodor Adorno, a major cultural critic of the century; and

Erich Fromm, who became one of the most popular writers in the United States.

In the early 30s, with the rise of Adolf Hitler and the Nazi Party in Germany, affectations toward communist ideas became somewhat, well, inconvenient. The Frankfurt School closed up shop in Germany and eventually made its way to Columbia University in New York City where it found a receptive home. When WWII broke out, some of its members went to Washington, DC, to contribute to the battle against fascist ideology, some went to California to explore expanded thought paths for the critical theory discipline, and some remained at Columbia.

So what exactly was the Frankfurt School of thought about? You are going to recognize it as familiar instantly. Their goal was to develop "critical theory," a comprehensive method to change society as a whole. It embraced everything from literature to philosophy to economics to sociology to psychology, and more. It drew from the work of philosophers as diverse as Georg Hegel, Marx, Friedrich Nietzsche, Sigmund Freud, and Max Weber. The Frankfurt School members synthesized philosophy and social theory to develop a critical theory of contemporary society that would combine all the above-mentioned elements into a new interdisciplinary theory. The goal? To advance us more quickly into Marx's utopian end phase of history, a communist society.

If you wonder if this is where critical race theory (CRT) is derived, the answer is yes. Critical race theory can be thought of as a "thin slice" of critical theory, as can critical legal theory from which arose CRT. In America today, one of the most triggering concepts for conflict and chaos is anytime CRT is mentioned in schools or in the workplace. One of the problems is that most of the people fighting about it do not even know where it came from or what it really means. No matter. The term has spread, and its use has been weaponized.

The founders of the Frankfurt School would be proud. Their intention was to tear down established constructs and make way for a communist future. What the future holds is uncertain, but the tearing down part is well underway. The influence of the Frankfurt School in American education is far more pervasive than was the COVID-19 pandemic in spreading illness. The intellectual ship that landed at Columbia in the 1930s has been churning our students and new disciples for a century. The influence is everywhere. This is why our education system is such a mess. All our teachers are trained or indoctrinated under the same theories, hence they are doing the same to our unwitting children.

What is important to keep in mind is that while this book is about positive engagement, it is also built around a principle of individual self-determination. The Frankfurt School ideas are meant to lead us along a socialist path until utopia can be reached. We are skeptical about utopia and very much against any compulsory move toward it. So are, we believe, most Americans if they stop to think about it.

The Frankfurt School, and its many derivations and academic spin-offs and inspirations, has been the single most important intellectual driver of collectivism and division of the past century. That sort of drive toward collectivism has played into the hands of the global oligarchs who want us to be more reliant upon something bigger than ourselves and turn to some sort of authority to "fix" things. This collectivist, Marxist philosophy basically rests on the concept that the greater good must prevail. The individual is essentially expendable for the greater good. Conversely, most Americans were brought up under a foundation of individualism and self-determination where strong, healthy, and productive individuals are the key to a strong, healthy, and productive society. Structurally, these societal foundations are in opposition and this is where we find ourselves.

Academics, however, typically hide within hallowed halls and deliver lectures from podiums in theater-seating auditoriums. They don't usually go out and "do" anything; they don't make anything except more poisoned minds. Turning ideas into actions requires activism, the next piece of the trilateral puzzle that has led to our division and has operated in a manner that is somewhat secretive, if not at least difficult to clearly see.

ACTIVISTS

The actions of activists are divisive and troublemaking almost by definition. The goal of an activist is to upset the status quo and create change. Activism is disruptive. Martin Luther King Jr. was an activist who upset the status quo and led to reforms that increased the rights of Black citizens. Susan B. Anthony was an activist who disrupted conventional notions about women and their rights and value as members of American society. These were courageous people who placed themselves at significant personal risk, King paying with his life, in order to change the system. Their activism led to something positive.

Why, then, are we pointing to activists as part of the cause of our conflict and chaos addiction in America today. It is because we are drawing a distinction between King, Anthony, and others like them to the kinds of activists who have operated with a darker, more sinister set of motivations. The distinction is clear and non-arbitrary. King and others have worked to create change within a system. Other activists have been working just as hard to try and destroy the system.

To begin, let's return to the campus of Columbia University in New York where in 1966, two professors in the School of Social Work, Richard Cloward and Frances Fox Piven published an article in *The Nation* titled, "The Weight of the Poor: A Strategy to End Poverty." They wrote their piece after having been inspired by the race riots in Los Angeles. The two proposed a guaranteed annual income program and urged the Democratic party to push for it. They calculated that an enrollment push for welfare benefits would create a sort of mass collapse that could lead to a sort of socialist solution.

The Cloward–Piven strategy can best be summarized as:

- Overload the system
- Create mass panic and hysteria as the system is overloaded
- Oversee the destruction of the system
- Replace the former system with a new system

Cloward and Piven were not just creating a method for welfare reform, they were creating a paradigm that would be adopted and used time and again by radical elements in the hopes of destroying the American system. Their method has even come to be known as the "Cloward–Piven Strategy." While Cloward and Piven made a huge contribution to the minds of those who seek to divide us, even they must bend the knee to perhaps the most, certainly one of the most, destructive Americans of the past 150 years. That person is the "father" of community organizing, one Saul Alinsky.

Born in 1909 in Chicago, the son of Russian-Jewish immigrants, Alinksy attended the University of Chicago where he was taught by professors that social disorganization was the cause of poverty. By 1938, Alinsky set aside notions of a conventional professional life and entered the world of political activism. He would remain in that field until his death in 1972.

In 1971 he published his seminal work, *Rules for Radicals*. This book was a sort of guide on how to wage war against America from the inside. Alinsky wrote the following regarding what "radicals" believe:

> The Radical believes that all peoples should have a high standard of food, housing, and health.... The Radical places human rights far above property rights. He is for universal, free public education and recognizes this as fundamental to the democratic way of life.... The Radical believes completely in *real* equality of opportunity for all peoples regardless of race, color, or creed. He insists on full employment for economic security but is just as insistent that man's work should not only provide economic security but also be such as to satisfy the creative desires within all men.

That is a very collectivist, non-American, non-natural law, view of a just society. There is no real way to reform America to get to that place. You have to tear it down. How does Alinsky propose that be done? That is where his thirteen rules come into play.

In his prelude to offering those rules, he writes this about the very pragmatic Niccolò Machiavelli, the Renaissance Italian who is considered by some to be the father of political science:

> "What follows is for those who want to change the world from what it is to what they believe it should be. *The Prince* was written by Machiavelli for the Haves on how to hold power. Rules for

Radicals is written for the Have-Nots on how to take it away." Alinsky was a sort of sociopath, a man who in one paragraph talks in glowing idealistic terms, while in another he coldly and clearly discloses just how far he is willing to go. Alinsky enjoyed conflict. He has inspired generations to crave it in the same manner. The greatest trick radicals like Alinksy can ever play is to convince the world they are lovers of peace and tranquility.

Here are Alinsky's thirteen rules for radicals:

1. Power is not only what you have, but what the enemy thinks you have.
2. Never go outside the experience of your people.
3. Whenever possible, go outside the expertise of the enemy.
4. Make the enemy live up to their own book of rules.
5. Ridicule is man's most potent weapon.
6. A good tactic is one that your people enjoy.
7. A tactic that drags on too long becomes a drag.
8. Keep the pressure on.
9. The threat is usually more terrifying than the thing itself.
10. The major premise for tactics is the development of operations that will maintain a constant pressure upon the opposition.
11. If you push a negative hard and deep enough, it will push through into its counterside.
12. The price of a successful attack is a constructive alternative.
13. Pick the target, freeze it, personalize it, and polarize it.

Notice his use of terms like "enemy" and "target." Those enemies and targets are also known as American citizens with whom

Alinsky and his disciples might disagree. Pay special attention to rules number eleven and thirteen. These are simply monstrous. More than any other one person and more than any other single document, this is the battle plan for collectivist and authoritarian radicals of every persuasion and subdivision. Don't think for a minute that the oligarchs looking to control us haven't been feeding off the results of Alinsky's sown divisions for decades now, or that they, as we know with at least Hillary Clinton openly idolizing the man and his tactics to the point of writing her thesis on his work, aren't aware of the fact that he dedicated his book to Lucifer himself with a wink and a nod. The original radical for which he writes:

> Lest we forget at least an over-the-shoulder acknowledgment to the very first radical: from all our legends, mythology, and history (and who is to know where mythology leaves off and history begins—or which is which), the first radical known to man who rebelled against the establishment and did it so effectively that he at least won his own kingdom—Lucifer."
>
> —Saul Alinsky, *Rules for Radicals: A Pragmatic Primer for Realistic Radicals*

Some people reading this book might find what I have shared above illuminating. They may have been totally unaware of these types of plots and people. To you, as I always say, go out and research for yourself. Knowledge is power and a vaccine against manipulation and control. We have only scraped the surface here. Although it may feel to be a deep cut, it is not. Others reading this book might have their own list of these people and their organizations that have helped to tear our nation apart and who have kept secrets from us for the purpose of controlling us. Don't be offended if you think we "missed" yours. We are and have been under a massive, well-planned, thought-out attack and we must prevail as the stakes of this "game" could not be higher for you, your family, and our way of life globally.

COMMUNIST GOALS
CONGRESSIONAL RECORD—APPENDIX,
PP. A34-A35 JANUARY 10, 1963

EXTENSION OF REMARKS OF HON. A. S. HERLONG, JR. OF FLORIDA

IN THE HOUSE OF REPRESENTATIVES

Thursday, January 10, 1963

Mr. HERLONG. Mr. Speaker, Mrs. Patricia Nordman of De Land, Fla., is an ardent and articulate opponent of communism, and until recently published the De Land Courier, which she dedicated to the purpose of alerting the public to the dangers of communism in America.

At Mrs. Nordman's request, I include in the RECORD, under unanimous consent, the following "Current Communist Goals," which she identifies as an excerpt from "The Naked Communist," by Cleon Skousen:

[From "The Naked Communist," by Cleon Skousen]
CURRENT COMMUNIST GOALS

1. U.S. acceptance of coexistence as the only alternative to atomic war.
2. U.S. willingness to capitulate in preference to engaging in atomic war.
3. Develop the illusion that total disarmament [by] the United States would be a demonstration of moral strength.
4. Permit free trade between all nations regardless of Communist affiliation and regardless of whether or not items could be used for war.

5. Extension of long-term loans to Russia and Soviet satellites.
6. Provide American aid to all nations regardless of Communist domination.
7. Grant recognition of Red China. Admission of Red China to the U.N.
8. Set up East and West Germany as separate states in spite of Khrushchev's promise in 1955 to settle the German question by free elections under supervision of the U.N.
9. Prolong the conferences to ban atomic tests because the United States has agreed to suspend tests as long as negotiations are in progress.
10. Allow all Soviet satellites individual representation in the U.N.
11. Promote the U.N. as the only hope for mankind. If its charter is rewritten, demand that it be set up as a one-world government with its own independent armed forces. (Some Communist leaders believe the world can be taken over as easily by the U.N. as by Moscow. Sometimes these two centers compete with each other as they are now doing in the Congo.)
12. Resist any attempt to outlaw the Communist Party.
13. Do away with all loyalty oaths.
14. Continue giving Russia access to the U.S. Patent Office.
15. Capture one or both of the political parties in the United States.
16. Use technical decisions of the courts to weaken basic American institutions by claiming their activities violate civil rights.
17. Get control of the schools. Use them as transmission belts for socialism and current Communist propaganda. Soften the curriculum. Get control of teachers' associations. Put the party line in textbooks.

18. Gain control of all student newspapers.
19. Use student riots to foment public protests against programs or organizations which are under Communist attack.
20. Infiltrate the press. Get control of book-review assignments, editorial writing, policymaking positions.
21. Gain control of key positions in radio, TV, and motion pictures.
22. Continue discrediting American culture by degrading all forms of artistic expression. An American Communist cell was told to "eliminate all good sculpture from parks and buildings, substitute shapeless, awkward and meaningless forms."
23. Control art critics and directors of art museums. "Our plan is to promote ugliness, repulsive, meaningless art."
24. Eliminate all laws governing obscenity by calling them "censorship" and a violation of free speech and free press.
25. Break down cultural standards of morality by promoting pornography and obscenity in books, magazines, motion pictures, radio, and TV.
26. Present homosexuality, degeneracy and promiscuity as "normal, natural, healthy."
27. Infiltrate the churches and replace revealed religion with "social" religion. Discredit the Bible and emphasize the need for intellectual maturity which does not need a "religious crutch."
28. Eliminate prayer or any phase of religious expression in the schools on the ground that it violates the principle of "separation of church and state."
29. Discredit the American Constitution by calling it inadequate, old-fashioned, out of step with modern needs, a hindrance to cooperation between nations on a worldwide basis.

30. Discredit the American Founding Fathers. Present them as selfish aristocrats who had no concern for the "common man."
31. Belittle all forms of American culture and discourage the teaching of American history on the ground that it was only a minor part of the "big picture." Give more emphasis to Russian history since the Communists took over.
32. Support any socialist movement to give centralized control over any part of the culture—education, social agencies, welfare programs, mental health clinics, etc.
33. Eliminate all laws or procedures which interfere with the operation of the Communist apparatus.
34. Eliminate the House Committee on Un-American Activities.
35. Discredit and eventually dismantle the FBI.
36. Infiltrate and gain control of more unions.
37. Infiltrate and gain control of big business.
38. Transfer some of the powers of arrest from the police to social agencies. Treat all behavioral problems as psychiatric disorders which no one but psychiatrists can understand [or treat].
39. Dominate the psychiatric profession and use mental health laws as a means of gaining coercive control over those who oppose Communist goals.
40. Discredit the family as an institution. Encourage promiscuity and easy divorce.
41. Emphasize the need to raise children away from the negative influence of parents. Attribute prejudices, mental blocks and retarding of children to suppressive influence of parents.
42. Create the impression that violence and insurrection are legitimate aspects of the American tradition; that students and

special-interest groups should rise up and use ["]united force["] to solve economic, political or social problems.
43. Overthrow all colonial governments before native populations are ready for self-government.
44. Internationalize the Panama Canal.
45. Repeal the Connally reservation so the United States cannot prevent the World Court from seizing jurisdiction [over domestic problems. Give the World Court jurisdiction] over nations and individuals alike.

What we have tried to do here is make a compelling argument that there are, and have been for some time, sinister forces at work trying to undermine America. While these somewhat different ideologies, motivations, and goals might be quite different, we are at a point of convergence whereby the globalists have recognized these power struggles, harnessed them, and are driving them towards the ultimate goal of chaos and societal collapse to be reimagined and built back better.

All of them have sought to divide us. It is empirically impossible to deny their success. All of them have also kept secrets. There are two ways to keep secrets. One is to hide facts and the other is to hide intentions. The people intent on fomenting division in America have been masterful at employing both as needed. Hatred can be so blinding it is very difficult to sometimes just shake your head, gather your thoughts, and realize that you have been played and manipulated. It has been said that it is easier to fool a man than to have him admit that he has been fooled, but this is not a winning mindset. That is what has been happening to us in America and quite frankly globally. Make no mistake, we let it happen on our watch, but unlike someone addicted to drugs or alcohol who really has nobody to blame but themselves, we have been deliberately led down this path toward conflict. This is why we must recognize the problem. We must all be humble but with righteous indignation. I am an American and I have a problem. Now, it will require us all—every living, able-bodied citizen who cherishes freedom—to be deliberate among ourselves to collectively turn around, reverse course, and do better as if our lives depended on it, because unfortunately, they very well might.

CHAPTER 3

DOING BETTER:
AN AMERICAN RECOVERY

find it interesting that the near-total degradation of civility, rules, and norms in our political discourse, business decision-making, and judicial processes has an interesting parallel to that of the lore and functioning of the Mafia. Much has been written about the founding of organized crime and their codes of conduct. As these codes began to be discarded for power and profit, the organization began to falter and lost its way. The same can be said for the codes, norms, and values in much of society. We have lost our way, our moral compasses, and any sense of fair play or ground rules in the way we operate in society. It's a world where anything goes and the winner takes the spoils. Today there seems to be a total breakdown and anarchy in the sense of the stability of the societal structure.

As many of my listeners know, I have interviewed many of the J6 prisoners who were standing for their right to peacefully protest and to address their grievances with their government. One of those interviews was with a gentleman named Jeremy Brown. Jeremy's story is extraordinary and clearly a miscarriage of common-sense justice, but he continues to stand strong in his belief in truth and justice even from jail. One of my last questions to him was, "What would you like to tell my audience as we wrap up here?" and his response was, "Don't do nothing." So this is where we are. Please don't do nothing.

It is most likely the case that anyone reading this book is doing so because they have a sense that Americans can and must do something—something that works. We must do better when it comes to having civil discourse with one another. In the first two chapters, we have pointed out that we believe that Americans have become addicted to conflict and chaos. We have also shown how we came to develop that addiction and illustrate some of the institutions and systems that drive this demoralizing and dehumanizing agenda. Now let's take a look at what recovery from that addiction can look like.

We start with one of the most commonly used, and always abused, phrases in American culture, which goes, "It's not personal. It's strictly business." I guess our culture has in fact adopted much from the Mafia. The fact that the phrase comes to us from Mafia lore and *The Godfather* film series ought to be warning enough as to its insidious nature. The fact that the phrase was only introduced into our American lexicon in 1972 and has become almost universally recognizable since then is a testament to its appeal, but what exactly is that appeal?

"This isn't personal…" is typically pulled out and used by someone when they are about to tell somebody something that they themselves are not really comfortable saying. The employer uses it when he lays off an aging worker. The supplier uses it when he cuts off a slow-paying, but loyal and longtime customer. It is even used in variation when someone is, in fact, ending a personal relationship because of some sort of inconvenience it causes to them. "This isn't personal. I just don't have any other choice," or, "It's not you, it's me."

In short, the "this isn't personal" construct has become a rationalization tool for people to use in order to somehow detach themselves from responsibility for their actions. It is a way to indicate to the recipient of uncomfortable, or even unfair, news that this just isn't your fault. There's nothing you can do. In the famous words of John Malkovich's character in *Dangerous Liaisons*, "It's beyond my control."

You can reasonably ask, "What does this communication turn of phrase used to rationalize behavior when getting rid of something or someone have to do with civil discourse in the private room or public square?" The answer is that the removal of personal responsibility from our actions is habit-forming! If we can convince ourselves that the actions we take are not something for which we can be held responsible, that excuses us somehow when we engage people on any level and in any situation. We detach our words and actions from their impact or consequence. This is a bad habit and opens us up to conflict addiction.

What does "doing better" in this regard look like? We need to realize that everything is personal! We are all people. Walls, machinery, and organizations don't hear words or feel actions. People do. We need to be vigilant in remembering that all, not most or some, of our actions and words are personal to the recipient.

This means that the absolutist will never be able to find peace in this life if they are going to insist upon demanding absolute agreement from others or otherwise they will turn to conflict. None of us can even get absolute agreement within ourselves as we always have that little voice in our head or heart that questions everything, even if we don't choose to acknowledge it in our discourse. I am sure that you have noticed that in today's public square if someone is part of an identifiable ideological "tribe" they will immediately get criticized by other tribe members if they deviate from orthodoxy. We referenced this in the first chapter. Why on earth would somebody lash out at somebody else who agrees with them on ninety-nine out of one hundred points simply for one simple variant of opinion? That isn't rational. Exactly! Addiction isn't rational. We are actually hunting for that one single point of contention. We are primed for that trigger so that we can kick in our addictive tendency toward conflict. No matter how broken the addict is, they can always scrape together enough coins to buy a baby-pint of bottom-shelf vodka at the liquor store or a lottery ticket. The absolutist can always find that one point of disagreement so that they can purchase a shot of conflict.

If we can recover from this addiction to conflict, part of what we will find is that we will have a spiritual awakening as to the difference between principles and preferences. A phrase that people use quite whimsically is "It is a matter of principle with me." The question the good skeptic needs to ask themselves when those words leave their lips is, "Is it?" Many people use the phrase so frequently that you would think of them to be pure, righteous, and steadfast in their character, but then their behavior betrays the words. They don't seem to be too terribly principled at all. What they are really saying when they state their "principle" is that they would prefer something to be a certain way. Of course, to the absolutist, there is no difference between a principle and a preference, at least to them. That lack of introspection opens them up to being susceptible to conflict addiction.

With honesty and introspection, we can come to learn through recovery that we likely have a small handful of true principles and an enormous library filled with preferences. I would argue that even principles can be compromised if the stakes are high enough. Yes, murder is wrong as a principle, but if someone is seeking to kill your child then you might very well murder the attacker compromising your principles. Those things which we prefer, and sometimes even our principles, are things where we can constructively engage with others to attempt to persuade them, but not to demand that they yield. This single element alone can lower the temperature in every issue-driven room to seventy-four degrees with circulating fresh air. In reaching across the cultural divide, we need to find common ground with principles and preferences, such as liberty as a principle. But as we said, the nuance lies in the stakes of the game and an introspective understanding of negotiation.

PRINCIPLES, PREFERENCES, AND PRACTICAL CONSIDERATIONS TO NEGOTIATED SOLUTIONS

With regard to principles, convey them openly and honestly and hold as fast as you can, but understand that sometimes the stakes of the game are so high that there may be a higher order principle that takes precedence.

With regard to preferences, be willing to adjust as might be appropriate and necessary. This is one of the basics of negotiation.

Search for the wisdom to know the difference between the two, understanding your goal is not to win an argument but to win the war.

If that brings to mind the Serenity Prayer then you are on the right track.

> *God, grant me the serenity to accept the things I cannot change, the courage to change the things I can, and the wisdom to know the difference.*

What does "doing better" in this regard look like? It means that we have to come to understand that tolerance and surrender are not synonyms. We can be accepting of disagreements with others because most of those disagreements relate to matters of preferences and not our firmly held principles. We must also understand that some may not fully understand the ramifications of holding firm on principles if they do not understand the stakes at hand. We will also need to surrender our quest for absolute ideological purity and full agreement on every aspect of every topic. That can best be accomplished by remembering we don't even agree with ourselves all the time, or even most of the time if we really are honest.

Anyone who ever bought anything from a used car lot or a knockoff purse on a Manhattan street corner knows about what some call negotiating but what is really just haggling. This is when the used Mustang dealer has a sticker on it for $15,000, you offer $10,000, and the salesman says, "Let's split the difference." By meeting halfway, the buyer walks away feeling satisfied, not ever stopping to realize that the used car dealer still just made over $5,000 on the sale and likely would have gone further down in price if the buyer had been a negotiator and not a haggler.

While professional negotiators know that "splitting the difference" or meeting in the middle is a bad tactic, regular folks view it as something that sounds fair and reasonable. Indeed, it does give the feeling that both sides are compromising by the same amount and if everyone had that attitude maybe things wouldn't be so bad.

The problem is that for conflict addicts the "middle" is subjective and they tend to want to have the bigger piece of the remaining wishbone. How can we know what the "middle" even is in our disagreements? If there is a middle, how could we see it through all of our anger?

In an America, where recovery is our goal, people should not be focused on finding a middle. Instead, what they should focus on is understanding exactly where they are, where the other person is, and what the most reasonable place is to rendezvous that makes sense from a variety of aspects, not simply subjective distance.

To stay with the metaphor, imagine you are planning a get together with ten friends and they live in various parts of the country. Someone very good with math could find the equidistant point that would be optimal in terms of distance for everyone. The problem is that the point might be located in the middle of a quarry or a restricted government army base. In reality, what you do is take into account all sorts of factors, one of which would be nothing if there is a place that one or more of the members simply would not be able to get to if it were chosen. "Not able" would be a big consideration if you wanted that person(s) to attend. Ultimately, your group would weigh all options and choose the best place for everyone. For one, it might be an hour's drive and for another it might be a cross-country plane ride. The point is that distance isn't all that matters in making the choice.

Another problem with relying on distance is that, even on their best day, people tend to overestimate the distance between themselves and others. The problem gets even more acute when they are in conflict. Said plainly, if Americans are golfers, we keep choosing the wrong club. Because we don't measure distance well, and because we tend to overestimate it, we easily get frustrated and turn to conflict. We need a "fix." There goes meeting in the middle.

The use of social media has made finding a satisfactory meeting place all the more difficult. Engagement has become impersonal and also lacks the need for continuous back-and-forth. Specifically, the problem is that I can send you, or the world, any sort of nasty or saucy message and then step away from the engagement for as long as I want. This gives time not for cooler heads to prevail, but for the conflict addict's anger to build. In business, there is an unwritten rule that when you get some angering news you wait twenty-four hours to respond. The reason is that it promotes a more rational and less emotional reply. For the chaos addict it can yield just the opposite effect. If you say that when we people get into heated quick exchanges that is also something bad, you're right. The problem for conflict addicts is that they will get their drug any way they can, whether it is in an instant or tomorrow.

In short, social media has become anything but social, and has turned into perhaps the most obvious and damaging expression of our addiction to conflict. We need to move into a place where the users of screens can place themselves in a frame of mind that puts the person(s) with whom they are communicating right in the room physically next to them. We also need to have people realize that when they are communicating with one person on social media they are actually communicating with the world, and their addictive behavior is triggering the addictive behavior ripple effect in an untold number of others.

Finally, we want to get to a place where we can "own our 1 percent" of every disagreement. Before we can bridge a divide between us and someone else, we have to be willing to acknowledge that we created at least some portion of it. When it is sincere, there are few things more powerful than someone acknowledging their role in a misunderstanding or disagreement. As Americans, we have increasingly become less and less willing to take blame ourselves—even 1 percent. Part of an American recovery will have to include people being willing to say that what aggrieves another party isn't just a figment of their imagination. In virtually every grievance there is a bit of justification, even if it's only 1 percent of it. We all need to be willing to own our 1 percent, 10, or even 100 percent for that matter because the only thing that matters is a solution to our national problem.

What does "doing better" look like in this regard? It means that we develop the right mixture of humility, awareness, empathy, and compassion to treat every encounter with others as an event that is important to us because we want it to be important to them. We need to remember that it's only people, real people, who feel, who hurt, who need to engage positively and productively. There is no Twitter, Facebook, Instagram, or TikTok person. There are only people who are using those platforms. We need to learn how to treat every individual as though they are our significant other, we love them, and they just told us they are leaving. Because in that moment, no matter who or what we normally are, we will grab their hand, look them in the eye and say, "Wait a minute. Tell me what's wrong. I want to listen. I don't want to lose you."

While there's a well-known phrase that seems to date back to the 1400s, it became more prominent in a well-read novel of its time authored in 1896 by Charles Sheldon. That book was titled *In His Steps*, but it was the subtitle that would become famous: *What Would Jesus Do?* That phrase circulated for over one hundred years before a Baptist school teacher in Holland, Michigan, decided there needed to be a way to get her students to embrace the message. From that idea, WWJD bracelets were born and for nearly a decade they could be found almost everywhere.

Jesus Christ is a figure viewed by different people in different ways. To Christians, He is the Son of God and God incarnate. To Muslims He is a prophet. To some of the Jewish faith He is also a prophet or rabbi while others see Him as heretical. To an atheist, He is likely seen as part of the great opiate of religion created to delude the masses. This is not a religious text and so we leave that debate to readers and theologians. What we do want to point out is that whatever you think of Jesus Christ from a religious perspective, we hope that everyone can agree that His teachings were filled with love and wisdom.

There is a passage in the Christian Bible, Matthew 22:34–40, that describes the Pharisees trying to "trick" Jesus by asking Him a question as to which of the Ten Commandments was the greatest. Jesus confounded them with His answer which, while often translated with variation, always comes out to this:

> Thou shalt love the Lord thy God with all thy heart, and with all thy soul, and with all thy mind. This is the first and great commandment. And the second *is* like unto it, Thou shalt love thy neighbor as thyself.

The first of those two we can respectfully set aside and let readers of all belief systems have at it (although, civilly please and without conflict). The second commandment Christ cites is something that Americans would be well advised to contemplate regardless of their stance on faith. We as a people have seemingly lost our way in terms of just being willing to start from the premise of loving our neighbor. In the literal sense, think of how you might react by watching the new neighbors unload their truck next door as they move in. Do you start to judge their art choices? Do you look for bumper stickers on their cars with a message with which you don't agree? Do you start to assume that their large shaggy dog is going to make a daily mess of your front yard? We have replaced "love your neighbor" with "size up and judge your neighbor."

We do this wherever we go and while it isn't new, it's human nature. What has changed is our burning desire to confront our neighbor preemptively, assuming that he or she is someone with whom we not only *might* take issue, we *want* to take issue! Christ wouldn't do this and it has nothing to do with whether or not He is God. It has to do with something that our grandparents taught us. It has to do with simply being decent. The Golden Rule of treating others as you wish to be treated. We as a society need to revisit and re-embrace the Golden Rule.

You could make an argument that the two most impactful people in all of history, one on the secular side and one on the religious, were Socrates and Jesus Christ. They share two things in common. The first is they were both forced to give their lives for their teachings. The second is that they both changed the world not by arguing with others in heated exchanges, but by asking them questions.

The best way to have someone come to see your point of view is to have them voluntarily come to have it as their point of view. The religious might call this a conversion. Conversions come through contemplation, revelation, and self-awareness. This can best be generated by asking questions of others and by letting them hear their own answers. You don't talk them into something, they end up talking themselves into it! There is no greater evidence of conversion than to have someone with whom you are talking to tilt their head, scratch their chin, and say, "I never thought of that."

Another interesting thing about "conversions" is that they only stick if they are voluntary. You can shout someone into submission, but not into lasting agreement. Even little nuances in our conversations can make a huge difference. Consider choosing the phrase, "I think you're wrong," versus saying, "I see it differently." The former leads to conflict, while the latter leads to open listening and contemplation.

Socrates knew that. Jesus knew that. They asked questions that changed the world. If you start by loving your neighbor, if you start by asking yourself, "What would Jesus do?" it gets much easier to engage them with an open mind and start to have a positive question-and-answer exchange. Who knows? You might even get a conversion as you do your part to build a better society.

What does "doing better" in this area mean? It means that Americans will become more willing to live Martin Luther King Jr.'s words of judging people by the content of their character and not anything else. It means taking the time to learn and understand what is inside each person and where they come from and why they believe what they believe. It means asking questions. It means keeping four simple letters in mind: WWJD?

When Sir Thomas More penned *Utopia* in 1516 about this sort of idyllic place of cooperation, it was lost on many that the word "utopia" comes from the Greek language and means "nowhere." Perfect places, like perfect people, simply don't exist.

We the People need to understand that if true recovery is possible, we need to learn this process and we need to understand that perfection is not a goal of the process, it is unattainable. People in recovery simply start from the premise that their lives have become unmanageable owing to their addiction. A common phrase within the "rooms" of recovery is "Together we do get better." There isn't a person who has successfully worked a program for thirty years and remained sober who would tell you that their life is perfect.

What they likely will say is that their life has gotten better, and it is no longer unmanageable.

If we were seeking perfection in our interactions with one another that would make us a sort of absolutist, and we already have made clear that the absolutist will face no happiness in this life. What we do seek, what is reasonable to seek, is that we make our lives with one another manageable again, no matter our differences.

So, if you are willing to leave your red and blue banners at the door, forget the R or D false choices by dropping the idea that there are actually sides at all, walk into the church basement or community center room with us, and get prepared to pick up a white chip or key tag to commemorate your willingness to humbly take action to improve your life and your nation, then you already completed the first step towards healing. White is the symbol in recovery for someone who is just getting started. All that is required to get that white-colored trinket is a wanting and willingness to get sober, to find a better way, to do better, to heal your addiction to conflict and chaos and help heal our nation.

We have shared our thoughts as to the nature of our addiction, how it developed, and what a life free from addiction to conflict and chaos filled with constructive engagement can look like. The question remains: How do we get there? In the next twelve chapters, we will attempt to answer that question by giving you a process through which you can walk the walk and take that journey with others. I am confident that America can work again if you are willing to work this program. I have also come to understand that, quite frankly, we don't have much of a choice as the stakes of this game are so high at this point for both the individual and the future of our county. We can no longer "go along to get along" or simply put up our dukes and start fighting. We need solutions. What we are experiencing today in our country is simply unmanageable, unhealthy, and will ultimately lead to our own destruction. We believe this is not our destiny, and while God wins, it's up to each and every individual citizen to get actively engaged and do the work. We have as individuals and as a society the ability to change course; certainly the need is apparent as well, but we must decide we truly want to.

Finally, they say in recovery of the addict who simply refuses to pursue sobriety that they will always face one (or more) of three eventual outcomes: jails, institutions, and/or death. You can make your own sort of metaphorical translation as to what those outcomes might equate to on a national level. Whatever you come up with, they won't be good. Join us on the road to recovery. Let's all try to do better and save our nation and humanity worldwide!

PART 2

AMERICANS ANONYMOUS—THE AMERICAN RECOVERY PLAN STEPS

WE HAVE A PROBLEM: ADDICTION TO CONFLICT AND CHAOS

WE ADMITTED THAT WE HAVE NOT TAKEN PERSONAL
RESPONSIBILITY FOR NOR UPHELD OUR DUTY AS
INDIVIDUAL AMERICAN CITIZENS TO PRESERVE OUR
NATION AS FOUNDED, AND AS A RESULT OUR COUNTRY
AND OUR LIVES HAVE BECOME UNMANAGEABLE.

WE THE PEOPLE MUST FIRST RECOGNIZE AND
ADMIT THAT WE HAVE A PROBLEM.

The date was November 7, 2017. It was early evening in Midtown Manhattan as a major snowstorm began pounding the city. I was working on a chaotic film set with a massive crew and an all-star, high-maintenance cast at the Apollo Theater in Harlem. We were running behind as usual when so many artists and egos are involved, and were told we would have a significantly shortened dinner break. A few of my politically astute friends and I rushed to bundle up for our brisk run/walk to the nearest Midtown polling station. We could eat anytime; we could not bear one more term of Mayor Bill de Blasio! This was our chance, as a group of New Yorkers who watched our city sliding into a dystopian socialist disaster, to save our city from the nightmare we all knew would be coming if he were to remain in power.

From a national standpoint, 2017 was an off year, with the major presidential election only a year behind and what is commonly called the "midterm election" still a year away. In New York, as in many other states, other elections take place during that in-between year. One such election was for that of New York City mayor. At the moment, that post was held by Bill de Blasio and he was up for reelection. I had watched since my first year in college to date the glory of NYC during the Giuliani years, and the unfathomable total decline towards untenable during de Blasio's first term. The city was a part of me, and I felt that another term would irreparably destroy Gotham.

Bill de Blasio had been anything but a popular mayor. As recently as a year earlier he had a disapproval rating of 51 percent. And I would say that's generous, as we know how manipulated polls are. That said, in May when the primary was held, only 15 percent of registered New York Democrats showed up and when they did, they re-nominated him with a whopping 74 percent of the vote. Something was off.

Worried we would not get through the line to vote fast enough to be back on the movie set in time, we were stunned when we got to the polling place. It was virtually empty with literally no line at all. This was Midtown Manhattan! Nothing in Midtown Manhattan is ever empty. After we voted and began walking back everyone was uncomfortably silent for a while until my friend said in disgust what we all knew, "De Blasio is definitely going to win. Goodbye New York."

When the dust settled, de Blasio did, in fact, win, and did so by a margin of 66.2 percent to 27.6 percent over the other major party nominee. More telling, however, was the fact that only 25 percent of New York voters had turned out to vote (only 8 percent of the population).

This begs the question: How does a mayor who has more than half of his voters disapprove of him end up winning by almost 40 percentage points? There are a number of terms that come to mind: apathy, disengagement, disenchantment, possibly fraud, and so on. Perhaps the best words that can be found that explain not just the results of the 2017 election in Gotham, but also the general condition of America today are these:

Neglect or abdication of personal responsibility.

Americans by and large have become neglectful of the opportunity, codified into a system by our Constitution, given to us by our Founding Fathers. We have taken for granted our liberties and simply assumed that they will always be there—a sort of given like the sun rising and setting. We refer again to Ben Franklin's warning when asked what sort of government had been given to the newly formed nation: "A republic, if you can keep it." The phrase "We the People" is often spoken but seldom actualized. We were supposed to take ownership of this country and treat it like a family-owned business that needs to be constantly managed to make certain it is staying on track. Businesses that aren't well managed soon go out of business. Franklin and others knew that we could keep what they had given us only with vigilance and participation.

Then there is New York City with the pathetic turnout in 2017 for a mayor who many believed was abysmal. Vigilance has clearly left the building. Participation was delegated to the other guys who would surely go vote. What has led to this general malaise of personal responsibility for the piece of America that each citizen should take as personally as they do their job, business, land, or home? What has caused our country to hit the addict's bottom to the point of not even realizing their country had become unmanageable? The short answer is that we have surrendered our civic obligations and public-mindedness in pursuit of materialistic and hedonistic pleasures. We have also gotten lazy, distracted, and frankly worn down.

At this moment in time, the United States is the place where we can find the greatest level of material wealth and physical comfort that has ever existed in all of human history. There is no past place that has risen and fallen (that we know of) that offered what we now have, nor is there any country on earth today that compares. This is arguably the most opulent society that has ever been seen. This should, of course, be nothing but positive insofar as most of man's existence has been spent struggling for the basics of food, clean water, safety, and shelter.

Unfortunately, as with so many other things in man's existence we seem to have found a way to turn the blessing into a curse. A number of different problems have developed as a derivative of our comfort, each of which has contributed to our becoming conflict addicts.

The first is our move toward consumerism. The "ism" suffix when attached to a word simply definitionally changes it into a distinctive system, practice, or philosophy. It can also be thought of as a sort of religion. If you think that in making this claim we are somehow coming out against free enterprise, think again. No less an authority than the "father of capitalism," Adam Smith, author of the 1776 book, *The Wealth of Nations*, warned of what could happen to people when they developed an obsession for "stuff." We have become increasingly preoccupied with preserving the things we have, accumulating more things, and disregarding others in the process.

One of the most disheartening jobs anyone can have is being a consultant or counsel for a family-owned business. The difficult part of that job is dealing with the family dynamics when a member of that family business passes away, especially if it is a parent. Suddenly, spouses and siblings who had worked well together for years are at each other's throats trying to make certain they get as much as they can or believe they should have. Just think of families you know, perhaps even your own, where you have witnessed this same sort of greedy, almost vulture-like, behavior. Take that family situation and extrapolate it out across a nation. We can't seem to get enough stuff. Our entertainment and advertising culture contributes to this "ism" (Smith also identified that problem way back in the eighteenth century). Almost everywhere we turn we are faced with an image designed to create a sense of need that is insatiable. You could say that we are addicted to getting "stuff." That isn't the specific addiction this program is trying to address, but those who are recovering from addictions to drugs or alcohol will tell you that addicts are addicts. One addiction feeds another.

Another problem that has led to our neglect is what they call in economics the "free rider problem." In that discipline, the problem refers to people being able to take advantage of something that is being provided to them without actually having to directly pay for it. The most common example used in classrooms is that of a highway that the government provides but that any motorist can use regardless of where they are from or how frequently they might travel on it. This is why you see the argument made for charging tolls for the use of roads. You use, you pay.

Translating this problem into American society isn't a large leap. With 330 million of us, we have taken on the attitude of "let somebody else do it." This has devolved into an even more perverse variation, which is along the lines of: "There are so many others doing it, why should I even bother? What difference could I possibly make? Plus, I'm busy accumulating and enjoying all my stuff."

This leads to nobody bothering to show up to vote in New York against a mayor of whom they don't approve. Somebody else can just take care of voting for me. What's the point anyway? It doesn't matter. This doesn't just happen at big elections. It happens everywhere. Why run for school board? Susie's mom can take care of it. Why join in a fight against a new local restrictive ordinance? My voice won't matter. By the way, I have one thousand streaming shows to watch on my ninety-five-inch 4K flat screen with surround sound. What people lose track of when they become free riders is that they aren't paying attention to who is actually driving. We have a natural tendency to assume that the people who will carry the burden are people just like us. After all, aren't we all sort of the same? The answer is an emphatic no! Our neglect has provided the opportunity for people who do not have Americans' best interests at heart, a focused minority of people who want to divide us, to step in and take charge.

Days prior to the 2020 election, I was on a Zoom with about twenty other content creators and personalities who, regardless of background or identification, were committed to the fight for America's future. When I asked the group how many of them were going to vote in a few days I was shocked that only one other person raised their hand. One person said, "It doesn't matter who we vote for. The elections are all fake. Nothing changes no matter who wins." This is a free rider problem devolving into hopelessness and inaction.

How do these joint tendencies toward consumerism and free riding contribute to our addiction to conflict? The answer is that by getting lost in our playthings and by failing to contribute, we can't stop what is happening in the world around us, and because we have excluded ourselves from trying to constructively help shape it, we get angry at the results. When you have a problem, action is the key. If you are not active your passivity often devolves into anxiety, fear, and chaos because you lack control as you realize you are on a runaway train and at great risk. Specifically, our consumerism leads us to focus on material items and to competitively compare what others have that we don't. We have not just been trying to keep up with the Joneses, we have found ourselves increasingly envious of the Joneses and envy breeds contempt and bitterness. We want what others have and we judge our own happiness vis-à-vis the possessions of other people.

Regarding the free rider problem, just because we are leaving something to be done by someone else doesn't mean we are going to be satisfied with the results. In a less serious way, anyone in a relationship with a significant other knows the routine of them saying to you, "Just figure it out and I will be fine with your decision." Then, after you have completed your "mission" they tell you all the things you did wrong and what they would have done differently. This is a problem sometimes solved by anything from flowers to couple's counseling, but when it happens between strangers, reconciliation becomes more challenging.

Americans have surrendered the idea of being "We the People" to being only "Me the Person." There is a misunderstanding that commonly takes place between the two, especially with people who are very much concerned about having the right to do their own thing. It is true that our Founding Fathers created a system designed to maximize and promote individual liberty. There was, however, a catch. In order to preserve individual liberty, we needed to exercise collective responsibility to safeguard it. Joining together isn't a surrendering of individual freedom, it is necessary to keep it. The stakes are so high that we need to compromise on our principle of individual freedom to actually maintain it. This type of compromise takes a level of humility and understanding that we need more of in society. Our extraordinary levels of comfort and wealth, combined with a feeling that somebody else can take care of it…whatever "it" is…have caused us to lose our vigilance.

We have come to care little about what gets done next, but we are very quick to point out what isn't done well. We are also always comparing what we have versus what others have. Envy is one of the seven deadly sins for a reason. Whether you believe in the notion of sin or not, there is nothing good that comes from feeling envious (focusing on what others have that you want), nor does anything come from its sister emotion of jealousy (focusing on what another has that you think is rightfully yours). There is also a bit of learned helplessness at play in our having moved away from our obligations as We the People. We live in a nation of large systems. It is easy to feel powerless when you are surrounded by big government, big business, big education, big medicine, and so on. We have to remember that if things seem to be too big, we were the ones who allowed them to become too big. We did this. We are not victims, we are volunteers. People joined together to create these big systems, we can just as easily join together to figure out how to constructively engage with and change them.

Together we can do better. We should not neglect our own self-interests; we just need to understand that the best way to pursue those interests is to join together and engage in a constructive manner to preserve the system that was designed to allow our own individual selves to flourish. We also must remember to never do so at the expense of others.

———

Ready to work a First Step? Here are some ideas for you or members of your group to discuss and implement:

1. List three things about America that you are grateful for and how they enhance your life on a regular basis.
2. List your unique skills or gifts and how you could put them to good use in the fight for freedom and liberty.
3. Understand that local action is where you can have the most profound impact. Make a list of three actions you will be taking in your local community or neighborhood and give them deadlines.
4. Trust yourself. Take the time to go inward, grab a pen and paper, and handwrite old-school style who you are, what you believe, how you feel about your life and your nation, and what you hope for in the future. Update regularly. Journaling works.
5. Don't feel you have to do everything at once—make a list and check off your progress as you go. Action is a powerful cure for anxiety and helplessness.

WE ARE THE SOLUTION: UNITY, COMMUNITY, AND ACTION

WE CAME TO BELIEVE THAT A POWER GREATER THAN OURSELVES, AS AN INDIVIDUAL AND AS A NATION, COULD AND WOULD RESTORE US AND OUR COUNTRY TO OUR FOUNDING PRINCIPLES, STABILITY, AND SANITY.

WE CANNOT DO THIS ALONE. WE NEED THE POWER OF FAITH, UNITY, AND COMMUNITY.

R easonable people can differ.

In our country today there are many debates that rage about the proper role of not just the federal government in relation to individual states, but to the role of government in general in governing the lives of its citizens. There are many disagreements. Should banking be centralized? Should the federal government commandeer the economy or should each state have the right to set its own policies? Should we be more of a "democracy" where the general population decides upon matters or should we be more of a constitutional republic as our Founders intended where decisions are entrusted to our states and elected officials?

These are issues that are hotly contested anywhere from dining room tables to coffee shops, from college classrooms to the halls of Congress. The most vitriolic engagements take place across all the various social media platforms, where often supporters of any one particular view are openly hostile to anyone out there who takes an opposing side and where hating in the third person, hating the "theys" and "thems," comes with virtually no personal cost to the hater. We have even created a whole new class of people organized and paid to parrot a particular viewpoint that often stirs division without any sort of academic or thoughtful pedigree. We call them "influencers" and their reach can be significant in today's world of social media fame and worship. The interesting thing is that most of the issues we fight about today have been issues of disagreement for a very long time.

How long? How about going back to our Founding Fathers? They, too, disagreed on many major issues and yet they were able to come together, air their differences, and form an entire new nation from scratch.

The major division in philosophical approach came between those who were called "federalists" and those who were simply called "anti-federalists." The federalists favored a strong central government while those opposed wanted decentralization. You will recognize the names of key members of both points of view. For the federalists we have the likes of James Madison, Alexander Hamilton, and John Jay. For the "antis" we have Samuel Adams, Patrick Henry, and George Mason. There was also the lesser-known but influential New York governor George Clinton, the attributed writer of *The Anti-Federalist Papers*, published in a New York newspaper.

The differences ran deeper than just pro- and anti-federalism. Within each group there were mini factions (the kind of division against which Madison warned in his contributions to the more widely known *Federalist Papers*). For example, Jefferson and Madison disagreed with Hamilton over the assumption of state debts by the feds and over other various economic issues. The men who came together to form a federal republic were divided themselves, some being more federalist and some being more "republican" (more states' rights oriented). Jefferson was more of a democracy proponent than was Madison. There was a big division, and then there were further significant divisions within those divisions.

While our purpose isn't to write a book on the founding of our country, it is extremely important for anyone looking at the conflict in today's America to understand that conflict within our country isn't new. Conflict has always been with us, even before we existed as a nation. The reason it is worth referring to our founding when discussing the power of coming together is that these were not just people who didn't agree on a few things sitting in a room to try to solve some single problem. These people were coming together to try to create a brand-new nation! Moreover, they not only didn't agree on a few things, they disagreed on a great number of things, many of which were highly significant.

Some of their disagreements didn't even exist when they started because the issues upon which they would come to disagree had never before been contemplated. They were creating new disagreements in the process of trying to resolve whatever one was in front of them in the moment.

Here is a very important question for you to ask yourself: If we were to try to form a new nation today, in our current environment with our addiction to conflict and chaos so pervasive, would we be able to come together and make it happen?

Our answer to that question is no, we could not. We have lost our ability to come together and resolve even the smallest of differences, let alone the kinds of major ones required to form a new nation. Those who fault our Founding Fathers for what are now clearly perceived imperfections in their design, the continuation of slavery chief among them, need to recognize just how fundamental and numerous were their many disagreements. Slavery was the most blatant example of something that needed to be changed, but what is lost in its criticism is that the Founding Fathers gave us a system that allowed for it to ultimately be changed. No United States? No end to slavery.

Our Founding Fathers understood the importance, the necessity, of coming together. While each of them had different ideas about what a new country could and should look like, they knew that they needed to engage in a constructive manner or nothing would get done. This needs to sink in. Are any of the things over which we are warring with each other today of anywhere near the significance of trying to form an entire new country? The question is rhetorical. Clearly, the answer is no.

We have been moving away from our ability to constructively come together to promote positive change for a long time, but there is no question that our deterioration as a people in this regard was greatly accelerated during the pandemic time and its associated lockdowns and policies of isolation. We all know the stories about the increases in addiction to substances, the rise in behavioral disorders, and the wave of suicides that corresponded with people being kept away from others and then being told to fear contact with others when they were around them. As bad as all those things are, there was another price that we are paying that hasn't been alleviated just because the end to the pandemic has been declared.

When the government ruled that we lock down, socially distance, and mask up, we got out of the habit of getting together. Now, some would argue that we got together more. We used the pandemic to start online video meets with people, some of whom we maybe had even lost track of over time. This seems to be a positive. In some sense, in terms of reconnecting, it certainly was. Something, however, was and is missing from those engagements that is both literal and metaphorical. Engagements on a computer or phone screen lack depth.

When we see someone on a screen, we are only able to see height and width. Depth is missing. Depth is not just an element of physical time and space; it is something spiritual we encounter when we are in the physical presence of another person. We are able to better grasp their essence—what's inside of them. We don't just get to see them in three dimensions, we get to look behind the curtain allowing us to read and feel them on an emotional level.

That look inside makes it harder to get into conflict with them. The engagement becomes more personal. We also can't just hit the "end" button for a conversation and sign off. If we really feel the urge to disengage when we are in person, we have to either physically get up and walk out of the room, or we have to order them to leave. These actions are uncomfortable to us, and they should be. A key tie that binds us together is actually being together.

During the pandemic, America got used to working from home. With the pandemic behind us, many people have adjusted to continuing to work from home. There are advantages, to be sure. Your refrigerator is close. The dog can be let out. You can take an afternoon nap if you don't have an appointment. These are pluses, but the minus is the loss of the forced and spontaneous collaboration that takes place in the office by having someone step into your doorway and ask, "Do you have a minute?"

Volunteers who work in traditional recovery programs will tell you that the online meetings that took place during the pandemic were only partly successful. They were attended, but not at the same level as are conventional in-person meetings. They also did not have the same kind of raw and open sharing commonly found in the actual physical rooms of recovery. Lots of reasons can be thought of for that. One problem is as simple as many people are camera shy and just don't feel comfortable sharing and being portrayed on screen by others. Whatever the reason(s), the meetings lacked some depth.

One of the unintended, but inevitable, consequences of isolation is that it breeds unrest. We have too much time to spend "in ourselves." We start to use our imaginations to conjure up all forms of thoughts—some good, some not so good. Sometimes we may even lean towards conspiratorial or slightly paranoid, sometimes simply dwelling on dark thoughts. Humans are naturally social creatures and, left only to ourselves, we can travel to bad places without ever leaving a chair. Not being social can make us antisocial. The pandemic operation led us down this path toward isolation. Once the lockdowns ended, many of these temporary bad behaviors had turned into permanent habits. Habits, as we know, are hard to break.

To the extent that we do still come together, we tend to come together with other people who agree with us. Again, social media has made this type of exclusive, like-minded association easier. Think of anything you feel passionate about, then go online and search for some kind of digital-based group that is centered around it. We guarantee you can find one. When you join the group, you will find yourself in an echo chamber that will spend much of its time taking shots at anyone who isn't in the group. Whether it is political issues based, or any affinity group whatsoever, you will find a place to comfortably share commonality and anonymously hate on others.

One of the key attributes and best parts of a traditional Twelve-Step meeting is that the groups are never homogenous, except to the extent that everyone shares an addiction. You will find yourself in rooms at the same time with people who range from millionaires to stay-at-home moms to blue-collar workers, to veterans. Some even might be homeless or living in care homes or halfway houses. What's more, don't be surprised when the millionaire is being sponsored (led through step work) by the factory floor worker. It happens all the time. Class disappears. Politics disappears. Religious distinctions disappear. Everyone just wants to stop their addiction.

It's similar to those who showed up at pubs and churches under cover of night, many of whom became known as our Founding Fathers, gathering together just wanting to form a new nation based on freedom and liberty. Just imagine what they accomplished despite serious differences. Imagine us trying to accomplish it today. You will have to imagine it because we are not there yet.

Many Americans today share the desire for our nation to come together. I am firmly convinced that We the People are the answer and we need to find the solutions. Unfortunately, many lack the initiative to pick up the phone, grab a coffee, or organize a community meetup to discuss our concerns. Instead, most people stay in their comfort zone to their own detriment, and increasingly people don't even know their neighbors let alone the officials in their communities making choices for their family and friends locally. The people you don't know may end up being your best partners on the journey to take back control of your surroundings, life, and future destiny.

For an addict the decision is often between, "Do I have a drink or call someone who is supportive and sober?" For many Americans today, the decision is, "Do I shut down and put my head in the sand or do I reach out to someone like-minded and supportive?" Or, unfortunately, it's becoming much more common to forget having a real conversation with a supportive friend and just hit social media to consume and spew hatred or vent frustration with anonymous avatars with whom we have no human connection. This is not how we grow our circle of influence, our fellowship of friendships, or a local community of patriots. In order to unite, We the People need in-person fellowship with diverse and accepted differences and ideas to truly live a textured, fulfilling existence to reach productive lasting outcomes. In-person meetings can change everything for the individual who walks through the door a stranger and leaves a welcomed new friend. We need more of that, much more.

That said, we need to choose to reach out, be brave, and be the one who sets the date, puts up the flyers, makes the calls, and takes the lead to start groups and meetups to facilitate community. We can't fear no one showing up or thinking we are crazy. We the People must build the bridges to fight for liberty and freedom together. We may make uncomfortable associations and then turn them into comfortable alliances. That is what our Founding Fathers did. Many of the ideas that launched our society emanated in the taverns of Philadelphia, such as Tun Tavern and City Tavern. Ben Franklin referred to the group as the "Secret Society of Social Drinkers." We aren't able to go back and listen in at those tables, but we can guess that they didn't agree on every point of every topic. It is certain they had some conflict and chaos during those discussions, but they stood bravely together, united under the promise of freedom or the threat of death.

They didn't, however, become addicted to conflict and chaos. Our existence today is proof. We are left to wonder what would America have looked like, would America have ever existed, if the Founding Fathers had tried to build it over Zoom?

The father of modern physics, Sir Isaac Newton, had as his second law of motion, $F=ma$. That means force equals mass times acceleration. Step Two is all about the m in the equation. Coming together creates mass. We need to come together as differing components of that mass so that the force we create is a constructive, not destructive one. The acceleration will need to come from constructive engagement, not further conflict and chaos.

Ready to work a Second Step? Here are some ideas to discuss and implement:

1. Start or join a local group or meet up with the cause of liberty and freedom as its focus.
2. Reach out to friends or family and express your concern for our nation and society and see how they feel. Listen.
3. Think about and start friendly conversations when appropriate about universally important issues that nearly everyone can agree on like ending war and preserving free speech.
4. Go to events and local meetings where decisions for your town or county are being made, even if you are alone, and sit in the back. See how the room looks and feels in person. Next time bring someone else.

5. Challenge yourself to interact casually with strangers in stores, restaurants, or the local gathering spots without an agenda—just casually being friendly and spreading openness and light rather than head down and only interacting when necessary. Smile and make eye contact whenever possible.

MISSION OVER EGO: RESTORING OUR FOUNDATION

WE DECIDED TO TURN OUR LIVES AND OUR WILL
OVER TO LIVING UP TO OUR FOUNDING PRINCIPLES,
THOSE THAT CAME FROM GOD'S GRACE AS WELL AS
THOSE THAT CAME FROM MAN'S WISDOM. WE SOUGHT
TO EDUCATE OURSELVES ON OUR FACTUAL HISTORY,
OUR CONSTITUTION, OUR FOUNDING DOCUMENTS,
AND OUR BILL OF RIGHTS, COMMITTING TO USING
THIS DEEPER KNOWLEDGE TO INFORM ALL OF OUR
AFFAIRS AND ACTIONS GOING FORWARD.

MISSION OVER EGO.

There is a phrase that is common in the rooms of recovery that instructs us to put "principles above personalities." The phrase is as simple as it sounds. Addicts are being warned to not get distracted by what they might think of any one individual in the room, but instead to focus on the principles that the program is trying to convey. If they can do that, then they can perhaps achieve their primary purpose, which is to get better.

In the context of this book and the attempt to try to work through and conquer our addiction to conflict and chaos, we are going to modify that phrase to suggest that in order to be in the process of recovery, you will need to put "principles above policies." This is not a program designed to figure out what to do about education, healthcare, welfare, or any other issue that creates division within America today. It is about restoring the principles of constructive engagement between people so that they can sit down and address policies together in a positive manner. We must remember that the mission is to save our country and not to debate policies. How do we save our country? I feel strongly that by bringing as many people as possible under the tent of nearly universal human principles of a good, just, and healthy society. Focus on the Ten Commandments and Golden Rule tenants versus the seven deadly sins that much of society seems to be drawn into in today's world.

With that noted, while we are not advocating policies, we are advocating a premise. That premise is that we want everyone in this country to be able to live a free life absent as many constraints and restraints on their individual behavior as possible in a society that needs to recognize that, left to live without rules, humans are inclined to sometimes do harm to other humans. Some restrictions are necessary, but we want every American to face as few of those as possible so long as they do not interfere with the rights and freedoms of others. Hence the Golden Rule as a principle and the Ten Commandments as guardrails.

That is what America's Founding Fathers wanted for us and that is what we are trying to help people restore through coming together and having positive engagements. Step Two gave as an example how our Founders, despite serious differences, were able to do exactly that. In Step Three, we need to understand what it is that they gave to us by coming together and from where their ideas originated. We can't preserve or restore something if we don't truly understand what it is that we are restoring. This is why we have included the Declaration of Independence, the Bill of Rights, and the Constitution in our appendix. These foundational documents as well as the biblical, moral structure of one nation under God are critical to understanding our founding principles that built and will restore the greatest nation on earth.

Before getting more specific about some of those ideas, a couple of more general points need to be made. The first is that the United States was the first, indeed only, nation ever created based upon a combination of ideas and empirical experience. It is commonly accepted that the Founders were all very familiar with the great ideas about governance and political theory that originated in Ancient Greece, especially with Plato and Aristotle, and continued through our Founders' time in the European Enlightenment. They were particularly influenced by one of the last consuls of Rome, Marcus Tullius Cicero (106–43 BC), the French philosopher Montesquieu (1689–1755 AD), the English jurist William Blackstone (1723–1780 AD), and, above all, by the early father of the Enlightenment, John Locke (1632–1704 AD, more on him shortly).

They were also very familiar with another famous English philosopher, the sort of "prince of darkness" about human nature, Thomas Hobbes (1588–1679 AD). It was Hobbes who took a very dim view of man's inner self and who felt that man's nature could only be controlled through the rule of a strong monarch. If the Founding Fathers were a computer, Hobbes's ideas were running in the background memory while their word processor was creating our founding documents.

These ideas allowed them to construct a nation not built on rules, but on a theory. That theory was that there was a way to structure a nation that allowed people to be free, while at the same time safeguarding them from themselves and their tendencies to exploit one another when given the opportunity—especially to exploit people from positions of power within government.

If theory was important to our Founders, then so were the actual results of the human experience over the past two thousand years, and especially their own recent experiences, and seeing what had been learned. They had witnessed firsthand the excesses of an unchecked monarch. They had examples of what happens when a nation's army is allowed to be used inside of its own borders to control citizens. They had scores of examples of the kinds of policies that led to revolts and civil war.

Much of what works and doesn't work in terms of nation building and maintenance has already been learned, experienced, and revealed. It was their job to try and make sense of it all, learn from mistakes made by others, and to do better.

The other important general point to keep in mind is that our Founding Fathers were greatly influenced by the idea of God. One of the things that can cause some people to turn away from the rooms of recovery is the focus of some fellowships on how turning to God is necessary in order to remove our weaknesses of character and make our lives manageable. For some, the "God thing" is simply too much and they abandon the program, leaving their fate in the hands of the very person who got them into trouble in the first place: themselves. The way I might look at the importance of God in this, for those for whom the concept is less clear, is as the concept of a higher purpose and power. A selflessness that occurs when you fully understand that that higher purpose and power ultimately serves you and all in the great ark of our own existence and humanity as a whole.

We said in chapter 3 we were not going to take on theology, and we are keeping that promise. We are not trying to tell you that in order to recover from our national addiction to conflict and chaos that you have to accept God. What we will say is this: if you want to embrace the ideas of liberty embedded in our founding, then you do have to accept that the idea that God or the belief in God played a major role and that a higher moral foundation and purpose is critical to creating societal harmony as best it can be achieved and maintained.

Our Founding Fathers came from a mixed bag of religious beliefs, from Christian to Deists (those who rationally deduce the likely existence of a God) to many variations on the personal belief and understanding of God. What is key is not their individual beliefs, but the fact that Judaism and Christianity had been impacting civilization for millennia before they ever came along. It would literally be impossible for men of European lineage to not construct a new nation that was not influenced by what we call Judeo-Christian values. Judeo-Christian values had been influencing every philosopher and every leader since the Roman Empire, even if they were in rebuttal to them.

Regardless of whether or not you feel God is a part of you, to be intellectually honest you have to acknowledge that the idea of His existence is a part of the collective us. Let's take an honest look at four key elements of our heritage for the purpose of understanding what our Founders had in mind and why we should all be able to unite around the principles while engaging in the process of creating policies.

FOUNDATIONAL IDEAS

As noted, the Founding Fathers were influenced by the ideas of the many great thinkers who had come before them and drew up their plans for a new nation by taking the ideas that they liked and leaving the rest behind (a great concept straight out of the rooms of recovery). Of all those ideas, none were more impactful than those of John Locke and his work *Second Treatise of Government*, published anonymously in 1690 (the *First Treatise* was an argument against absolute monarchical power).

The *Second Treatise* was Locke's vision of a just form of government in which the obligation of the state was to protect the life, liberty, and property rights of the citizens, rights that Locke referred to as "natural rights." In calling them natural rights, Locke was saying that these were rights that man held that existed objectively regardless of any form of government. This is also sometimes referred to as "natural law."

Natural law theory has its roots in Aristotle, who felt that man had rights that could logically be traced back to an "unmoved mover" who started all things. Aristotle's writings, like many others from ancient times, were lost to much of civilization for centuries before being rediscovered and translated into the original Greek in the thirteenth century. That was the same time period when the great scholar of the Catholic Church, Saint Thomas Aquinas (1225–1274 AD) began his writings. Aquinas adopted Aristotle's idea of an unmoved mover and replaced it with the Judeo-Christian God. He said that man's right to freedom came from there, and he used the term "natural law" as the descriptor.

Locke, a man of a sort of mixed religious background, secularized the work of Aquinas and applied natural law, or natural rights, to the idea of a just way to organize society. Locke felt so strongly about the limited role of government that he even condoned revolution in extreme cases should a government stray too far from its only legitimate function of preserving life, liberty, and property rights. To gauge the influence of Locke on our Founders one need look no further than our Declaration of Independence, which states that our unalienable rights are those of "life, liberty, and the pursuit of happiness," Thomas Jefferson's near direct lift from Locke.

Perhaps a close second to Locke in terms of influence was the previously mentioned Roman consul Cicero, who, like Aristotle, had his writings lost in history. For centuries. They were discovered in 1345 by the Italian scholar and poet Petrarch. Cicero is credited by many as posthumously launching the Renaissance because of the power of his works (to this day, Cicero's writings are used in classes that teach Latin language because of the brilliance of his prose).

The specific contribution of Cicero was that he wrote extensively about the proper structure for people to use if they wanted to establish a republic. Writing decades before even the birth of Christ, Cicero mapped out a system that looks almost identical to the one our Founders created with its separate branches and division of power. The Founders referenced Cicero frequently.

So it is the case that a man who had been dead for approximately 1,800 years, and another man who came from the country against which we fought a war of independence, were two of the primary contributors to what is now the United States of America. Neither could have envisioned it, but it proves the power of powerful ideas.

DECLARATION OF INDEPENDENCE

We celebrate July 4, 1776, as the birthday of our nation. Of course, it depends upon how you define "birthday." The first shots of the Revolution were fired in 1775 at the Battles of Lexington and Concord. Our Constitution was not created until 1787, ratified finally in 1788, and the first Congress convened in 1789. Perhaps we got betrothed to revolution in 1775, pregnant in 1776, and then, well, a long labor from 1787 to 1789?

Regardless, our Declaration as an independent sovereign nation, its structure, and its founding ideals, was a historic moment for Americans in particular, and possibly even more so for humanity in general. It was drafted as a sort of legal complaint, the kind found in a lawsuit. It listed twenty-seven separate grievances against the British Empire and monarch and as "damages" it demanded separation. Its structure and language were significantly influenced by yet another Englishman, William Blackstone (Blackstone's published works and teachings on common law also served as the standard within our legal system for more than a century after our founding).

The Declaration famously opens with the following:

> When in the Course of human events, it becomes necessary for one people to dissolve the political bands which have connected them with another, and to assume among the powers of the earth, the separate and equal station to which the Laws of Nature and of Nature's God entitle them, a decent respect to the opinions of mankind requires that they should declare the causes which impel them to the separation.

We hold these truths to be self-evident, that all men are created equal, that they are endowed by their Creator with certain unalienable Rights, that among these are Life, Liberty and the pursuit of Happiness.--That to secure these rights, Governments are instituted among Men, deriving their just powers from the consent of the governed…

You can see the influence of Locke and you can also see the influence of a belief in God. Anyone is free to dispute the propriety of the references, but it cannot be disputed that they are there in plain sight for all soon-to-be new Americans and the world (especially King George III) to see.

Also note the deliberate use of the term "unalienable" (inalienable in today's English). Something that is unalienable means by definition it cannot be given back by the possessor. In plain language, our Founders said that we are stuck with the rights to life, liberty, and the pursuit of happiness and we can't give those rights away even if we want to. That does not mean, however, that we can't have them taken from us if we don't remain vigilant.

THE CONSTITUTION OF THE UNITED STATES

In Step Two we learned that agreeing to a constitution for this new nation was anything but easy. Debates were robust, disagreements abundant, and vitriolic language, both on the floor of Independence Hall and in print, was common. Despite all of that, these brilliant, courageous, strongly opinionated men managed to come together to create the most extraordinary document ever written (excluding the Bible for simple reasons of avoiding distracting debate).

That document opened as follows:

> We the People of the United States, in Order
> to form a more perfect Union, establish Justice,
> insure domestic Tranquility, provide for the com-
> mon defense, promote the general Welfare, and
> secure the Blessings of Liberty to ourselves and
> our Posterity, do ordain and establish this Consti-
> tution for the United States of America.

The question we need to ask today as we find ourselves mired in conflict and chaos is this: Do any of us, regardless of our opinions on anything, disagree with the intentions of what our Founding Fathers said they were trying to do? If we don't disagree, then we should be trying to maintain what they started. We can't do that without doing what they did.

A common expression in recovery is that we can't give anyone else the results of our own recovery. We can, however, share our experience and hope that others can benefit from it. The Founders shared their experience with us. What will we take? What will we share? And what will we leave behind?

THE BILL OF RIGHTS (AND OTHER AMENDMENTS)

Many Americans are likely more familiar with the first ten amendments to the Constitution (Bill of Rights) than they are with the actual core document itself. While we have a total of twenty-seven amendments added (one to repeal a prior amendment, that of Prohibition) to the Constitution since inception, the first ten happened almost concurrently with its original adoption. Here is what you need to know about those first ten from the perspective of trying to cope with a conflict and chaos addiction.

The battle that took place to get the "basic" Constitution finished for submission to the thirteen colonies for approval didn't end when the document was finished. The anti-federalists, led by men like George Mason and Patrick Henry, felt that the Constitution didn't go far enough in limiting government. The federalists thought the job was done. Eventually it was agreed to compromise and send twelve amendments out to the states for ratification (yes, twelve, and before that number was reached it started at seventeen). Two of those didn't make it through the ratification process. Compromise was found layered in compromise wrapped in compromise.

Over ten thousand amendments have been proposed since 1789 with only a small number making the cut. What is key to remember is that every single amendment to the Constitution is fully part of the Constitution without any kind of subordination to prior existing text. That means that with regard to something like slavery, present at the beginning but made unconstitutional by the Thirteenth Amendment, it is fully part of who we are and is just as much a part of the Constitution as is the First Amendment. There are no "lesser" parts.

The key here is not to memorize our founding documents but to internalize the spirit, the ideas, and the context in which those documents were written. If you can get familiar with the ideas that developed over a two-thousand-year period, if you can appreciate the debates that took place between the Founders, if you can sense the intellectual and emotional stretches that had to be made in order to move beyond differences and create a brand-new nation, then you are ready to embrace their work product. After that, you can go ahead and memorize the documents if you like because what you are memorizing will make sense.

Finally, you will hear politicians and experts use the terms "republic" or "democracy" when describing our country. Sometimes the same person will use both terms but in two different sentences. So, what are we?

To be comprehensive and inclusive, think of us this way: We are a democratic (from Greek meaning "people rule"), federal (from Latin meaning treaty or alliance between independent states), representative (from Latin, show or display for others) republic (from Latin meaning the state or commonwealth). Simply said, we are a nation where people are supposed to be free to elect people to represent them and where the states in which they live also have the right to govern themselves and be represented at the national level.

We believe we are not any of those things anymore. We have surrendered our power by failing to understand our founding principles and instead have turned or, more appropriately stated, been turned on each other ravenously. While we are having at it with each other, a large handful of powerful and sinister people, both inside and outside our borders, have used our anger against us and have exploited an opportunity to take power. They have become a sort of international oligarchy, ruling elitists with their own interests in mind, not those of American citizens.

Why do we stand for it? Would our Founding Fathers have stood for it? In fact, they refused to stand for it! Gaining a better understanding of what they were thinking would be helpful in conquering our addiction to conflict and chaos.

Ready to work a Third Step? Here are some ideas for you or members of your group to discuss and implement:

1. Define your mission. What does it mean to you to save America?
2. Try to imagine what it would be like to lose our country and freedom to a global governance model rather than the constitutional republic we live in today. What are the

stakes we are facing individually and as a nation if that happens? Write them down.

3. Talk about each founding document. Understand key concepts and purpose, preferably with another person or even better, a group. Why was it written? Why is it important in the present? Is it being implemented and respected currently in America? If not, how?

4. What does the Golden Rule mean to you in terms of life, liberty and the pursuit of happiness?

5. Compare and contrast the ten commandments with the seven deadly sins (in appendix).

AN HONEST ASSESSMENT OF PERSONAL RESPONSIBILITY AND ACCOUNTABILITY

WE LOOKED INWARD AND MADE AN HONEST ASSESSMENT OF HOW OUR OWN INDIVIDUAL BEHAVIOR OR LACK OF PERSONAL RESPONSIBILITY HAS CONTRIBUTED TO THE SITUATION IN WHICH WE FIND OURSELVES AND OUR NATION.

HONEST ASSESSMENT OF ACCOUNTABILITY FOR PERSONAL BEHAVIOR.

n the rooms of recovery, the way that many addicts describe themselves is to say that they are "restless, irritable, and discontent by nature." Another related description that is often used is to say that the disease of addiction is really a function of "disease." Choose which you like best, both phrases make it clear that there is much more that is wrong in a person's life than the actual addiction. The condition is more than genetic tendencies and acquired dependency.

Likewise, with our current national addiction to conflict and chaos, far too many Americans are restless, irritable, and discontent. It is clear that if someone is in a state of dis-ease that they are going to be more likely to turn to a substance to help steady their nerves. They are also quite susceptible to triggers that draw them into feelings and behaviors that keep them in the dis-eased state.

Traditionally, addicts have been generally understood as those who excessively and compulsively abuse intoxicating substances or activities as an escape from some form of pain and suffering. While that remains true and all too common today, another avenue of escape has emerged: the addiction to conflict and chaos. This addiction leads many to partake in similar destructive feelings and behavior not the least of which is of irrational disdain for thy neighbor.

The question is: What has led us to develop that addiction and are we aware of what we are doing? Are we aware of our personal contribution to this problem? Just like the drug addict who has to take responsibility for their actions in order to overcome their problem, we have to take responsibility for our own behaviors that have divided our nation and made civil discourse so difficult. We are going to identify several different contributors causing Americans to use their new drug of choice, which is conflict and ensuing chaos. Before we do, however, you really do need to be ready to be brutally honest with yourself. We will help you do that by focusing on understanding the difference between intentions and actions.

Anyone who might have seen the classic 1995 movie *Leaving Las Vegas* is familiar with Nicolas Cage's character who just surrendered himself to the depths of his addiction, and for all intents and purposes drank himself to death willingly. In that case, his character married intentions to actions. While that happens in real life, it isn't normally the case.

Very few addicts intend to become addicts. In the case of alcoholics, it's not uncommon to hear someone say, "I really shouldn't drink but…" Or, "I don't have a problem, because I don't use every day." In both cases, you are seeing a form of denial. In the former case, you have someone denying their ability to make a change they have acknowledged they need to make. In the latter case, they are denying they have a problem at all. What do these polar opposites have in common? In both instances the person is expressing their knowledge that they do in fact have a problem but it's not that bad.

If both are addicts then they shouldn't use at all, but their actions are betraying their intentions. We are seeing that now in our behavior towards others. No matter where you go, no matter what issue you are addressing, no matter the position of the person you are addressing, you will almost always hear them say that they are not intolerant but that all sorts of other people are. If you ask an audience at speaking engagements to raise their hands if they think they are decent, ethical people, everyone always raises their hand. If you then ask them if there are people in the world who aren't decent and ethical, again, everyone raises their hand. How is it that nearly every room is filled with decent and ethical unicorns?

The point is this: very few people intend to be intolerant of others and create conflict. That said, nearly everyone acknowledges that we are living with an ever-increasing level of conflict and chaos in the public square. People's intentions must not be lining up with their actions. Ask yourself, are your intentions lining up with your actions, especially in light of your mission to help save our nation?

If you are willing to get honest, I mean really honest, with yourself, the answer to the above is likely a sort of sheepish, "Not always." That means you are behaving differently than you intend to, even while noticing or, more likely, being bombarded by that distasteful behavior in others. In traditional recovery programs, this is called a defect of character. It isn't acceptable, nor is it accurate, for any of us to say that we don't have any character weaknesses, but everybody else does. If we all said that, it would mean that nobody has these weaknesses of character, and, if that were true, we wouldn't be in the mess we are in and I wouldn't have even considered writing this book.

Let's take a look at some personal weaknesses of character that may have led us to become conflict and chaos addicts. These are not excuses. They are explanations.

We allowed ourselves to be swayed by the narrative and adopt a victim mentality: For decades within America there has been an increasingly aggressive narrative construct of oppression and victimhood of us or the other. We have been told, cajoled, or incented to identify as something and that something qualifies you as a victim. Whether you are oppressed or an oppressor, you are a victim in some way. There are many categories of identity, such as race, class, religion, education, gender, and the list is growing exponentially and getting sliced thinner and thinner. You name a characteristic of a person and the powers that be will find a way to identify it, corral its members, and define the nature of its victimhood status. This is a vicious cycle because victims seek justice and restitution to feel that they are being heard and being treated fairly.

The problem with a culture of victimization is that while most people naturally feel sympathetic toward those who truly have been oppressed or denied in some way, nobody feels sympathetic about being a victim. Victims are typically angry about their status. This very human trait is being used against us by those in power. It's an old tactic called divide and conquer. So if a certain person or group of people want more control or power they can gin up anger, conflict, and chaos within a populace. This tactic is well documented and there is no better way to do it than by making its members feel like they are victims. Victims of what? Doesn't matter. The people who are consciously trying to break apart our country, the ones we wrote about earlier in the book, know that if they can get people to feel this way then they can count on disruptive behavior from that point forward. In fact, that disruption has and can lead to overthrown governments, genocide, and societal ruin. These are the stakes we are fighting for. A chance at stability and harmony in society or ultimately anarchy, chaos, and enslavement. If this sounds a bit hyperbolic then you need to go back and review your history books. It has happened many times before and it is happening to us right now.

Allowing yourself to be cast in the role of a victim and then embodying that role is a defect of character and it says that you don't value yourself for who you are. You are not on a path to betterment. You are just a victim in need of redress for no fault of your own. It leads you to a path of resentment and anger because you can't take something to which you feel entitled from someone who has it, or worse, you do take it and conflict erupts. This purposefully and inevitably leads to massive and sometimes unrecoverable societal problems. The plan was executed, the results are unmistakable, and if taken too far, inevitable collapse occurs.

It is also important to note that if everybody is a victim, then there can be no real victims because the victims are being victimized by more victims. Until we see the true victimizers, the real enemies of We the People, we cannot find our bearings and fight back appropriately and with real positive results. The real enemies know this well and hide in the morass of victimhood, oppressors, and emotions as they push their agendas forward. This is why anyone who questions the narrative is called an aggressor, a racist, a misogynist, a climate denier, and so on. No one wants to be labeled as such and this keeps dissent in check. And until We the People figure out their game and learn to play it to win—not play into their hand to just get along—we will continue on this destructive path.

When we actually lose track of people who truly have been wronged in a society because everybody claims to have been victimized then there is no actual justice and justice is perverted in the truest sense of the word. One needs to just look at our actual justice system today and you can see perversions of justice everywhere. This perverted justice environment makes healing impossible and further leads to conflict, chaos, and ultimately destruction of societal fabric.

We believe we are morally superior: There is often a relationship between certain behaviors or feelings that can sometimes be found within our character weaknesses. Something that can happen when we feel we are a victim is that we can then automatically think that we are morally superior to the people we see as oppressors. Sometimes these two character weaknesses go together.

Not all the time, though. We don't need to feel like victims to feel morally superior. Going back to the show of hands exercise mentioned earlier, it seems that most people have a fairly high opinion of themselves and their own "goodness." That can easily translate into thinking that others who don't see things their way don't just disagree with you, they are morally inferior. This sort of attitude gets reinforced on social media where we tend to self-select our groups and thought leaders who can get very hostile, and very personal, when attacking people with whom they disagree.

We can also slip into this feeling of being morally superior if we learn that we are, or think we are, in the majority on an issue. A friend had an experience once while sitting on a jury in a criminal case where when the members took the original vote it was eight-to-four guilty. He noted that from that point forward the eight felt like there was nothing left to discuss. There were eight of them and only four of the others, so they were right and the others were wrong. You can guess the result: a mistrial followed a day later. Compromise is elusive when moral superiority clouds the goal of true justice for the greater good.

America's survival can't endure mistrials where we get to have new jury members to start over. We are stuck with each other in perpetuity and this issue must get resolved to save our nation. Ask yourself, when you find you are in the majority on some matter, do you really feel like you need to engage with someone from the minority constructively? Do you ever just find yourself getting angry and resentful of them because they aren't "smart enough" to see things your way?

Feeling morally superior breeds contempt for those who you feel just aren't as good as you. The question is: Are you really as good as you think you are? And, if you are, shouldn't you view that as a gift to be shared with others instead of treating them with hostility? Again, remember the mission of saving our country. Good leaders lead by example, build consensus, or drive to success any way they can to accomplish their particular mission. Failure is not an option and hope is not a strategy.

We allowed ourselves to sit idle while judging others: One of the advantages of technology and social media is that it's easy to sit in an easy chair and follow the news and pundit commentary. Whether that information is true or not is another topic, but there is certainly plenty of content to consume at our fingertips and plenty of opinions to be formed and espoused.

The problem is that many people are armchair quarterbacks or worse yet, just put their head in the sand and go along to get along. Much of their opinions comes from propaganda media, curated feeds, and watching the actions of others. They then sit back and critique them. "He should have done more." "She should have done less." "They are idiots for saying that." So it goes that they spend their days sitting in judgment, playing Solomon without his wisdom.

Modern technology, which ironically has increased our ability to get involved in a meaningful, constructive manner like never before in history, has led us to the point of becoming actively inactive. We spend an inordinate amount of time watching others do things instead of doing them ourselves, and then harshly judging them for what we see as missteps.

A great saying from scripture reads, "Judge not, that ye be not judged." (Matthew 7:1) The problem here is that in our chaos-and-conflict-addicted society, everybody is judging everybody else and rendering harsh criticism and an infinitely negative loop of judgment and inaction.

I know plenty of people who know all sorts of things about nearly everything. Many of them know a whole lot more than I know about any given topic. They have strong opinions to go along with all their knowledge. That is why I seek out many experts on my show and relish those that I can learn from. One thing I do focus on is experts who not only educate and inform but also focus on solutions and action. My friend Cathy O'Brien, who is a well-known CIA MK-Ultra whistleblower and trafficking survivor, always says don't voice a problem without also adding solutions and action steps. Ultimately the key to healing and progress is action.

The key to getting out of this mindset and actually understanding the world and the challenges we face is to be engaged, activated, and working to solve the issues you care about. Getting active is an antidote to frustration and anger. Don't do nothing.

We allowed ourselves to lose personal contact: While this process had been well underway prior to the pandemic operation, there is no question that the government and institutionally forced COVID-era lockdowns, social distancing mandate, and the work-from-home nonsense was a massive acceleration in the march toward personal isolation. Not only were people forced to cease nearly all in-person societal interpersonal engagement, but we were driven by the government and the media to fear each other and the physical world in general.

Now, since the lockdown pause, which one should view as a normalization phase of societal control mechanics, hotels, stadiums, and restaurants—the ones that survived—are once again crowded with people back in public places and everything looks to be normal. The thing that you have to think about is this: Is being surrounded by people the same as being engaged with people? Have you ever been in a crowded room and felt entirely alone? Everyone has. The fact is that the government used the COVID to force people to isolate themselves physically, and when their doors opened back up again many people were still isolating if not physically than emotionally. The new normal they promised is a newfound sense of being surrounded by the other. People watch what they say, where they are physically, and are easily distracted by unexpected stimuli. The new normal is not normal at all. We are being herded literally and figuratively into a contrived prison state and we don't even see it. The security and trust of our sur-roundings, and those surrounding us, seems very different in their new normal to many people we meet.

We can retreat to a literal cave or to a metaphorical one just as easily, as many of us felt we had during the COVID lockdown. Our own homes became part of an imposed new normal in many ways as well. Losing interpersonal and meaningful physical engagement with others has heightened our lack of connection to our respective souls, our inner voice of wisdom, understanding, and discernment. That doesn't go away with a repeal of an emergency order or a tem-porary all clear from the Great Reset orchestrators and their enforc-ers. The retreat into ourselves makes us vulnerable to the many other negative forces outlined in this book. This isolation opens a gateway to other transgressions which, in turn, lead us down the path toward heightened conflict and chaos addiction.

> "What prepares men for totalitarian domina-tion in the non-totalitarian world is the fact that loneliness, once a borderline experience usually suffered in certain marginal social conditions like old age, has become an everyday experience of the ever-growing masses of our century."
>
> Hannah Arendt, *The Origins of Totalitarianism*, 1951

In this isolation, many of us were led by propaganda media into narratives without personally seeking and finding the truth. Many of us got lost in fear and confusion, and have abandoned our gut instincts and critical-thinking skills.

During this time of mass societal propaganda, manufactured fear, and confusion, the concepts of misinformation, disinformation, and malinformation have been introduced by the powers that be to dissuade the masses from believing what they see, hear, and learn. This psychological war tactic is a critical tool for narrative control to hide the true nature of what is happening all around us. They want to keep us frogs in our slowly heating cauldron so we don't notice that we are being cooked.

Labeling information sources as misinformation, disinformation, malinformation, or conspiracy theory purveyors blunts their effectiveness, creates division, breeds mistrust, and is a time-tested tool of totalitarian control against the masses. The war on truth is real and it is up to We the People to arm ourselves with truth and facts, which are the greatest inoculation against propaganda manipulation and control. There's a reason that the "ministry of truth" type operation has been rolled out so pervasively in this heated narrative battle for our minds.

You should all be aware that the term conspiracy theory was developed and weaponized by our CIA to be a pejorative or insult when anyone questioned the JFK assassination *Warren Report* findings, then the 9/11 commission findings, or even Barack Obama's origin story and background. All these narrative control trigger words are used to discredit or malign the information source and are tools of the oligarchy and media to silence the questioning of their chosen narrative. When the public begins to look at a government narrative with skepticism and reasonable people suspect a cover-up, the media and government propaganda machine goes into overdrive to discredit the source, destroy its reach, or censor their voice completely, sometimes going so far as eliminating the source, all in the name of protecting the people. What I believe is that this censorship-industrial complex is in fact simply protecting the institutions of power and the individuals doing nefarious things in the cloak of darkness to protect and advance their agenda. It is far beyond the scope of this work to talk about all the true or questionable conspiracies that are circulating today, but it is fair to say that over time we come to learn that many of these conspiracy theories turn out to be facts and truth—that timeframe is compressing as We the People wake up to the lies we have been fed. We do, however, want to focus on how these ideas and inquiries, whether true or far-fetched, are being used to feed and stoke our addiction to conflict and chaos.

We all need to hone our critical-thinking skills and our internal moral and ethical compass to survive this information war.

Pick your favorite conspiracy and deconstruct it. You will find all sorts of data or information, scattered about the internet media or in conversations, all of which seem to point in a certain direction. We then take all of that information and say that it must mean this. We then call this a theory. It is not. It is a hypothesis. It is an assumption we made using inductive logic (creating the general from many specifics).

Everyone ought to remember from high school science that once you have a hypothesis you have to test it. That's the scientific method. The problem with most conspiracy hypotheses is that they are difficult to test. That doesn't mean they are wrong; it just means it's difficult to prove them. Often, when you get to the deepest place of connecting the dots, you find information missing, intentionally hidden, or classified for "reasons of national security" or some other term used by the government to say it's none of the public's business or nothing to see here. That itself leads to more speculation, and thus more conspiracy hypotheses are formed. See how that works? This is part of the mass media psychological warfare operation to sow confusion, fear, and doubt, and to discredit truth.

We have all lost friends over our failure to accept someone's hypothesis as being true these last several years. When totally locked in to a belief for survival, some people become too attached to even entertain that they may be wrong or could have received faulty information. If maybe we presented ideas to others as possibilities, instead of definitive truths unable to be proven but worthy of being considered, the process would be far more constructive. Instead, we are presenting inferences as absolutes, and they become just another way for us to generate conflict. Posing questions as opposed to statements of facts has diffused many conflicts, and forces critical thinking and constructive dialogue in most cases. Demanding someone adhere to your ideas ends the possibility of constructive examination before it begins.

Going back to antiquity, the four cardinal virtues were known to be fortitude (or courage), temperance (or moderation), justice, and prudence (or wisdom). Think about your own behavior over the past however many years. How virtuous have you been under the simple terms noted above?

On the other hand, consider the seven deadly sins (think of them in a secular sense if more comfortable), which we seem to be elevating and celebrating as a culture today. Pride, greed, wrath, lust, envy, gluttony, and sloth. These are behaviors that contribute to the kinds of character weaknesses noted above. The ancients were on to something.

We owe it to ourselves first, and to our neighbors a close second, to try to become more virtuous. We need to look at our own personal behaviors that might fall into the categories identified here in Step Four and be honest about which ones are ours. We need to take ownership that we are part of the problem before we can become part of the solution.

Ready to work a Fourth Step? Here are some ideas for you or members of your group to discuss and implement:

1. Test your opinions with research. Try to not only look for sources you go to regularly, but look at opposing narratives, additional sources, or links in the bibliographies of the research, and discount that which cannot be proven. Learn to use critical thinking to discern for yourself, then eliminate that which is not provably true and factual without doubt. Only stand firm in that which you personally researched and your own subsequent conclusion.

2. Think of a friend or two you lost touch with over the last few years because of differences in politics or ideology or in the handling of COVID, climate, or election. Is it time to reach out or check in if the relationship was important to see what can be reconciled? Many people have had an earth-shattering experience the last several years totally unique to them, and are just starting to have the fog lift while facing new realities or consequences. You may be surprised. Many lost relationships are not really lost, just no one reached out so far. Do that.

3. What is something you changed your mind on recently that you believed for years or even decades and now know to be false. How did the lie affect you? How about the truth?

4. If you feel a victim in some way, define what exactly makes you feel that way? How does believing you are a victim help you become less victimized? Does defining yourself as a victim harm you in any way? Put yourself in someone else's shoes who you know who believes they are a victim.

Does their belief help and/or harm them in any way? Is your or other people's belief that they are a victim the real problem? Who would you or they be if they weren't caught up on the ideas and resentment associated with identifying as a victim?

IDENTIFYING THE ROOT CAUSE OF OUR PROBLEM

WE SHARED IN BOTH PRIVATE CONVERSATIONS AND IN PUBLIC FORUMS THE EXACT NATURE OF THE PROBLEMS THAT PLAGUE OUR NATION TODAY, AND WE DID SO CLEARLY AND PRECISELY, WITHOUT BLAME OR BIAS, AS AN INDIVIDUAL CITIZEN NOT A MEMBER OF A COLLECTIVE.

SHOW UP, STAND UP, AND SPEAK UP.

What are some of the real root causes of this dis-ease of addiction to conflict and chaos from which we suffer? Many will likely have their own particular ideas about what is behind our division. Given how dynamic societal movements are, and given the complexities of living in a country with 330 million people, there is going to be at least some truth in every explanation that is offered as to why we fight. The challenge for us is how to narrow it down and give the recovering American citizen specific and useful tools towards our desired outcomes.

We are going to try to focus on some big, but specific, categories and then rely on the people who enter the rooms of societal recovery to further thin slice those categories in order to effect change in their own particular groups or communities.

CENTRALIZATION OF POWER

In 1789, the First Congress of the United States authorized three executive departments: Foreign Affairs (which became the State Department), Treasury, and War. It also authorized an attorney general and a postmaster general. In 2024, the year in which these Steps are being written, there are some 438 agencies and sub-agencies in the federal government. You cannot have this kind of growth in size and scope without some corresponding increase in the power and control that the people within those 438 entities have over your daily life. The Federal Register (the "book" that contains all federal government regulations) continues to grow its many tens of thousands of pages and adds anywhere from 3,000–4,500 final new rules each year! We have so many rules that unless you remain locked in your house each day with the power turned off you run the risk of violating something just in the course of following your everyday routine.

We learned earlier that our Founding Fathers had disagreements over many things, one of which was how much power should rest in the hands of the federal government. While those discussions were serious and with clear differences, there can be little doubt that if Hamilton and Jefferson were alive today, both would agree that adding three-thousand-plus new rules every year at the federal level would be unbelievable, outrageous, and, in their eyes, unacceptable.

Centralization of power in America is not confined to the growth in the federal government and its thousands of rules.

Everywhere Americans look, power has been, and continues to be, consolidated. State governments have exerted more control over counties (or parishes) and large corporations have gotten larger as industries "scale" and one business gets swallowed up by another, even larger, competitor. Everything has gotten bigger. America has super-sized power, influence, and control, and consolidated it into the hands of fewer, larger entities. This institutionalization of control is a cancer that must be reversed.

Is "bigness" badness? Not per se, but in this case, the centralization of power that has occurred in America over the course of several generations, and at an increasing rate in recent times, has clearly had a causative impact on our addiction to conflict and chaos. Here is why: when we are confronted with something very large and very powerful it creates a feeling of helplessness and hopelessness when it comes to dealing with whatever "it" is for any purpose. Have you ever had to deal with a problem with the Social Security Administration? How about with your state's Department of Motor Vehicles? Have you had to try to get your airfare refunded lately for a trip you couldn't take? If any of those experiences have felt frustrating and hopeless, you can always do something easy like getting a large bank to reverse an erroneous service charge to your account. Ha ha, yeah right. Now with the trend of virtual AI support it is getting progressively more difficult and dehumanizing to interact with any business or institution.

When power is centralized instead of being dispersed it becomes easier for that power to be wielded arbitrarily, abusively, and without conscience. This is what everyday Americans are encountering now in almost every facet of their daily lives. Reasonable and rational questions as to why something is a certain way are met with answers like, "Because it's our policy," or, "It doesn't matter if it doesn't make sense to you. It's the law." Even worse is no person at all but some artificial intelligence or some programmed machine telling you to "press one for yes or hang up."

Those kinds of answers lead to frustration which, in turn, develops into anger. The problem that gets created with regard to becoming addicted to conflict and chaos is that while you can get angry with Social Security for denying your claim, or you can become outraged at a bank for not reversing your fifty-dollar fee, you can't actually express anger toward an agency, a business, or a machine. You can only express anger toward another living, breathing human being. Much like an old, overworked engine releasing steam, our frustration with centralization and automation has led us to release our anger by lashing out at those around us because we lack a reasonable avenue to air our grievances and no one cares or listens. We get frustrated a lot. We release it a lot. We have turned it into a habit. We call it addiction. When every one of our daily interactions is depersonalized and automated through immutable policies or, worse, artificial intelligence built on inane rules, this breeds massive anger.

LACK OF ACCOUNTABILITY

A derivative of centralized power, but still its own separate cause of frustration, is a lack of accountability, both in others and in ourselves.

Think of how any time we see something happen that is tragic and outside of an act of nature (although, increasingly we are doing this with those kinds of events, too) we can hear ourselves saying, "Somebody needs to be held accountable." Human nature seems to have us needing to have somebody blamed or punished for things that go badly. Perhaps this stems from the previously identified classic virtue of justice. We need things that seem to be unfair to be answered for by someone.

This can be, and often is, taken too far in the sense that sometimes s*#t just happens and there really isn't anyone to blame. That said, in cases where some sort of perceived wrong has been committed, we do naturally search for someone to hold accountable.

In our country where large and impersonal systems have evolved, where power has been centralized into very large entities, it has become very difficult to find anyone who is accountable for anything for whatever has happened. As a corollary, it has become increasingly easier to hide our own accountability when we are buried deep within those large systems. After all, the person who feels like they have been the victim today might well become the victimizer tomorrow simply within the context of "just doing their job." I speak often on my show and in speeches about one of my favorite authors, Hannah Arendt, who wrote about the banality of evil of the Nazi soldiers just doing their jobs. The abdication of responsibility for doing evil because it was your job as a cog in the wheel of some institution or government can longer fly. It is evil on top of evil and accountability must be demanded.

A phrase that has become as common as, "Some weather we're having," is, "Hey, it isn't my fault." We live in a country where saying that we are "just following orders," or, "It isn't my decision," have almost become axioms. When you are frustrated with something, it is difficult to find someone who will take responsibility, and when you are being called out for something that has happened, it is easy to deny responsibility.

But our nature demands accountability! We can't escape it. When we can't find it, we get angry. When we shrink from it ourselves, we make others angry. When we recognize it in ourselves, hopefully we feel shame and guilt, but alas in today's immoral winner-takes-all world, we are losing that moral compass as well. Everyone says that something is someone else's fault, or that it is their agency's fault, or their company's fault. We crave someone saying, "It's my fault." This lack of accountability in our society has left us simultaneously trying to desperately assign responsibility while running away from responsibility ourselves. From this, the natural progression to conflict and chaos is easy to understand.

MAINSTREAM MEDIA AND "ANTI" SOCIAL MEDIA

Social media's impact gets a mention in virtually every one of our Twelve Steps. I feel that it is not only something that has facilitated and deepened our addiction, but it is clearly causative and it's not an accident. The people who own and run the various platforms know full well that there is money to be made by instigating hatred. Hatred creates intensity and intensity creates what they euphemistically call "engagement" on social media platforms. That engagement then begets traffic and traffic begets advertising revenue.

The people that run these platforms make money from us hating one another. They are the dealers and they have us hooked. But who are the suppliers? It is not hard to trace nearly all the major social media platforms to some form of government development funding. It is my firm belief that the powers that be created these platforms to not only make money off taxpayer-funded development, but also to use for data collection, propaganda proliferation, psychological manipulation, and control, as well as to sow division among the masses. It is social engineering at a global scale. It's also interesting to note that the dealers have amassed immense wealth and power and regularly cycle in and out of government and other supplier power circles. This is a very dark and deep rabbit hole but it's important to understand the scale and scope of the manipulation that feeds our addictions.

We talked early on about how my work has shown me that we are being herded towards neural pathing to crave conflict and chaos. Social media is likely the leading path-blazer for such brain activity. It makes it literally physically comfortable to sit on your bed, place an ergonomic pillow behind your head and neck, and just consume and share hateful thoughts. In the good old days, you had to put on a coat, hop in your car, and drive somewhere to argue with someone in person. That was a lot of work. Not anymore. Social media is an all-inclusive resort for exchanging insults, often anonymously, which is an entirely new level of perversion of human interaction.

So many lines within this program are devoted to social media that it is not necessary to devote more within this section. Suffice to say a major part of a successful American recovery is going to have to involve each and every person re-examining their own personal use of social media platforms and being willing to push back against those who create and control those platforms in an effort to defeat their deliberate attempt to manipulate, divide, and control We the People.

CHINA (CCP)

The nation of China or, more correctly stated, the Chinese Communist Party should be viewed as a mighty adversary and possibly a clear and present danger to the free people of our country and all people of the free world. To what extent is debatable, but the CCP does openly state their objective of replacing the United States as the main world superpower, and much of the globalist-controlled organizations and multinational corporations and banking institution seem to be just fine with that. In fact, many of the self-anointed elitists, from Rockefeller to Kissinger to Bill Gates and Eric Schmidt to Larry Fink of Blackrock and Klaus Schwab, his fellow board member at the WEF, all espouse that the CCP has the most effective and efficiently run society on the planet. Full totalitarianism and track-and-trace surveillance with zero freedom, but these American educated billionaire oligarchs openly praise their handling of their citizenry. They are seemingly aligned at the very top with the global public-private partnership and multinational corporations beyond what most people realize as well.

Make no mistake, The CCP are a main power player in the war to control humanity and, make no mistake, they are cunning, organized, and have a stated plan for world domination. They have also, basically unchallenged, succeeded in significantly building out their Belt and Road Initiative, which serves as both their control mechanism of many international supply chains' routes and resources, as well as the key to their strategic military plan for worldwide domination. The CCP has also been able to lead the BRICS nations' move away from the West, while courting many nations to lean more and more towards the Chinese currency, the yuan, as the dominant world currency for trade.

Napoleon has been attributed as having said variations of the following: "Let China sleep, for when she wakes, she will shake the world." Whether it was Napoleon or not, since President Richard Nixon opened the blinds on the America-China trading floor, the sun has shone brightly on this nation of 1.4 billion people and they are definitely wide awake…and adventurous. The CCP and its reach must not be understated.

For starters, China is not, strictly speaking, a communist country despite it being referred to as such by the entire world and even its own governing party. There is nothing about China that Karl Marx would recognize were he to come back to life today and see it. China calls itself a communist country, because, thanks to Marx, the concept of communism still has some utopic cache among world academics and elitists, as well as among young people. China is a fascist country, a term with no positive spins left on its board. It features a strong centralized government, large, siloed industries, and its academia joined together to accomplish a single mission: to weave itself so thoroughly, from every possible angle, through the Western economic fabric so that every Western nation comes to depend upon it and cannot sustain their lifestyles and systems without it.

Once they accomplish that mission, the West will no longer be able to live without them. When that happens, China controls them, and when that happens, China wins.

The single greatest impediment to China reaching their goal of world domination is the United States of America. In the free world, the United States is the economic and military powerhouse. Economically, they are better able (although less so with each passing year) to work around Chinese dependence, while militarily, they are an adversary so capable that an actual war could likely lead to the annihilation of the planet.

How then does China take down its primary adversary? The answer is simple: they let us take it down ourselves, through infiltration and manipulation from the inside by creating so much conflict and chaos among the American populace that we rot to our core from the inside out until the outer layer, our national structure, systems, and ultimately our sovereignty collapses.

In a 1984 interview, KGB defector Yuri Bezmenov described the four stages of subversion through psychological warfare used by the Soviet Union to try to take down America. Those four stages were:

1. Demoralization, which would take an estimated fifteen to twenty years to execute and uses the educational system as its foundation.

2. Destabilization by attacking the essential structure elements of the nation such as the economy, foreign relations, and defense systems.
3. Crisis, which can be used over and over and can happen quickly once the first two stages are complete and leads to a planned or organic violent overthrow of structural elements.
4. Normalization, where everyone settles into a "new normal" that bends to the wishes of the enemy.

Have you heard the term "the new normal" lately, or "reimagining" this or that? They are planting these linguistic seeds so that the new normal seems common and expected and that predictive linguistic programming attenuates resistance because we expected it and well, now it's here. These tools can be repeated and recycled until the goals are reached and we are well down that road.

The Soviet Union did a lot of damage to the United States during the Cold War, but the old Soviet Union ended over thirty years ago. China continues, and China, along with the globalists, has adopted the tactics of the Soviets and they have been much more effective. My research has helped me to understand that the USSR and the CCP are likely the front groups implementing the globalist agendas for the power players that have been planning global domination for a very long time. Whether it's the Nazis, the USSR, the CCP, the US government, or the tech giants, the tactics, goals, and damages to a populace seem eerily similar. You can decide for yourself where we are in Bezmenov's cycle, but that the Chinese are using the same model now is not really up for debate. If you watch my show, you will learn how broad and deep the CCP infiltration is in our nation and that their stated goal of global domination is well documented.

Why is China doing better at doing damage? The answer is easy. Everyone knew the Soviet Union was our enemy and we had no meaningful ties with them economically. China, however, has been allowed to make us a very dependent trade partner and they have deluded Americans, especially American businesspeople, that they are really just like us and only want to do business. A close friend has spent decades working with American companies doing business with the Chinese. He has seen this delusional denial surface repeatedly. How have we as a country allowed nearly all our manufacturing and critical supply chains to be nearly totally dependent on China? Much of our computers, microchips, drugs, and pharmaceuticals, among other critical assets, depend on China. How is that not a national security concern? We as a country have been sold out by our leaders to the highest bidders and China has a big checkbook.

It was the Soviet Union's founder, Vladimir Lenin, who said, "The capitalists will sell us the rope with which we will hang them." In the case of China, we have designed the rope, shared the design; they have manufactured the rope off-brand, and we have been purchasing it cheaply for decades and fitting it around our own necks.

Meanwhile, they sow seeds of dependence and division. Whether it is through their presence on college campuses, use of their TikTok platform, investments in American companies, use of American mainstream media, or a myriad of other ways, the Chinese are making shocking inroads in destroying our country and it's hidden in plain sight. They are currently a chief architect and implementer of much of the strife in our country and we don't even realize it. Worse than that, we are buying it like candy!

DEPENDENCY

Today in America too many of us have allowed ourselves to slip into varying levels of dependency. We all lived through COVID and the unemployment-palooza and stimulus checks into our accounts that led many people to give up old goals and ambition and become dependent on the government though never before would we have even considered it. It presented itself, and even with the dystopian threat of universal basic income for all looming, many, many people figured why not? Many are still unable to go back to being free and productive without dependence on the government check, which inevitably is limiting to one's own liberty and fulfilling one's potential and has many strings attached. Once the government has total hold over your ability to buy food or house your family, life becomes very different from what could have or would have been if you were forced to rely on yourself. Relying first upon ourselves has been replaced to a large extent with reliance first upon others or worse, our government. Just like with social media and its ravaging effects, this is not entirely our fault.

Generations of leaders in America have purposefully tried to make us become dependent. It is a natural extension of dependency to become easily controlled by those upon whom you are dependent. Tyrants, dictators, and totalitarians—often under the guise of helping people—offer universal basic income or communism flat out, but this never does nor has it ever in history proven beneficial or to be a solution for free people who crave purpose and want to see their full potential. It's a trap. Always has been and always will be. The goal of temporary help, or a hand up, should always be short term in a healthy, thriving free society. As Ronald Reagan said, "We should measure welfare programs' success on how many people leave it, not how many people are added. Welfare's purpose should be to eliminate, as far as possible, the need for it in the first place."

Nobody likes being controlled. When you are controlled, you have an awareness of it that is either conscious or subconscious. That leads to resentment and that leads to anger and a tendency, that can easily turn into habit, to quickly lash out at others. The others don't have to be anyone associated with your dependency. Again, like that overburdened engine, you are letting off steam.

Centralization of power, lack of accountability, "un" social media, China, dependency, and other factors are all ills from which we suffer in today's America. There are no easy cures for these societal afflictions, but there is treatment for them, and the primary combatant is awareness. These five forces are at work in all of our lives, some directly and some through others. Be aware. Be vigilant.

———

Ready to work a Fifth Step? Here are some ideas for you or members of your group to discuss and implement:

1. Centralization: Think about how you allocate your time, money, and vote towards liberty and freedom. Make every effort to support decentralized players and small, self-supporting businesses. Step out of the control matrix everywhere and anywhere you can.
2. Accountability: When looking at problems in your life or our nation, first look at the systems but then focus on the individual or individuals who are actually causing the problems. Are there key players harming the bigger group or organization? It's very difficult to apply blame and

accountability to an institution or system. Look to the actual people creating the problems and exactly what they are doing or not doing that makes them responsible.

3. Media: Evaluate your media and social media consumption. Unplug from these systems often, and set limits on your usage. Do more in person and in nature on purpose. When you're disconnected for a period of time, consider what lingers from the information you've consumed and why. Is it something you feel passionately about when removed from the screen or only in the moment? Is it propaganda being used to sway your thinking or behavior? Learn to decipher patterns and triggers used to manipulate you. Propaganda doesn't work if you recognize it.

4. Recognize that there are significant geopolitical malevolent forces in the world that seek to repress and control you as well as disrupt or harm our nation. Be aware and vigilant of these forces, and do your best to protect your family and community by pointing out these forces when appropriate and explaining their agendas and why we must be aware of them.

5. Dependency: It's normal and OK to need support or help, but it's very destructive to be dependent or codependent with other people or with the government. Work to be independent in every element of your life as best you can, and avoid the big systems of control in favor of personal sovereignty. We all need a hand up from time to time, but realize the more you take from anything or anyone that can control your behavior the more freedom and personal liberty you give away.

BELIEFS, KNOWLEDGE, TRIGGERS, FEAR, AND ACTION

WE TOOK THE STEPS NECESSARY TO BECOME REAL
AGENTS OF CHANGE AND PUT OUR WORDS INTO ACTION
IN OUR SPHERE OF INFLUENCE AND BEYOND.

KNOWLEDGE, UNDERSTANDING, COURAGE, ACTION.

What you need to know going in is that if you want to be a real agent of change, you are going to need to get comfortable with being uncomfortable. If addicts have an advantage over We the People working to restore our union, it is that addicts are trying to change their own personal behavior and right their lives in a society one might view as not as sick as the individual. They are the masters of their own successful recovery process. In our case here in American society, we individually not only seek to change ourselves to heal ourselves, but our broader overriding mission is to heal society as a whole by helping to impact the behavior of others. That is an entirely different endeavor. It's less about a specific behavior and more about finding common ground and harmony creating a virtuous cycle of healing and unity among We the People.

It seems strange to use a warring metaphor in a program that is designed to get people to reduce their level of conflict and chaos, but you are going to need to don your battle dress, consider your strategy and tactics, and get yourself ready to engage an enemy. You just need to remember that the enemy isn't other people, the enemy is the implanted demon inside them. The psychological manipulation and programming that led them astray resides in actual people and somehow we must reach as many as we can to save ourselves. In all cases, the goal is to save the host so we can dismantle the war machines and save ourselves.

Here is a five-part process to work through so that you can become a real agent of change:

Know what you believe: In America today, the media and academia have created an environment where people are encouraged to see extremes and label oppositional voices or with whom we don't agree as being either "far right extremists" or "far left loons." The right and left labels get tossed around so arbitrarily that no two people even have the same definition as to what they mean.

What the powers that be want us to believe is that in America today we have "team right" and "team left." Our two-party political system has been usurped by the globalists' uniparty of power and they have obfuscated that agenda and actively promoted a divisive form of two competitive units, each with different "platoons" that take the field against each other.

People tend to end up on one political team or the other based upon the messaging of the team they perceive is most important to them. As an example, someone who feels very strongly about a woman's right to choose "my body my choice" will tend to end up on team left. Someone who really cares about protecting all pre-born life will likely end up on team right. This is why the messaging and propaganda of specific issues is so important and powerful and why these divisive issues are used so aggressively and skillfully.

Once you end up on a team, you look to see who else is on that team and what the different platoons are about. If you want to be accepted by those around you, those on your team, what do you naturally do? You support your teammates! What this leads to is a reality in which all kinds of people are supporting all kinds of ideas and positions with which they might have quite limited, if any, knowledge. There is a literal sort of mindlessness to the positions they take. They become fans in the political stands, faces painted, jerseys ill-fitting, screaming at the top of their lungs, "Let's go blue" or "Let's go red."

We have become accustomed to supporting different ideas or positions with which we are not truly familiar. Do that often enough, do that with enough intensity and emotion, and you can very easily become unable to draw a distinction between what you truly believe versus what you have simply allowed yourself to be led to believe. Most people don't even realize that they are being propagandized and manipulated to choose a side and that the powers that be use this division to accumulate power, control, and money. This is why it's so important to know history, research for yourself to find the truth, and come up with your own beliefs honestly and without emotion so that you have a better sense of the truth and facts and a better sense of your own true beliefs.

Awareness of your own personally held beliefs is vital in becoming an agent of change. It isn't about forcing those beliefs onto others as that will just drive us deeper into our conflict addiction. What is important is when you understand the truth and honestly formulate the things that really matter to you, you will be better equipped to help others. You will be stronger in your stance and ability to articulate your beliefs and your authenticity will shine through as you break down barriers and bring more harmony to our country and world. Of course it is vitally important to begin with large, uncomplicated issues that nearly all can agree on like our Founders did with life, liberty, and the pursuit of happiness.

Think about how often in your life you have realized that you are getting "sucked into" something where you wake up one day and wonder how you ever let yourself get mixed up in it in the first place. This is what is happening today all across America as people are just blindly getting sucked into the beliefs and ideas of others because they are trying to be good teammates.

We the People need a team America, not team right or team left and certainly not team globalists. Know your beliefs so you can help get everyone on that team instead of the one they are on today. If we can make that happen, we won't need any teams anymore!

Know what you know: facts matter!

Facts are interesting and nettlesome things. Listening to others argue, you will be struck by some of the references and idiomatic phrases that are used regarding facts:

> "You have your facts, I have mine."
> "That's not what the facts are."
> "Those are lies, damned lies, and statistics."
> "They've done research that says..."
> "The plain, simple fact of the matter is..."
> "Look, facts are facts."

Facts are pesky. They get in the way of someone being able to quickly advance the correctness of their side. The issues presented by facts that make them so troubling are:

- You don't usually know how many there are.
- You don't know where to find all of them.
- It is time consuming to pursue them.
- They may not help support your opinion of the issue when understood.
- You aren't certain if you can trust them when you find them.

The one known element about facts in any situation is that there is a finite number of them. They exist objectively. There might be ten or there might be a thousand, regardless, there is a sum of certain facts.

Now imagine two well-intentioned participants with differing opinions regarding a particular event. They set a time in two days to discuss their issue and they want to be fully informed before the discussion begins so they can have a fact-based conversation. So they both set out on their own individual quest for facts.

Over the next two days, both of them will learn different things. Assuming that they are unfailingly able to uncover only true facts and are not fooled by "noise," when they sit down together for their showdown, the likely scenario regarding the two of them and the facts is that:

- Each of them found facts the other didn't find.
- They both found some of the same facts.
- Some facts remained undiscovered by both of them.

If our two participants are able to sit down and stick only to the facts, there is both good news and bad news. The good news is that they will be able to take what they have learned separately from each other, share it, and then have a discussion around the complete universe of facts as they have discovered them. The bad news is that no matter how cooperative and well-mannered they are, they are still not operating with all the facts. Since that latter point is almost always and unavoidably the case, this would be a realistic best-case, albeit imperfect, scenario for civil and productive conversation about the matter at hand.

Unfortunately, this is almost never the case. Doing the research is a painstaking investment of time hardly ever equally invested. When discovered, facts are not usually openly shared by each side and there are many problematic factors of perspective, prejudice, emotion, and noise, which are always introduced into the conversation. Once they enter (and they almost always do so without deliberateness or awareness on the part of the individual participant), the conversation rapidly deteriorates in both quality and civility with peaceful resolution no longer an option. When people begin to discuss issues, fact-based issues, they are often in possession of very few facts. On some level, consciously or unconsciously, they are aware of this.

Whether it is a bad lead guitar player turning up the amplifier's volume, or a poor chef using too much spiced sauce over dried-out ribs, everybody knows that loudness and spice can at least partially cover up a lack of ability. So, when two people sit to discuss an issue and neither one truly knows many facts upon which they can rely, they crank up the volume and the heat and they do it in a hurry. They are hoping that their demonstration of passion will distract the other party from realizing that they don't actually know what they are talking about.

For most people, when they are addressing a subject with which they are very knowledgeable, an almost scary sort of calm can come over them while they are discussing it with someone. So confident are they in their knowledge and expertise that they don't need to shout, they only need to inform and listen. The very best professors are like this in their classroom. It doesn't mean they don't vary their voice for impact and theatrics, it just means they keep cool while explaining the subject matter. These people are confident; they know what they know, and they know that they know it.

If people could do a better job of understanding the above-described knowledge-based process and the impediments to informed and productive conversation, then they would be less likely to elevate their voice and their blood pressure. Knowledge breeds confidence, which leads to calm. Ignorance is the father of petulance, which only leads to pointless conflict.

Investing the time to learn facts will make you a calmer, more effective, agent of change. This is why I do so much research and focus on truth and facts. It is also why one of the first things I did with *The Mel K Show* website was to add a resources page that I regularly update. This is an information war and We the People must cut through the noise and propaganda to seek and spread the truth and facts that many people are unfortunately unaware of.

Understand your triggers: We have discussed the idea of triggers in previous chapters and Steps. In the conventional world of addiction, triggers are those things which give your mind and body the cue that says it is time to use your drug of choice in order to become "comfortably numb." In our addiction to conflict and chaos, we also have triggers. If you want to be an agent of change, you will need to become familiar with your own triggers so that you can control or avoid them and stay mission-focused.

In the Twelve-Step world they look at three different realms that hold triggers for us in terms of kicking our addictive behaviors. Those three are people, playgrounds, and playthings. Let's look at each of these in the context of making ourselves change agents and what we might have to be cautious of to avoid falling back into bad habits.

First, people. Everyone knows about the problem of toxic relationships. We typically think of these with people in our lives who are in perpetual states of drama or who are just general downers on virtually any topic. These kinds of people are the ones we often try to avoid at the grocery store by going down a different aisle or whose call we ignore when we are in a good mood and just can't bear the thought of being brought down.

In the case of conflict addiction, we need to be wary of people who are so deep into their addiction, who are so lost that they don't believe in effective solutions or they don't recognize the problem and are just not ready to do better. Some of these people are so far gone or are so fixed in their narrative that they will only frustrate you to no end and will try to discourage you from even trying to make progress or reach out to others.

Even people on team America may say, "Why are you wasting your time? You can't reach them, you can't bring people together, the folks on the other side will never listen to you." Some people are so deep into their addiction that the only way they can stay happy is to keep other people down right alongside them or they just fight on without truly understanding how to accomplish the mission. Those are the kinds of people you need to be wary of and from whom you may well have to distance yourself.

Next is playgrounds. In the case of a person addicted to substances an obvious example is the local tavern where the same people have been sitting on the same barstool for twenty years. The serious addict who wants to get sober knows that they have to give up their barstool and maybe substitute it for a seat at the local coffee shop instead.

Think about your friends or groups to which you might belong that might be squarely on team America. Even here there can be fierce disagreements, but it is a space where you can practice your newfound skills and tools in relative safety and security. You can even share what you are learning here to drive toward solutions to build bridges to save our country. It is critical to have strong and resolute freedom-fighting circles but we also must find effective solutions to create more cohesion internally and to bring more people under the tent of positive social change.

It will also be critically important to get out of your comfort zone and approach those who may disagree with you. This is where it is most difficult and also where much progress can be made in our mission to restore our nation. Anywhere and everywhere you find yourself among others is an opportunity to listen, tactfully approach, and engage. I do this daily. In all my day-to-day interactions I try to sniff out the perspective of my fellow man. I listen, I ask questions, and if given the opportunity I engage thoughtfully and politely to plant the seeds of truth and knowledge.

Sometimes just being courageous enough to voice a non-mainstream thought or to share a story you experienced that points to a subject most shy away from will spur a very interesting discussion or even just an acknowledgment of the issue. We all need to stand up, speak up, and be courageous. I can tell you from experience that courage is contagious and that there is strength in numbers and numbers is what we need. Be a thoughtful and strategic leader in your own circles. Be courageous and watch the contagion grow.

Finally comes playthings. The most important example I can think of is the use of smartphones which is the largest plaything contributor to conflict addiction. This will also be the toughest trigger to manage, and the reason can be found in another famous addiction, that of overeating.

The people in Overeaters Anonymous have a much harder challenge to face than do their brethren in say Alcoholics Anonymous or Narcotics Anonymous. If you are addicted to alcohol or drugs the answer is to give them up entirely. That is hard, but consider the challenge of someone in OA. Those folks can't give up eating! They must learn how to responsibly manage and use their drug of choice, which is food. If they keep eating the way they are, they will die. If they stop eating, they will die. They need to find balance.

The same is true for change agents and their smartphones. It is virtually impossible to function in today's world without one. Yet, they are the most common plaything trigger for our addiction to conflict because of the continuous pouring in of social media content and other messages that can turn up our temperature. Setting some sort of boundaries for yourself for smartphone use will likely be necessary for you to be successful in helping yourself become ready to help others.

Be ready to conquer fear: Constructive engagement has become so rare these days that people almost seem to be afraid of it. It is as though we have become engageophobics, irrationally fearing to approach others in a direct, but positive way. But is it really irrational? Well, I would say yes and no. Yes because the world is very propagandized and polarized so there really can be a disdain for the other, and no because anything worthwhile is not easy nor without risk. If you want to help save our country and our global community you will need to take some risks and sacrifice now because it's likely that your sacrifice later will not be a choice and the sacrifice or loss will be much greater than you could ever imagine.

You are going to need to get over that fear if you want to help yourself and others. The best way to do that is to identify the fears that you might have. That can be difficult if you don't know what you are looking for, so here is a way to self-examine for fear using three categories very familiar to traditional recovering addicts:

- Fear of not getting something you want;
- Fear of losing something you think you have;
- Fear of not being liked.

In addition to understanding your fears it's important to know that this mission is greater than we can imagine and that courage is what people do when they act, putting themselves at risk, in the presence of fear. Fear is not exclusively a bad thing. When fear is recognized, understood, and overcome, it can be immensely rewarding. You can't really have a hero without the elements of risk and fear.

When it comes to fear of not getting something you want, have you ever said to yourself, "If I tell my boss his idea won't work, I'll never get my raise at the end of the year"? The examples of this kind of fear are infinite. What matters is that when you are getting ready to be a change agent, you need to be asking yourself, "What might I not get by entering into this action or discussion?" You can't overcome a fear without first identifying it.

Fear of losing something you think that you have is the opposite of not getting what you want. Instead of being worried about not getting a raise, you get worried about losing your job entirely. This fear can feel greater than the first one because we tend to be more concerned about losing the known things that we are attached to than of not getting the uncertain.

By far what seems to be the biggest kind of fear present in today's America is the fear of not being liked. "Like us on…" is perhaps the most common marketing message of our time, maybe of all time. We desperately want to be liked and the fear of not being liked is paralyzing.

In all instances of feeling fear the most important motivational tool is to think about what you gain by moving through your fear and what you will gain through that process. Ultimately the risk-reward choice is an individual one but just make sure you understand the stakes on the table. Your worst fears may be nothing compared to yielding to your fears. Action is bravery. And I will repeat…when fear is recognized, understood, and overcome, it can be immensely rewarding. You can't really have a hero without the elements of risk and fear.

If you become a change agent in the fight against conflict addiction, understand that people who actually want conflict between us are not going to like you. Does this mean you will lose friends? We aren't sure, but it's likely, at least until they realize what in the world is happening—or possibly they are so far gone you are better off without them. If you lose somebody because you were trying to make a positive difference, did you ever really have them as a friend in the first place? Beyond people you already know who might turn away from you, be prepared to be disliked by strangers, people who have never met you but who are going to be critical of you simply for committing the crime of thinking independent thoughts outside the mainstream narrative and trying to bring people together.

You are going to have to find a way to either not be afraid or push through the fear of people you know, and people you don't know, turning on you if you want to make a difference. Remember, if that problem didn't exist, there wouldn't be any need to launch a battle against conflict addiction in the first place. Any attacks or disdain of your new bold, nonconforming behavior validates your mission and should be worn as a badge of honor! And always remember the stakes of freedom vs. tyranny.

Plan to be passionately dispassionate: One key attribute of a successful salesperson is that they know how to care deeply and not care at all simultaneously. The great salesperson knows how to get themselves fully prepared and motivated to sell their product or service. They also know they will not sell everything to everybody. When they get a "no," they keep going and try to turn it into a "yes." If the answer remains firmly "no," then they are able to take a deep breath, gather their thoughts, and move to the next opportunity to sell to someone else.

If you want to make a difference, you are going to have to learn to care more about making a difference towards the mission than about winning any particular battle. Battles will be lost and soldiers will fall but the mission is paramount. There must be no ego in the fight. You are also going to have to realize that you may not be able to save the world alone and any intentions you have to that effect need to be moderated, but you can change yourself and those around you, and your power is likely much greater than you can imagine.

You need to be steeled and you need to be rational in order to be effective. Losing your temper, falling to pieces, getting despondent—these are all things that you need to try to avoid. Set high but manageable expectations. Become ready to shake off failure and smile softly at success. Be passionate but control how you release it. Passion is powerful—so powerful it can actually be dangerous if it is overexposed. Show just enough to others to have them catch it, not be repulsed by it. Leave your ego and labels out of the battles, understand the mission and soldier on to greatness.

You can do this. You can make a difference. I can point to specific, numerous, and significant ways in which many unsung regular people I know, including myself, have been able to make a large, positive, lasting difference in people's lives and the world as a whole. It hasn't been easy, but it has been very worthwhile and fulfilling. I want you to experience what I know and have been fortunate enough to have experienced. Be your own white hat and let's do this for God, family, and country.

———

Ready to work a Sixth Step? Here are some ideas for you or members of your group to discuss and implement:

1. List three universal beliefs you would fight for and why you believe they are universal to all people.
2. List one fact /statement to argue for each of your three universal beliefs.
3. List your biggest fears of speaking out and why.
4. List what stakes would motivate you to push through that fear.
5. Write out with pen and paper your personal life mission statement. What outcomes and goals will you achieve if you adhere to this mission in all of your affairs?
6. List topics that you believe most can come together on and discuss how to approach, such as:
    *   Stopping endless wars
    *   Protecting children
    *   The value of a secure national border
    *   Balancing the national budget

UNDERSTANDING THE GLOBAL POWER STRUCTURE AND PLAN

WE IDENTIFIED THE OBSTACLES THAT FACE WE THE PEOPLE IN CREATING CHANGE, AND WE SOUGHT TO EITHER REMOVE THEM OR WORK THROUGH THEM AS MIGHT BE NECESSARY TO ACHIEVE OUR DESIRED OUTCOMES.

UNDERSTANDING THE BATTLEFIELD AND STRATEGICALLY MOVING THROUGH THE CHESSBOARD.

A re we a sovereign nation with our own identity, constitution, borders, language, and culture, or are we a part of a globally governed one world conglomerate where we identify as borderless global citizens bound by a global one-size-fits-all constitution covering all humanity?

Earlier we talked about the things inside of us that make us susceptible to being drawn into the disorienting world of addiction to conflict and chaos. Think of those in terms of being narratives or controls that can be used by anyone who is trying to foster such an unstable climate. The next question is: Who is trying to use those tools to manipulate us and why?

We are going to focus on the "why" before turning to the "who." We have come to use a lot of different labels in our society today in an attempt to categorize people. Typically, we use labels to describe "other people" instead of ourselves, and we do so with the intention of making them distinguishable as "bad" when we are comparing them to ourselves. If you will ever notice, we do not often self-label.

Recently there has been a massive corporate, governmental, and entertainment industry push to slice and silo humanity into thinner and thinner categories, creating even more labels, new vocabulary, and continuously redefining basic accepted under-standings within society. There are so many, in fact, that they tend to lose their meaning to the point where no two people can agree on exactly what they mean or define terms once concrete and clear. Many people still cannot believe the question, "What is a woman?" could not be definitively defined by a Supreme Court justice candidate, or that the question would be controversial or debatable.

If there are too many labels overall, it begs the question of whether or not any labels have any meaning. We think that some still do. One of those who we identify as the highest level of dis-tinction in the current chaotic situation is the group known as the "globalists."

Globalists are those who are in favor of creating a world with-out borders or sovereign nation-states. Their "ism" is globalism. Globalism has turned itself into a new and very historically unique form of fascism, a term reflexively associated with early twenti-eth-century Italy, Spain, and, of course, Nazi Germany. Fascism has always been something that evolved at a national level. That is what has made this current form unique. This is the first time that fascism has been tried on a scale that does not involve geographic boundaries.

First, a quick working definition of fascism so that you can understand the argument. A fascist system is one where economic and political activity are organized around having a very strong central government that controls the law, joined together with large industry players who control economic activity, and then a compliant academic community and press corps that serve to reinforce and amplify the government's message. Fascism relies on creating some form of conflict within its territory that unifies people to fight against an enemy, either real or perceived. Said even more simply, a fascist system is a socialist system (centralized planning, management, and control of political, social, and economic activity) with an aggressive personality.

Based on my research and understanding of history, it is quite clear to me that we are witnessing a fascist movement, a form of Marxist revolution taking place on a global scale. A large handful of people, the international oligarchy referred to earlier, are attempting to place themselves in control over as many of the eight billion, or much less if they get their way, people who populate the planet as they possibly can. They want to centralize power and control all the resources. They want to dominate and rule.

This tendency is as old as mankind itself, the few wanting to control the many. What is different here is that in the past it has been the work of empires and nations. Nobody has attempted to do it universally because it simply wasn't imaginable. What has made it seem within reach in the twenty-first century that is different than in times past? We believe the answer is technology. We will come back to that.

We said that a fascist state requires the creation of an enemy in order to rally the people to support its efforts. What common enemy has the globalist fascist movement created?

There are a number of boogeymen that they have pushed but let's just look at a few:

- Anthropogenic climate change (human-caused climate issues)
- Healthcare and worldwide pandemic preparedness
- World food supply and supply chain weaknesses

Let's take these one at a time, beginning with climate change. It is well documented that the global elitists have targeted the use of anthropogenic, meaning human behavior caused, climate change to control the population. It started with global warming, which they couldn't really prove, and that switched to a broader threat of climate change which has since morphed into climate emergency and catastrophe. All of this as per the globalists is caused by humanity and irresponsible human behavior which must be eradicated and controlled. Which of course needs a global governance all of humanity solution. The control of this is centered in Davos and Brussels along with the UN and World Bank creating an all-of-humanity approach to reverse and cure. The unified globalist response also entails a huge consolidation of wealth transferred from sovereign nations to the same consolidated world governance group from all of the global economies. They seek to create a combined fund controlled by them to pay for the necessary implementations, estimated to be trillions of dollars, needed to reverse the course we are supposedly on to prevent global climate Armageddon.

Across the globe people have been propagandized and convinced that we are on the brink of an impending cataclysm centered around an imminent climate collapse of planet Earth. Most importantly, it's all our fault and people have been pushed to believe that this coming climate disaster is directly related to man's activities, in particular the burning of fossil fuels. This has been presented as "settled science" and that only radical changes in how we live in almost every aspect of our lives can prevent us from suffering the ravages of excessive heat, violent weather, disappearing shorelines, and ultimately the end of humanity on the planet. Some scenarios even have whole cities being swallowed up into the ocean, creating an Atlantis off the new shores of every continent.

It is beyond the scope of this book to address the various assumptions and theories surrounding these conditions. Suffice to say that the climate does and has forever changed and that there are many scientists that absolutely refute the claims of the climate change alarmists. It is also true that the governments actively engage in geoengineering of our planet, which many say is probably the most harmful human activity to our climate and planet. We can also look at big agriculture and their chemicals, the military-industrial complex and their wars, and many other activities of the globalists as the most harmful to our planet, but no, they tell us it's the common man and his personal carbon footprint that is killing our planet. This message from the very people who controlled and profited from industrialization who now want us to switch to their new "green" systems and methods that they also control and own. Isn't that special? The point here is that the changing climate has been used by the elitists in this globalist-fascist movement to convince people that we are in crisis and only the surrender to the wisdom, knowledge, and solutions of the global elitists can save them.

How about global pandemics? The threat of disease has been used before and it was planned to be used again. There were many plans, warnings, bioweapon developments, and dry-run simulations of a global pandemic and, well, we got one at just the right time for the globalists to seize power. If you haven't seen the videos of the Event 201 pandemic simulation, it will shock you—if it hasn't been scrubbed from the internet yet. Some of you may know that the ghettos of Nazi Germany and the quarantine/death camps were first set up because of the perceived threat of typhus. The story was that this disease was spreading quickly throughout the Jewish communities and that Germany needed to isolate the sick to protect the populace. There is a reason that they don't really teach history anymore. While some may find this information difficult to fathom, it is important to consider all the facts, data points, and players, given what we lived through on a global scale—who benefited, and what are the ultimate stated goals of the globalists and the stakes of this global power game?

In early 2020, the COVID operation, which I call the plandemic, was used to terrorize and control the global population in a manner and scale never seen in all of history. Did you know that the CDC changed the definition of a pandemic to exclude mass death in favor of mass sickness which was measured by a flawed PCR test? Did you know that there was no flu reported during the plandemic? Did you know that well-known viral therapeutics were forbidden to be used by our governments and the CDC, and that people who spoke about potentially safe and effective therapeutics were censored and attacked? All this fear mongering, lockdowns, masking, social distancing, and choosing essential businesses vs. nonessential businesses was despite the most recent pandemic being less lethal than most common flus. Consider also prior pandemics such as the Black Death of the 1300s and the Spanish flu of the early twentieth century that were far more lethal. But today, global communication and globalist propaganda created the "feeling" that this was the most serious health condition ever seen by mankind. This has given the globalist oligarchy the opportunity to use this manufactured crisis to convince hundreds of millions of people that somebody, or somebodies, has to take charge of health on a global scale to protect us from future outbreaks.

When we look at the food scarcity crisis and the globalists' push to control the world's food supply and eradicate poverty we see another psychological attack on the people. These two might seem to be two separate items but they are inextricably connected. Globalists have been very successful in pointing to impoverished conditions across the planet and telling people that changing what we eat and how it is grown and brought to market must be centrally managed in order to reduce world hunger, make the food supply safe, and reduce poverty in the process.

You don't need a pen and paper to connect the dots to see how this particular issue gets tied into the previous two noted above. Look at who controls big agriculture and the plight of small local farmers. Consider how small farmers are under attack and all manner of controls are being implemented to force them out of business. Who on earth kills their population's food supply? Well, the globalists do. Look at the control of meat production and the push to eat fake meat or, God forbid, bugs, and who owns those companies. Look at the use of GMOs and harmful chemicals in the food-industrial complex and you will clearly see that the globalists are clearly not looking out for We the People's best interests.

As I always say, do your own research and think for yourself. But if you really do the work and take a clear, honest, discerning look at the chain of events that we are living through you will understand that much of this is not an accident. There is a small group of winners and the rest of us lose. Of course there are real problems with the way we use or abuse our natural resources.

There are certainly problems with global health concerns and poverty. But it's important to recognize who is using these issues and to what end. You can look at any one of the issues identified above and say that these are all real problems. That isn't the question we want you to ask.

We want you to ask yourself: Why are these issues being used as a means by which to centralize global authority? Our answer to the why is that powerful people want to control us and to do that they have to frighten us. When people are frightened, the fight or flight response kicks in and when in a state of fear through conflict and chaos we cannot think clearly and are easier to manipulate. When conflict and chaos is amplified as in a color revolution it almost always leads to people turning to a strong central power to protect and save them. "Please just make it stop" becomes the cry of the masses.

Now let's look at "who" is doing all this nonsense. We have already addressed these power player oligarchs and their global confabs and meetings. It is always the same names and organizations hatching plans, proving it is a distinct self-appointed, coordinated effort by a specific, easily defined group. While some of the names change, they are nearly always the same philanthropic organizations, NGOs, corporations, and banking institutions. These elitist systems have remained the same for decades even if the players move around, usually within the same sphere, and meet several times a year to update and reinforce their plans and coordination.

As they have gained more confidence in their power and arrogance in their success, these groups and players are now easy to see. They do not function in the shadows anymore, like when they were conceived and started in the fifties or seventies, they are out in the open. They are loud and proud with their own websites, YouTube channels, social media accounts, and exclusive billion-dollar events in Davos and elsewhere covered by the society pages that remain and the mainstream media. They function as a world monarchy of elitists, celebrities, industrialists, bankers, kings, and queens we are to look to and admire in awe of their wealth and greatness. Luckily for us mere mortals, we see them as the opposite of what they see themselves. I call them the predator or parasite class, but you decide after you dig into the entire web yourself.

THE GLOBALIST BILLIONAIRE OLIGARCHY (THE STAKEHOLDERS)

Most of the grand master manipulators of global hegemony and division here and around the world are all hiding in plain sight. They have forums and meetings every few months in exotic locations where they refer to themselves as the "stakeholders" of the global public-private partnership namely of the World Economic Forum and their counterpart at the United Nations.

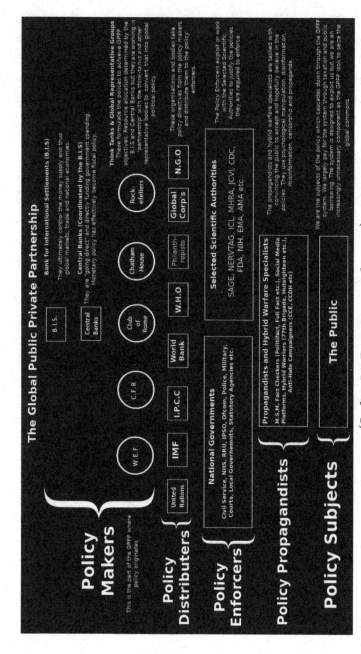

The Global Public Private Partnership

Policy Makers
This is the part of the GPPP where policy originates

W.E.F   C.F.R   Club of Rome   Chatham House   Rock-efellers

B.I.S.

Bank for International Settlements (B.I.S)
They ultimately control the money supply and thus global market, trade and national economies.

Central Banks

Central Banks (Coordinated by the B.I.S)
They are going direct and directly funding government spending. Monetary policy has effectively become fiscal policy.

Think Tanks & Global Representative Groups
These formulate the policies to achieve GPPP objectives. Resource allocation determined by the B.I.S and Central Banks but they are working in "partnership" with the think-tanks and other representative bodies to convert that into global political policy.

Policy Distributers
United Nations   IMF   I.P.C.C   World Bank   W.H.O   Philanthropists   Global Corp's   N.G.O

These organisations and bodies take policy directives from the policy makers and distribute them to the policy enforcers.

Policy Enforcers
National Governments
Civil Service, NHS, RRU, IPSO, Ofcom, Police, Military, Courts, Local Governemnts, Statutory Agencies etc.

Selected Scientific Authorities
SAGE, NERVTAG, ICL MHRA, JCVI, CDC, FDA, NIH, EMA, AMA etc.

The Policy Enforcers exploit or work with the Selected Scientific Authorities to justify the policies they are required to enforce

Policy Propagandists
Propagandists and Hybrid Warfare Specialists
M.S.M, Fact Checkers (Politifact, Full Fact etc.), Social Media Platforms, Hybrid Warriors (77th Brigade, Huteighteen etc.), Anti-Hate Campaigners (CCE, CCDH etc)

The propagandists and hybrid warfare specialists are tasked with convincing the public to accept and hopefully believe in the policies. They use psychological manipulation, disinformation, misinformation, censorship and propaganda.

Policy Subjects
The Public

We are the subjects of the policy which cascades down through the GPPP system. We largely pay for the system through taxation and public borrowing. The system is designed to exploit us but we are an increasingly unnecessary component as the GPPP look to seize the global common.

(Credit to Iain Davis at www.iaindavis.com)

The World Economic Forum's GPPP, global public-private partnership, is a self-anointed, obscenely powerful network of billionaires and probably trillionaires that manipulate the planet in the shadows from Davos, the City of London (not London the city), the Vatican, the vassal state that is Washington, DC, as well as by holding endless conferences in Beijing, Dubai, Wall Street, Aspen, Geneva, Brussels, Austria, and other enclaves where they and their loyal minions do their bidding in grand spectacle right in the public eye. This group considers themselves stakeholders of their, in their minds, wholly owned planet known as Earth, and all the things on this planet including eight billion human beings who inhabit it. They call us the resources to be managed.

These so-called stakeholders are made up of multinational corporations' board members, international central bankers, billionaire-oligarch-funded philanthropic foundations, globalist backed "think" tanks, unconstitutional government agencies, and never-ending nongovernmental organizations. These groups are staffed with many unelected operatives. Many of these organizations are covertly funded by taxpayers, dark money, and the same oligarchy behind the global domination plan. They include many heavily taxpayer- and predator-class-funded academic institutions and grant-making organizations, global-UN-affiliated organizations, and networks of unions that are in bed with politicians. They operate with very little if any oversight, and claim to be doing everything for the greater good, for the people, and the planet, but this is a massive fraud.

Many of these self-anointed, entitled elitists are selected through nepotism often channeled through private clubs, secret societies, leadership networking programs, or fellowship programs like the WEF Young Global Leaders or Rhodes Scholarship are groomed to assume positions of power and authority. They operate in a world where they confidently believe they are superior to the global population, who they might consider a peasant class, and they regularly skirt the laws or oversight that the rest of the citizens of humanity are bound by. Rules for thee but not for me. As expressed by Georgetown professor and insider architect Carroll Quigley's writings, they are a supraclass or superior class who deem themselves the important thinkers and thought leaders of their time, and are thus entitled to determine all aspects of human life and behavior to ensure that their power, privilege, and control be sustainable and appropriate to maintain order.

The GPPP or the global public-private partnership (they love their acronyms) appears to control all global finance and the world's economy to benefit itself, while keeping an outward appearance of working for the people of humanity. Opposite of what we have been led to believe for decades, my work has shown me that it is this group of elitists that controls all world, national and local policy, which they refer to as global governance. The term global governance and its directives and plans are all over their own websites. I encourage everyone to visit any of the entities listed on the above-referenced Davis's chart to see for yourself where it explicitly states that this new Great Reset to global governance will be the end of the outdated nation-state model. This includes ending national sovereignty, borders, and constitutions of individual nations to be replaced by a one world global governance model.

They have many global governance, Great Reset, *Agenda 2030* pieces coming together right now, all set to be presented and accepted if we do not get wise and change course quickly. They plan to accomplish this at the UN Summit of the Future in September of 2024 where America and other *Agenda 2030*-conforming nations will join something called *Our Common Agenda* which includes such features as a digital world ID and One World Health Pass. If you do not see all of this by now please be open and educate yourself before it's too late. I ask you to simply by visit the websites of many of the groups I am mentioning and type in their search area "global governance" or "*Agenda 2030.*" If you need even more proof that this the current plan, ask yourself why much of the controlled demolition of America is happening in lockstep in almost exactly the same way worldwide in supposedly free nations. Further consider that David Rockefeller—the original architect and founder of many of the GPPP controlling institutions including the UN, the CFR, the Fed, and the IPCC Club of Rome, to name a few—said the following:

> For more than a century, ideological extremists, at either end of the political spectrum, have seized upon well-publicized incidents, such as my encounter with Castro, to attack the Rockefeller family for the inordinate influence they claim we wield over American political and economic institutions. Some even believe we are part of a secret cabal, working against the best interests of the United States, characterizing my family and me as "internationalists," and of conspiring with others around the world to build a more integrated global political and economic structure, one world, if you will. If that's the charge, I stand guilty, and I am proud of it.

Or, as previously mentioned, he follows with:

> We are grateful to the *Washington Post,* the *New York Times, Time Magazine* and other great publications

whose directors have attended our meetings and
respected their promises of discretion for almost
40 years...It would have been impossible for us to
develop our plan for the world if we had been sub-
jected to the lights of publicity during those years.
But, the world is more sophisticated and prepared
to march towards a world government. The super-
national sovereignty of an intellectual elite and
world bankers is surely preferable to the national
autodetermination practiced in past centuries.

—David Rockefeller, *Memoirs*

As you can hopefully now see, we were all being herded,
whether you believe it or not, during the plandemic, to the new
model of centralized global governance. Their plan, run by intellectual elitists, titans of industry, and world bankers will oversee
all humanity and the planet from a centralized, technocratic,
totalitarian confab to ensure a sustainable future in line with their
open and public *Agenda 2030* and 17 Sustainable Development
Goals. They seek a form of worldwide socialism enforced by a
digital track-and-trace surveillance system being implemented
worldwide, ditching individual national sovereignty, autonomy,
constitutions, and borders of all nations who have aligned for the
plan. This is not hidden or a secret at all, in fact they just had a
big celebration in New York City honoring their halfway mark to
Agenda 2030 hosted by the UN, WEF, IMF, BlackRock, and other
GPPP partners, and even the Clinton Global Initiative.

Most Americans do not know or understand that Barack
Obama signed the United States on to the global governance
Great Reset plan in 2015, paving the way for America to adopt
Agenda 2030 and the 17 Sustainable Development Goals of the

UN/WEF/WHO and others. Even fewer know that the Biden–Harris regime recommitted with full gusto to *Agenda 2030* and the 17 SDGs in a ceremony in September of 2023, with a document easily found on the official White House website entitled *U.S. Action on Global Development*, which states, "The United States is committed to the full implementation of 2030 Agenda and the SDGs, at home and abroad." If you look at where we are and what that agenda truly represents, it is not symbolic nor a framework for idealistic humanitarian goals, it is in fact a clear and present danger to all Americans. The *Agenda 2030* implementation would override national sovereignty, our Constitution, Bill of Rights, and many other foundational American ideals. Everything we are experiencing now seeks to create order (a new world order) out of chaos. The American vision of our Founders, the rights endowed by our creator, and the concept of individual liberty and justice will be lost and history will be replaced to fit this new globalism model executed by the globalist elitists.

As the globalists describe it in their speeches, white papers, and other documents, you will see their new global model organizes a borderless world into what sounds like wards or sectors, eerily similar to the movie *The Hunger Games*, where everything is run on blockchain ledger technology. In their envisioned global utopia, they own, control, and develop nearly everything. All resources and assets, including humans, will be fully tracked and traced using various technologies, such as satellite, advanced networks, and Internet of Bodies implanted devices. AI and algorithms will allow them to facilitate mass management of all these assets in what they envision as articulated in the book by WEF figurehead Klaus Schwab called the Fourth Industrial Revolution. Their utopian vision of future global citizenship goals for a one world system superior to the past is humanity's worst nightmare.

The Build Back Better messaging we have all been hearing about is nothing less than a Marxist revolution via order out of chaos. It was rolled out by all complicit leaders globally including our own Joe Biden and Obama in concert with the pandemic operation leveraging in tandem the George Floyd BLM protests operation for a reason. What was America and the world and what worked needs to be destroyed and built back better in their dystopian vision. Only this globalist agenda and plans should be implemented going forward, by any means necessary and without the consent or even knowledge of the eight billion human beings being caught up in their plans.

I did not vote for this and I'm guessing you did not vote for this either, but the elitists are hell-bent on this plan and again, remember, by any means necessary. Obama, his cronies, and the many globalist oligarchs are all working in lockstep towards this agenda and the only thing that can stop them is us. This was a long game and although Obama officially signed on to the implementation of the global governance future, if we are to unravel this we must be fearlessly honest about its roots. In our mission of recovery, we must also accept that almost every president since George H. W. Bush has enabled and empowered the globalist consolidation towards *the Agenda 2030* model. This includes empowering China to replace us as a superpower, encouraging our manufacturing and supply chains to be offshored, allowing our financial system to be manipulated to consolidate money and power towards a one world financial system, and many other strategic moves needed to implement their 17 Sustainable Development Goals of this agenda. If you understand that, a lot more about what has happened to America and the world from 2015 forward makes sense.

Our Founders knew tyranny and multinational elitist control all too well as they experienced it firsthand and risked their lives to break those bonds of oppression. Because of their experience and wisdom, they came together to adopt a form of the Westphalian model of national sovereignty in which the government of one nation cannot make legislation or law in or for another. Unfortunately, through the machinations of well-known globalists such as the Rockefellers, Rothschilds, Henry Kissinger, and Zbig Brzezinski, along with the Crown and their cohorts, this model was infiltrated and subverted over time towards a global governance model. The globalist advocates used a long-game strategy of deception and strategic moves including war and financial manipulation on a grand scale to achieve their goals. Under the guise of creating a better world for the populace or as Kissinger described, the useless eaters and irresponsible breeding machines, we were slated to come under the control of those who deem themselves elitists. But now We the People are awake and we must radically course correct now to save what is good in this world.

While this is Americans Anonymous, this is in fact a global coup and a danger to all humanity. Their stated end goal is a one world, top-down global governance. Klaus Schwab of the WEF has claimed they have fully and masterfully infiltrated many governments and institutions all over the world. Schwab boasted of infiltrating the governments of Canada, Australia, the US, New Zealand, and elsewhere through his Young Global Leaders and Global Shapers programs. He further boasts proudly to have trained and indoctrinated many of those who run G7 and G20 nations as well as those who control Big Tech and dozens of multinational corporate boards and banks worldwide.

Some say they ensure compliance through legalized bribery, some say through blackmail, and others get stuck in untenable situations after taking loans they can never pay off from the IMF, the World Bank, or others. Lots of incentives and grants are doled out worldwide to get everyone in the same state of entrapment. These compromised leaders then enslave their own populations and businesses with the help of USAID, many UN-connected aid agencies, multibillion-dollar-funded international foundations, or NGOs. Ultimately all that money eventually goes through the opaque Bank for International Settlements in Switzerland, which enjoys complete immunity, has zero accountability, and offers no transparency. It's funny how we were conned into believing that Switzerland was the only true neutral nation, never to be questioned, yet many of the globalist power structures such as the World Economic Forum, the World Health Organization, CERN, and the Bank for International Settlements are all within driving distance of each other in Switzerland. Coupled with the endless pageantry of their many forums and globalist events culminating in their yearly Panem-like expo, the Davos WEF extravaganza, one can see that Switzerland is not what we were told.

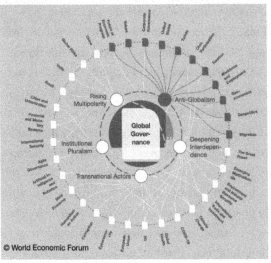

(Credit for graphic goes to World Economic
Forum Great Reset web page.)

At their yearly meetings and gatherings, be they at Bilderberg, WEF Davos Forum, COP events, in Jackson Hole or Sun Valley conferences, along with exclusive meetings in Manhattan, London, Brussels, Geneva, Shanghai, and the like, they figure out the goals that best suit them financially then implement the obvious problem-reaction-solution model we have been conditioned to follow time and again. That is best explained by David Icke as "Create the problem," "encourage the reaction that something must be done," and then offer the "solution." It is summed up by the nefarious motto "Ordo ab chao"—order out of chaos. Create chaos and then offer a way to restore order. The programming and propaganda begins, the cognitive warfare and technology ratchets up, and before the people know it everything is changed. They are trapped in the Klaus Schwab "new narrative." Fact checkers, thought police, and disinformation authorities remove dissenters and silence opposition, and all move forward without any pushback. This is the plan and that is what the Great Resetters and globalists of the *Agenda 2030* model are hoping for.

As I say, if the masses of the US citizenry were informed and aware that this self-anointed, outside, unified group of global billionaire oligarchs has planned, plotted, and is very close to implementing total global governance control by technocracy and digital surveillance control over all people without nation-states or constitutional protection, most would openly reject this and rebel. As we go through this recovery, this fact, once accepted, driven by ample evidence and their own provable actions, will likely be the most powerful unifier to heal the divisions they put in place to avoid detection. Understanding this agenda would serve as the one thing we can all agree is a no-go for our nation and our future beyond anything else. If we all understand the stakes as they are, we can come together as citizens of the sovereign United States of America, understanding that we are looking at the end of our freedom and liberty for all. As we come to realize the risks we all face, we will likely agree that we will not under any circumstance relinquish our privacy, self-determination, God-given natural rights, and individual sovereignty to a self-selected global cabal of unelected elitists who have no regard for any of us, our children, our families, or our futures.

In January 2021 Klaus Schwab of the WEF spoke about how it views stakeholder capitalism:

> The most important characteristic of the stakeholder model today is that the stakes of our system are now more clearly global....What was once seen as externalities in national economic policy making and individual corporate decision making will now need to be incorporated or internalized in the operations of every government, company, community, and individual. The planet is thus the center of the global economic system, and its health should be optimized in the decisions made by all other stakeholders.

This is all about centralized elitists controlling everything on planet earth by means of infiltration and dominion of all land, water, air, space, energy, food, property, internet, health care, and all life including your physical person. The globalist money men and corporate dictators do not hide their intentions. Please read their own words. Something these globalists love is telling us their plans, thus supposedly not circumventing free will. They will manipulate, starve, destroy, embattle, propagandize, brainwash, sicken, and do whatever is needed for the masses to, in their mind, lead us to welcome their totalitarian dictatorship without even realizing it. Read the WEF's own description of the ends justifying the means of their bought-and-paid-for destruction of humanity and freedom known as the Great Reset:

> To improve the state of the world, the World Economic Forum is starting The Great Reset initiative.... The Covid-19 crisis...is fundamentally changing the traditional context for decision-making. The inconsistencies, inadequacies and contradictions of multiple systems – from health and financial to energy and education – are more exposed than ever.... Leaders find themselves at a historic crossroads.... As we enter a unique window of opportunity to shape the recovery, this initiative will offer insights to help inform all those determining the future state of global relations, the direction of national economies, the priorities of societies, the nature of business models and the management of a global commons.

Not convinced? Why not look at the most recent opening remarks summary by WEF leader Schwab in May 2022 at Davos.

REMARKS DELIVERED BY KLAUS SCHWAB AT THE ANNUAL MEETING 2022

- *Davos 2022 is the most timely and consequential Annual Meeting since the creation of the Forum over 50 years ago.*
- *Davos will bring key global leaders from all parts of society together in person.*

- *The atmosphere in which Davos takes place will be welcoming but is also of the utmost seriousness.*

Under the theme "History at a Turning Point," the Annual Meeting of the World Economic Forum in Davos this year will be the most timely and consequential Annual Meeting since the creation of the Forum over 50 years ago.

The political, economic and social circumstances of our meeting are unprecedented. Davos will bring key global leaders from all parts of society together in person, and look at the consequences and repercussions for government policies and business strategies.

UKRAINE

Our first thoughts are with the war in Ukraine. Russia's aggression on their country will be seen in future history books as the breakdown of the post-World War II and post-Cold War order. This is the reason why we speak about a turning point in history. In Davos, our solidarity is foremost with the people suffering from the atrocities of this war.

This war is also personal to me. My earliest childhood memory is sitting in a shelter and hearing the bombs coming down. My life was and is devoted to reconciliation and bridge building efforts, and I never would have imagined that the unacceptable scepter of war in Europe would become reality again.

We will do whatever we can in Davos to support Ukraine, its people and its recovery. And the World Economic Forum hopes that – one day - the space for bridge building emerges once again.

There are additional reasons which make Davos 2022 so timely this year.

COVID-19

It is the first face-to-face reunion after what we all hope is the tail end of the most significant health catastrophe of the last 100 years, the COVID pandemic causing 15 million deaths according to the WHO. Thus, our big question should be: "How do we develop the necessary personal, national and global resilience mechanisms, to be much better equipped in the future, not only for a virus, but for any breakdown in our life-supporting systems?

A CLIMATE SUMMIT

Evidently, the protection of nature and climate comes first to mind. We all know that humankind has been left with only a few years to change course. The window of opportunity is rapidly closing. Thus, Davos 2022 must and will also be a Climate Summit. It will bring together the most relevant actors and it will drive action for all the Forum's initiatives in this field. That includes the First Movers Coalition launched at UN climate summit COP 26; the One Trillion Trees project, and many more. Moreover, fostering energy transformation will be at the centre of many discussions in Davos.

The return of war, epidemics, and the climate crisis: all these disruptive forces have derailed the global recovery. Inflation has not been this high in decades. What is so worrying about this, is the loss of purchasing power, particularly painful for those who had already difficulties before to secure their livelihoods.

GLOBAL ECONOMY

Our global economy is out of balance. There is too much debt, too much inflation, too much inequality, and not enough growth. Particularly worrisome, is that ever-larger parts of the global population are confronted with existential choices, or even fall back into extreme poverty or hunger. Those issues must be confronted in Davos and the global food crisis in particular needs all our immediate attention

HOW CAN DAVOS 2022 MAKE A CONTRIBUTION?

So how can Davos make a positive contribution to all those challenges in a world which is deeply stuck in crisis management?
The answer is threefold.

1. *Public-private cooperation*
    First. The challenges cannot be addressed by governments, business or civil society alone. The World Economic Forum is the international organization for public-private cooperation with official participation of more than 90 governments in Davos.
    Our multiple collaborative initiatives will drive progress by strengthening global and regional cooperation; by preserving nature and fighting against climate change; by developing new economic and social policies; by accelerating responsible ESG industry transformation, and by using the disruptive technologies such as AI, blockchain, and quantum computing, for the benefit of society. To remain ourselves at the forefront, the Forum will announce in Davos a new initiative: the Global Collaboration Village in the metaverse.
2. *Connect the dots - systemic complexity*
    There is another reason for Davos 2022 fulfilling a special function: Challenges have political, economic, ecological, technological and social dimensions and implications. Davos is the place to understand and see the world in its systemic complexity. Therefore, the program is so rich with over 400 sessions. It is the place to gain new insights and to connect the

dots, supporting more enlightened decision-making, collectively and individually.

3. *Stakeholder capitalism*

And finally. When it comes to business and economic activities, Davos is not a place for narrow self-interest. It is instead a place for the implementation of the notion of stakeholder capitalism, a concept I'm fighting for since 50 years.

A Forum partner is asked to value the contributions not just of shareholders, but of all those other stakeholders who are essential for business to succeed. As I wrote in my book Stakeholder Capitalism, Davos stands for a global economy that works for prosperity, people, and the planet.

We all are keen to see one another again in person. The atmosphere in which Davos 2022 takes place will be welcoming but is also of the utmost seriousness. There is no place for the frivolous fringe that seeks to distract and divert attention—and I condemn it wholeheartedly—particularly of those who have nothing to do with the World Economic Forum community and just to Davos to hijack our brand.

To summarize: in a world which is becoming more fragmented and more divided, and where many of the traditional multilateral organizations tend to become dysfunctional or at least mistrustful, a global platform based on informal, trust-based and action-oriented cooperation such as the World Economic Forum and Davos will be ever more needed.

Please visit www.weforum.org and look around. Please take the time to go through the individuals and corporations involved in all of the following: WEF Global Shapers, WEF Young Global Leaders, Schwab Foundation for Social Entrepreneurship, Centre for the Fourth Industrial Revolution, WEF New Champions, and especially Strategic Partners, Strategic Foundation Partnership, and Strategic Technology Partnership. All have pledged allegiance and sworn to uphold the goals to implement the orders of the global public-private partnership and international banking cartel in every corner of this planet from local communities to major cities to states and countries and everything in-between. They are spread everywhere, and we should know who they are and what they are up to wherever they may be.

To make it even more simple, back in 2016, shortly after Obama signed on to their agenda, they issued a document that made eight predictions of what the world would be like in 2030. If you visit their website, you'll see what the crystal ball of the WEF is showing:

1. All products will become services
2. There is a global price on carbon
3. US dominance is over—we have a handful of global superpowers
4. Farewell hospital, hello home-spital
5. We are eating much less meat
6. Today's migrants and refugees, 2030's CEOs
7. The values that built the West will be tested to the breaking point
8. By the 2030s we will be able to move humans toward the red planet

It is worth noting that this wasn't always the actual list. It has been modified and backdated much like an unscrupulous attorney might do if they realized they had made a mistake and thought they could fix it without anyone noticing by just altering some documents. Here is the list as it first appeared before it was scrubbed and cleaned up to make it more easily received by the public:

1. You'll own nothing and be happy
2. The US won't be the world's superpower
3. You won't die waiting for an organ donor
4. You'll eat less meat
5. A billion people will be displaced by climate change
6. You could be preparing to go to Mars
7. Western values will be tested to their breaking point
8. Fossil fuels will be eliminated

You can see from this list how the key factors being used to generate fear and conflict between people are in line with their globalist goals. This is closely tied to the *United Nations' 2030 Agenda for Sustainable Development*, created in 2015, that has been signed off on by 192 countries. Its preamble reads, in part:

> *This Agenda is a plan of action for people, planet and prosperity. It also seeks to strengthen universal peace in larger freedom. We recognize that eradicating poverty in all its forms and dimensions, including extreme poverty, is the greatest global challenge and an indispensable requirement for sustainable development. All countries and all stakeholders, acting in collaborative partnership, will implement this plan. We are resolved to free the human race from the tyranny of poverty and want and to heal and secure our planet. We are determined to take the bold and transformative steps which are urgently needed to shift the world on to a sustainable and resilient path.*

As we embark on this collective journey, we pledge that no one will be left behind.

All sound nice? The devil is in the details. This kind of positive-sounding language can all be boiled down to "you will eat insects." Do you think for a moment that these kinds of radical changes in global behavior can be accomplished without first generating conflict between peoples within nations to compel the change?

It is important to note that "these" people are very good at using or, more appropriately stated, manipulating language. There is a reason that there are so many lawyers in our government. They obfuscate what they mean with flowery language that often means the opposite. They use neuro-linguistic programming techniques and mass media to play on our emotions and most people's lack of intellectual curiosity to say what they will do without us noticing it, and therefore we accept it as it happens like it was preordained and not a big deal. But it is a big deal. One way to understand and therefore communicate and resist their plans and globalist goals more clearly to others is to understand their messaging and use of key phrases. What some common words mean to you is not what they mean when it comes to the stated goal of global governance.

Some of the most regularly used terms in their own documents including *Agenda 2030* and the UN Our Common Agenda are:

Stakeholders
Sustainable
Inclusive
Equitable
Developing countries
Governance

The Council on Foreign Relations is a US-based think tank designed to act in support of these initiatives. Its membership has great overlap with the WEF, and everything it recommends falls in lockstep with the UN and the WEF.

WHO has seen its prominence rise in the wake of the COVID operation. Despite its very sketchy track record in providing information at the start of the event and then during its life cycle, the fear created within people has only led to its elevation as we are drawn to the conclusion that we must have a world organization that is overseeing health in order to prevent something like this from happening again. Global problems require global solutions. Forget the fact that the WHO was already around for the beginning of the COVID outbreak and held wargames and simulations around such an event. As this book is being written, there is a movement to have the United States and other nations surrender their own national health sovereignty to the directives of the WHO.

Are you comfortable with that?

It is true that we live in a global community. World trade and the ease with which we can travel from country to country make that inarguable. But just because we interact with a larger community doesn't mean our local community, family, or individual sovereignty doesn't matter. Why is it that most people who own a home or live in a community have a fence around their yard or a locked door? If every country could use their own resources to be the best they could be and preserve their borders, language, and culture, the global community would be much stronger and healthier. This decentralized, sovereign-based philosophy can be extrapolated from country to state to municipality, community, family, and at the individual level. Strong pieces make a strong whole but strong pieces are somewhat independent and not as easy to control as broken, chaotic, conflict-ridden ones. The leaders of these global institutions are creating conflict and chaos and destroying all barriers to sovereignty so that we get to a place where the world is so dystopian that we plead for help to make the pain and chaos end. This strategy has a name and it's called the Hegelian dialectic. Simply explained, a problem is created, solutions are sought, and solutions are accepted, but the solutions are from the same people that caused the problem. Problem solved.

The hopefully obvious reason that all this manipulation and control is so dangerous for America and for each sovereign country and individual relates to the ideals and values that formed the foundation of the United States of America. Those concepts are not present in the agendas of the globalists of the WEF, WHO, the UN, the CFR, or any of the globalist entities. Their ideals, values, and goals are very different from and in fact antithetical to individual inalienable rights and natural law. They say they believe in the concept of the greater good or collectivist ideas, not the idea of individual liberty.

The truth is that they believe they are Gods, and that there is no one God or higher purpose. We know this because their "prophet" Harari says so on stage in Davos, and the room of about three thousand of the wealthiest people on the planet rise to their feet and clap wildly. Look it up—it's shocking. They have a winner-takes-all mentality and they do not consider We the People to be of value. In fact, they believe strongly in eugenics or a depopulation agenda. That's right! They want a lot less people on the planet so they can use the planet and its resources for themselves. These globalist elitists are, quite frankly, parasites and predators with a warped sense of their own importance, and there is no room in their agenda for natural law or natural rights favored by the free people of the world, which is why they are in a race against time to make sure they solidify total control and power as the world around them is waking up to their agenda and seeing them clearly all at once for the first time in history.

These people, their organizations, and their systems are international and they control the bulk of the money and resources. They are not American. They believe only in top-down global control and dominion. While these big global institutions can seem like they are outside of our control, the way they have achieved their goals so far is by infiltrating our systems. Most of our federal, state, and local governments, education, the arts, medicine, media, and so on, have been infiltrated for decades and hence the problems become very local and personal.

AMERICAN POLITICAL LEADERS

Many of the people, both public-facing and behind the scenes, are placed or groomed for these roles, and are actually required to be very much aligned with a globalist agenda. This can be done through indoctrination, blackmail, bribery, or just plain old stupidity. They support the globalists' agenda because it provides them virtually unlimited opportunities to grab one or more of the four "Ps"—power, profit, privilege, and prestige—as they assert themselves within the new governing world order. Many of these people also consider themselves Marxists, socialists, or communists, some openly and some more discreetly. Many do not believe in God, natural rights, or law, nor do they care about We the People very much. There is a reason that people who spend their entire careers in politics amass so much wealth and power on a civil servant's salary. There are perks to aligning with tyrants, and not caring about your constituents is often the result.

As long as they can keep us divided with the illusion of choice using team right or team left, they can take advantage of our conflict and chaos. Using division, they raise money and make new rules. They get us to vote for them by believing we vote for them so that they can "get" the other team through legislation and regulation, ultimately perpetuating the money and power grab for what I call the uniparty, which is controlled by the globalist elitists. For our political class, a unified America does not suit their agenda of the status quo that has enriched so many. These individuals must be exposed and weeded out in order to heal our nation and our communities.

EDUCATIONAL INSTITUTIONS

As we noted earlier, one of the key events that has driven us to the conflict addiction happened off our shores nearly a century ago with the creation of the Frankfurt School, which then migrated to the United States. This was a group of intellectuals with a vision of collectivism that has now permeated our educational system from kindergarten through college.

When people talk about indoctrination in our schools, all lesson plans can be traced either directly or with short deviations to this initiative. The collectivist influence is everywhere within academia and stands in stark contradiction to the ideas of our Founding Fathers that they memorialized. As a result, every year tens of thousands of graduates leave school with a collectivist view of how things should be. This leads to conflict.

This ideology is deeply embedded within our educational system by design. Any efforts to restore civil conversation and dialogue will have to take into account that young people are being taught just the opposite of our ideals and founding principles by many of their trusted teachers.

FEDERAL BUREAUCRACY

How does this monolithic presence fight to divide us? They do so by writing rules and exhibiting indifference. The two go hand in hand. We have mentioned the excessive amount of regulation that exists in our country today. Regulations are bureaucratic rules that take on the power of law. We, in fact, have a rule by bureaucracy. Every time a law is passed, by definition, somebody wins and somebody loses. There are people whom the law benefits and there are people whom the law restricts. The rightness or wrongness of any rule can be debated on its own merit, a sort of utilitarian calculation of total costs versus total benefits.

What cannot be debated is that we have too many rules, each one of them generating conflict seemingly by design (and sometimes deliberately and clearly by design). What is less known is that all these massive bills and laws are generally written by the think tanks, law firms, and special interest groups that funnel billions of dollars into the coffers of the political elite. This is a self-funding and self-perpetuating system of ever-increasing power and control.

Couple that with the indifference shown to citizens by members of that bureaucracy. Any American who must interact with the machinery that is the state knows of its cold and indifferent face. When you combine an enormous weight of unreasonable rules with the "let them eat cake" mentality of those enforcing them, you leave citizens in a permanent state of frustration and helplessness. That causes them to lash out. That kind of behavior can become addictive.

This kind of living environment helps the globalist agenda by leaving Americans so frustrated that they look for what might be an alternative, any alternative, to the oppression under which they find themselves. In time, if we don't stop them, it will get so bad that many will be begging for a solution, and that is the Great Reset, One World Order Global Governance plan.

MAINSTREAM MEDIA

Our mainstream media, which is losing its grip as a trusted source for many Americans, is firmly aligned with the globalist agenda. That lockstep support is easy to prove and abundantly clear with every news cycle and how they present stories to their audience. The ties between the media, government, and intelligence agencies are well known and documented. If you are not aware, the CIA infiltrated the media long ago through Project Mockingbird whereby the CIA had paid assets within the media to manage the narrative. Our Founders viewed an honest media to be a pillar of the ability to have a healthy constitutional republic where well-informed voters could make well-informed choices. If the voters are deceived, then we don't have the system most think we do. Add to that the fact that many, if not most, of those mainstream media journalists come out of and are indoctrinated at elite universities infiltrated with Frankfurt School ideology and their bias is a given.

The media doesn't just seek to divide us. Whether they individually know it or not they are destroying us and in the end they will eat their own. They do so by constantly lying to create false and destructive narratives and by delivering a message that can be summed up through saying that Americans who value individual freedom and national autonomy over collective, globalist ideas are thoughtless and selfish or racist or misogynists or whatever. There is a sort of liberty-, moral-, and values-shaming in how they present their news coverage. They are doing much more than dividing us—they are terrorizing the populous through psychological manipulation and creating an untenable social construct.

"C-SUITES," BIG TECH, AND BOARDS OF MANY LARGE CORPORATIONS

We have discussed the global fascist model that has been revealed broadly over the past few decades. This exact same model has also been uncloaked within the United States over the same time period. As companies have become larger and larger, they have acquired great power and global influence. Not only have they been infiltrated and controlled, but their economic strength allows them to work in collaboration with governments and other large institutions to exercise that power and to gain special privileges, typically through rich government contracts.

For very large companies, globalization means enormous opportunities for profit and wealth accumulation. We are firmly in the capitalist camp, in free market economies and meritocracy, but our current state is that of an unfair playing field and a lack of the rule of law that has created an ever-growing threat, a monster of power and control that consumes and harms society at will with no repercussions. The problem is that these large companies got large, and get larger, not because of free markets, but because of their special relationship with government and the privileges they are granted. We do not live in a capitalist, or free market, economy. We live in a mixed economy and the mix is getting filled by a few large players who have extreme amounts of control. One only needs to look at the tech giants or the commercial banks to find evidence.

Business used to be seen as a neutralizer of government power. Now it has become a partner in wielding that power. If you have a bit of difficulty truly understanding this, just consider the woke movement in business. Why would a men's razor company attack masculinity? Why would the bestselling everyday American beer promote a trans influencer? Why would a health and beauty company promote morbid obesity? Why would Disney, a family-friendly company, promote values that are not family-friendly? Are they driven by profits or something else? It really is not that hard to figure out—just look at their actions and corresponding results.

We said earlier that this is not a book about policies and that we are not promoting an ideology. We also said that we are supporting a principle and that is one of individual freedom. We want a free America and we think that most people do too. They just might not be aware of the forces that are trying to change it. This Step is intended to identify the impediments we have in taking back our country, restoring first principles, and reducing conflict in the process.

To state this as simply and clearly as possible, there are people scattered across the globe, firmly placed within organizations and governments, who are wanting to take control of humanity and manage our daily lives "for our own good" like we have never seen before. Technology has made it easier for them to both spread their messages and to censure the messages of dissent. Their size, scope, and power leaves many to feel hopeless about being able to fight back against them so we fight with each other instead—a sort of release.

We need to learn that there are more of us than them, and if we can stop fighting among ourselves and start talking, we can join together to push back against the global collectivist threat.

Ready to work a Seventh Step? Here are some ideas for you or members of your group to discuss and implement:

1.   Study the global public-private partnership chart of stakeholders on my resources page at www.TheMelKShow.

com. Do you know the origins, history, and financial backers of each group?

2. Identify WEF Young Global Leaders, then see if there are any graduates of these groups in your local, state, and federal government.

3. Go to each of the websites of each of the top-level groups identified on the chart on my website mentioned above and search for "global governance" and "*Agenda 2030.*" Does it appear they are all aligned in the ending of nation-states, the need for global governance and agreed-upon global rules, a desire for global surveillance and identification systems, and in supporting a unified enforcement of the same exact 17 SDGs regardless of national government or constitutions? Who is defined as the authority and enforcer of the global goals? Who is overseeing the financial and human resources on the global level?

4. Define global governance and what that means. Do you prefer this to the idea of sovereign nation-states governing within their boundaries while working towards peace and cooperation with the rest of the world, or a top-down world government coordinating from a joint platform to the rest of the nations' governments so all countries function in the same manner regardless of location or historical culture or background?

5. List the top five accomplishments of the top tier groups on the chart. If you are unfamiliar with the financial institutions listed or the BIS, please take some time to define these and who controls them and how they affect the global system.

6. When, how, and why was the United Nations formed? Who funded the United Nations? What specifically has

the United Nations achieved in terms of its stated goals at its founding? Has the United Nations been effective? How? Has it been ineffective? Why?

I know this is a lot to take in and there is so much to learn. Do your best to research for yourself, as knowledge is our best inoculation against the globalists.

VICTIMS OR VOLUNTEERS: DO NOT COMPLY—THE STAKES ARE EVERYTHING—THE TRUTH WILL SET YOU FREE

WE THE PEOPLE ACKNOWLEDGE THAT WE ARE IN AN ACTUAL WAR FOR OUR FUTURE, AND ARE FACING A DETERMINED ENEMY. WE ACCEPT THAT WE ARE THE VICTIMS OF A GREAT GLOBALLY COORDINATED DECEPTION, AND IT IS A REAL AND PRESENT DANGER TO OUR FREEDOM, OUR LIBERTY, AND THE SOVEREIGNTY OF OUR NATION.

WE HAVE COME TO UNDERSTAND THAT WE CAN RESCIND OUR CONSENT AT ANY TIME, AND REFUSE TO PARTICIPATE IN ANY AGENDA THAT DOES NOT ADHERE TO OUR OWN BELIEFS AND PRINCIPLES OR THAT OF OUR NATION.

WE UNDERSTAND THE STAKES AND DO NOT COMPLY.

WE ARE NOT VICTIMS, WE ARE VOLUNTEERS. YOU CHOOSE TO PARTICIPATE.

We previously identified our culture of victimization as being an impediment in our own lives as we get ready to become agents of change and help our fellow Americans recover from their addiction to conflict and chaos. The idea is that by holding onto a feeling of victimization, it is very difficult to shed our own anger and resentments and work toward living our life in a better way.

That would indicate that we see clinging to victim status as a sort of weakness of character, a term used in conventional recovery. That can be true if we are trying to cling to that victim status and use it as an excuse to lash out at others. It is similar to a pattern found in alcoholics or drug addicts when they profess to be trying to get sober. Somebody can do something that upsets them and then they will use their drug of choice almost as if they were using at that person in order to get back at them.

Being a victim is a very personal thing. Yes, there are people who either are or have been real victims of something. The question is how do they handle that, what do they make of that experience, and how do they move forward. We have all had bad things happen to us. Some modest grievances and some horrific and evil. Of course there should be acknowledgment, help, justice, and hopefully healing to those truly victimized. This should be an innate characteristic of a healthy community or society. But what about the perceived or self-defined victim, somebody who isn't truly a victim? This mentality is pervasive today, driven by social and media narratives and this perceived status, if you can call it a status, can often become that person's perceived reality. It is a debilitating condition, a form of disease.

That means that we must conquer the notion within ourselves of being victims and become warriors. And as warriors and agents of change, we need to reach out to the conflict addict who is still suffering and help them see the bigger picture if we can. We need to give them some form of acknowledgment for their feelings while at the same time showing them a pathway out of their deep and dark well of victimization. Some of the most horribly aggrieved people I have met are also the most happy and successful because they rose above their challenges. Perspective is critical, and understanding that positive action and attitude can and do lead to change is a powerful tool.

What we are asking you to do is to momentarily drop the distinction between real or perceived victims in your own mind and come at this from the premise that if somebody feels like a victim then it is real to them and has to be addressed in a positive and compassionate manner, not one in which you try to "prove to them" through argument that they are wrong. That just kicks in the fight or flight response, and you will have lost your opportunity.

An example of just how complex this victim culture has become in our country can be seen in a current event that is in the entertainment news as this book is being written. Disney is coming out with a new live-action version of the classic fairy tale "Snow White." In it, the lead character with skin as "white as snow" is being portrayed by a Latina actress. The seven dwarves are being played by non-dwarf adults, save for one actual dwarf. The outcries of victimization are everywhere. Some are pointing to white actresses being victimized by reverse discrimination. Disney is saying they are not using dwarves because it victimizes them by exploitation. Some members of the dwarf community are saying they are being victimized by Disney because this is one of the few roles that would normally be available to dwarf actors. The film project has turned into a hologram for victimization because depending upon which way you turn it, a new victim's image takes shape.

This might seem like a trivial example, and perhaps it is. But it is also representative of how deep the notion of victimization has been implanted throughout our culture. Remember, if everybody is a victim then nobody is. The corollary relevant to our work in trying to conquer conflict addiction is that since nearly all feel like victims in some way or another, we have to acknowledge it and address it.

It is our hope that you will start to be more aware of how you look at people and their situations and the various groups to which they might perceive they belong and try to understand why they might feel the way they do—why they might feel like victims. Be armed with acknowledgment, compassion, and kindness. At the same time, do your best to find common ground, as we all have grievances, and explore ways that we overcome our challenges in life. When someone overcomes a challenge, they can feel an immense sense of accomplishment, power, and joy. While pride is a deadly sin, being proud of overcoming an obstacle and achieving something is satisfying, rewarding, and uplifting, leading to greater and greater accomplishments.

Finally, remember that there are victims among us. These are real people, in real situations, being treated unjustly. Whenever someone is being treated in an unfair manner that they don't deserve, they are a real victim. Even when they have done something that led to their treatment, they will probably still perceive themselves as a victim. Either way, it serves us to try to reach them if we can.

On a personal note, I have been one of those "victims among us" at varying times in my life. Sometimes it was by my own hand and other times I was gratuitously and seriously attacked and harmed by others without any cause or provocation. In that state of depression and victimhood I needed support, tools, and the strength of will to climb out of that deep well of victimization.

My understanding of my own weaknesses, faults, and perceived victimhood helped me to understand where our country is today and how we have been led to become addicted to conflict and chaos. What I have learned through my life experiences has given me tools, strategies, resources, and the strength to overcome challenges and harness the warrior spirit. My goal in writing this book is to help our nation by sharing my understanding of the mess we are in and the ways we can dig ourselves out to heal and prosper again as a people and a nation.

Ready to work an Eighth Step? Here are some ideas for you or members of your group to discuss and implement:

1. Define the terms victim, participant, and volunteer. Do you fit in any of these categories when it comes to our culture, society, or nation?
2. Define manipulation and coercion.
3. What are some strengths you have that keep you from being manipulated or coerced? What are some of the weaknesses you can work on?
4. When was the last time you did something you did not want to do and regretted not saying no or not participating. What was your thinking before you made that decision? What can you do next time to choose a different path?

MAKING AMENDS AND LETTING GO: STRENGTHEN THE TIES THAT BIND US TOGETHER

HAVING IDENTIFIED WHERE WE HAVE NEGLECTED OUR DUTY OR RESPONSIBILITY FOR OUR SITUATION, WE SOUGHT TO HUMBLY MAKE AMENDS IN CASES WHERE IT WOULD NOT BE HARMFUL OR COUNTERPRODUCTIVE TO OURSELVES OR OTHERS.

BUILD BRIDGES TO AMASS A FORCE FOR POSITIVE CHANGE—THE RIPPLE EFFECT.

Traditional recovery programs speak to humbly making amends with those the addict has harmed as long as it does not hurt that person or others. For the purposes of saving our society, we must consider others and ourselves very differently in the equation, which is materially different in many ways from traditional recovery.

You will note that we do not want to unnecessarily harm ourselves in the process. This is not part of the traditional recovery program because there is a notion within those Steps that the addict has to be held accountable for what they did while in the depths of their addiction. In some cases, this even means turning themselves into the police for a crime they might have committed, or admitting to a spouse that you have cheated and accepting the consequences. My view of Americans Anonymous is that we have all been harmed and manipulated by forces often beyond our control or understanding, and the concept of personal blame or accountability is not as important as personal awareness and then taking action to reclaim our sovereignty.

First, in order to be successful in this process, you are going to need a few things:

> **Honesty:** No BS is going to be allowed in this process. You have to be honest with people if you want them to be honest with you. Just remember that your honesty can't be used to injure them further. That's not being honest; that's just having plain bad manners. Be honest, but do no harm.

> **Open-Mindedness:** You have to bring an open mind to this process, and you have to be willing to get comfortable being uncomfortable. You are going to hear and learn things from and about people that don't necessarily fit with your preconceived notions. No confirmation bias allowed. Don't go searching for the answers you want; search for the real answers and be willing to deal with them when you get them.

Willingness: This is going to take some work. You are not going to be able to do this just sitting comfortably in that ergonomic chair of yours. You will have to be willing to get up, get out, and get involved. That requires energy. Just get yourself started and watch how inertia can build.

Persistence: It took a long time to lose our way and we have been propagandized for a very long time from many sources. Winners win often through dogged persistence and the unwillingness to accept defeat. It can take years to deprogram individuals, and wars are not won in a day. Be strong, patient, and persistent, always keeping in mind just how important the stakes are.

The next thing to try to keep in mind is a phrase we have already used: as long as the ties that bind us together are stronger than those that can tear us apart, all will be well. We need to remember that whatever our differences and whatever our perceived notions are about injustices, we are all still Americans. That should create a positive tie between us that allows us to work through anything if we are simply willing to do so. If you want to look at it another way, you could say that we are stuck with each other, on the same boat if you will, so we ought to make the best of it and at least try. Either way, we are all tied together—will sink or swim together—so let's use and build on the strength of those ties that bind us.

Here are some suggestions for being a positive agent of change and helping save our nation as you reach out to others:

Don't recklessly martyr yourself: The way to address the grievances of others is not to destroy yourself. Here is what you have to keep in mind about people who perceive themselves as or have been conditioned to believe they are victims: victims tend to feel entitled to something. That means that if you try to do or say something that sacrifices your personal situation, it might not be appreciated the way you hoped it would be. The other person might just feel as though you were supposed to sacrifice for them, and then start looking for something else to satisfy their need because it is not really coming from a place of truth. Feeding into their victimhood narrative will not be productive, but understanding it and finding common ground from which to open the door and open minds will.

Avoid defending yourself or justifying yourself to others—it's a trap: It is almost a reflexive action, when somebody is sharing with you that they feel they have been victimized, to look at them and say, "Well that certainly isn't me. I do not…" We always want to instinctually defend ourselves. While it might very well be true that we are not part of some particular problem, going out of our way to say that is counterproductive. It creates a feeling of insincerity on the part of the other party. You are not building bridges but creating divides. If you are not part of the problem, don't tell them, show them! They will come to know you through your actions, understanding, resolve, and steadfast beliefs in positive change for all.

Ask questions of those who are closest to you—don't argue with them: When you are with friends, family, classmates, coworkers, or anyone who you find is sharing their victim status, ask them questions. Ask why they feel that way. Ask them if they can give specific examples. Get them to choose words to describe their circumstance. Don't try to prove them wrong or minimize their concerns. People who feel as though they are victims tend to feel less-than and apart-from. Arguing with them won't get them to that place. Remember, you can never win an argument with a victim. Often just asking and listening leads to an unexpected realization or breakthrough.

Work within the limits of the system (and work to change it in the process): We have all sorts of systems in this country, some legal, some deliberately structural, some simply organic and long-standing. In trying to create change and help people who feel victimized by any one or more of those systems, it is necessary to try to do it by working within its confines if you hope to get something done quickly. Working within an "unfair" system doesn't mean giving up and surrendering to it. It means that you are acknowledging that the best way to change it is to have new positive elements replace the bad ones from the inside out. A positive change within a corrupt system today can lead to a necessary erosion or even collapse of the diseased system, leading to replacing or rebuilding a better system for tomorrow.

Understand that your focus must be forward: Look where you are going, not where you have been. Those who feel like they have been victimized like to spend time talking about and focusing on the things that have happened that created their victim status. Said differently, if victims drive like they view their circumstances they will immediately get in an accident because they will only be looking in their rearview mirror. Without passing judgment on any of their claims or beliefs, you need to suggest to them that if they want real change, dwelling on the past will not help their cause. Use the future tense when engaging them, not the past. Focus on moving forward.

Do not expect instant gratification—steel yourselves for a long process: We got to this point in America over a very long period of time. We will not reverse this in a couple of years. Pace yourself. Find ways to savor the gift that is life while still acting as a change agent. Enjoy the journey. It does no good to abandon the joy of your life while trying to improve your life, the lives of others, or this country in general. We all know that caregivers have to take care of themselves first. Be good to yourself along the way!

Consider yourself a change agent and wear the label with honor: Those trying to divide us have long been winning the battle of language. It is time for us to take some control. Let us take the term "change agent" and ignore however and whoever else might have used it before for less-than-noble ambitions and claim it for our own. We are the people who are truly trying to change the direction of the country. We are the ones who are truly trying to reach others, hear their stories, and effect a positive change. Let us be united, clear, and unapologetic. Let us come under one term so we can speak with one voice and create a unified front for all other Americans to see. Whatever that term is, live it, love it, and be proud to be a part of the solution.

Recruit and inspire others: There are millions of people who will agree with us, but many lack the willingness to seek out active groups or do not see the opportunities around them. We need to attempt to recruit them. Individually, in small groups, through our community meetings, we can inspire others to find the will inside themselves to join. We need to constantly offer others the opportunity to join us in finding solutions together. We need to go forth and bring others in wherever and whenever we find a willing and able partner. Having their active assistance can be the winning edge over time.

Make those newcomers feel welcome: Have you ever gotten talked into going to a party by a friend where you don't know anybody, but they assure you that they will stay with you and make you feel comfortable? What happens when you walk in the door? Your friend takes off immediately and leaves you standing alone wondering where to hang your jacket. It is a lonely, uncomfortable feeling and it makes you want to just turn around and leave.

As change agents, this is something we can't allow to happen to new people who walk into our "party." We need to make certain that they are welcomed warmly and introduced to the crowd. We don't want them to leave. Every new entrant is a VIP upon arrival. That is how the traditional recovery program works, and it is how ours can if we work it properly.

Share our stories: We need to share the nature of our own personal stories of both overcoming our own trepidation before getting actively involved, and how our lives and outcomes improved once we did. Share what putting purpose into action ignited within us and others. People love stories. Sharing stories of learning, growing, and success builds a kind of enthusiasm. It makes people feel as though they are not alone, that something is really happening, and that they can be a part of it too.

Learn to dine with new "friends"—remember they do not eat red meat: We are in the habit of mostly communicating about issues and ideas within the safety of our own ideological and philosophical circles. This is comfortable for us. We are going to need to get uncomfortable and start to engage people who do not generally agree with us (whoever "us" is and whatever it is that we agree upon). That means that the kinds of things we might typically share among like-minded people, and the tone that we choose, not only will not work but will be counterproductive. "Red meat" can be served only to those who have a taste for it. Content and ideas that are both "leaner" and "sweeter" will be more appealing to the people we need to engage.

This Step truly requires a mixture of determination, steadfastness, perseverance, and compassion. These are difficult ingredients to blend, but nothing about recovery is easy. The hardest part is to keep your side of the street clean. Don't let yourself fall into a defeatist or negative mindset. The active addict can't very well help another active addict get sober. Be the example, and others will follow.

Ready to Work a Ninth Step? Here are some ideas for you or your group to discuss and implement:

1. Develop three questions that you can ask anyone that would be universally acceptable and can open doors. Asking questions honestly interested in the answer with no agenda works to open dialogue up.
2. List three things you believe are common-sense issues the majority of people would want fixed moving forward regardless of background or personal history.
3. Consider three people in your life you think you can reach that may join you in the mission to preserve freedom and liberty. Start the process of connecting to suggest teaming up to solve shared concerns and aim to put in some time preferably in person.
4. Start looking around for local meetings, or consider what your own meeting would look like. Write it down. Consciously continue formulating what a productive meeting would look like, and continue to consider where, when, and other aspects.

ETERNAL VIGILANCE AND A COMMITMENT TO DOING BETTER

WE STRIVE TO CONTINUOUSLY EXAMINE OUR OWN BEHAVIOR TO ENSURE WE ARE CONSTRUCTIVELY ENGAGING OTHERS AND NOT SLIPPING BACK INTO OLD HABITS. WE ACKNOWLEDGE WE ARE ALWAYS AT GREAT RISK OF RELAPSE TO OLD DESTRUCTIVE BEHAVIORS, AND REGULARLY COMMIT TO NEW BEHAVIORS AND WAYS OF THINKING.

BE SELF-AWARE, STAY MINDFUL, AND REGULARLY CHECK YOUR BEHAVIOR.

If you are familiar with recovery meetings, it's not uncommon that someone who has been around for a while, maybe even someone who has been a leader within that particular group, walks in uncharacteristically quiet, grabs a seat in the back of the room, head down, and later shares that they just used yesterday for the first time in years. It happens.

When it happens, that person has to start the Step Program all over again. How can any addict prevent this from happening to them? One answer is for them to constantly stay vigilant and constantly assess how they are doing in working the Program.

Likewise, our Tenth Step is designed to help you not slip back into your addiction to conflict and chaos. To that end, we are going to share a handful of tips that we think will be useful.

Most people will acknowledge that being sober wasn't achieved without many stops and starts along the way. Many relapse often before finally (to the extent there is a finally) figuring it out. What is interesting about relapses isn't the number of them, it is the fact that relapses occur for different reasons and with very different surrounding circumstances. The lesson is clear. If you think that there is only one thing that you have to avoid in order to not get sent over the edge, think again. You most likely have more than one trigger.

In today's world of twenty-four-seven propaganda media and divergent opinions, there is no shortage of platforms and people that will pull those triggers. Remember everything we have learned up until this point. Your political and cultural leaders are deliberately trying to keep us angry so that they can capitalize on that anger by having you "follow" them against your "enemies." It will often be very tempting to fall into old habits, but you must do your best to resist to accomplish the desired mission to save our country.

The media platforms bombarding us with hostility aren't going away, nor are friends, family, or coworkers who vehemently oppose our viewpoints, just don't get it, or are comfortably numb to the massive dis-ease that afflicts our society. Wherever you go in this conflict-addicted country, you are going to run into triggers. Let's start our Tenth Step helpful reminders by talking about triggers—avoiding them when you can and dealing with them effectively when you must. This will be the most fundamental requirement in your attempt to stay "conflict sober."

Know your triggers—avoid them, or confront and redirect them: Remember our introduction to the idea that addicts need to change their people, playgrounds, and playthings if they want to remain sober. You are going to have to do the same thing. Each one of the concepts listed below actually serves as triggers, but the general notion gets singled out here because it is really the key to maintaining conflict sobriety.

Triggers are about habits. Some addicts will say that smoking makes them want a drink or watching a football game makes them want to bet or feeling down makes them want to eat. These are the kinds of triggers that an addict comes to understand and seeks to avoid when possible and to reframe their thinking when faced with them.

Only you can know your triggers—what leads you to conflict and chaos with others. At the end of this Step you are going to be asked to make a list of what you believe are your triggers. This is important as it forces you to be introspective and honest and to evaluate your processing of external stimuli and resulting behaviors that may be harmful or clearly not productive. Ultimately We the People must form new habits and take new actions to achieve better outcomes!

No more secrets: As I have been saying on my podcast and in my speeches, we, as a country, are as sick as our secrets. And if you haven't noticed, we are currently living in a very sick society and that sickness has manifested itself in conflict and chaos. We the People need and must demand transparency, honesty, and disclosure from those in positions of power. One might say, "Be careful what you wish for because you may learn something you can barely handle." That is true but we must take the chance to save our nation.

Unfortunately, many will be shocked to learn what governments, corporations, institutions, and others in positions of power have done to We the People under the guise of protecting our safety and security over the years, but again this is part of the healing process. Transparency from those in power will lead to trust and we will be a more cohesive and stronger nation for it. We will also identify and weed out those conspirators that have acted in their own self-interest to the detriment of those they are supposed to serve and protect. Of course, not everything needs to be exposed, especially if it is truly a matter of national security. But covering up crimes that should never have been perpetrated, especially against We the People, is a crime in and of itself and we must rid our nation of this criminal pattern and practice.

There are so many things that have not been fully explored nor disclosed in the last fifty years in our country that it would be too much to list. Even if we go back just a few years and revisit some of the big events in our country that would probably suffice to help heal the nation. There seems to be a pattern and practice on the part of the elitists in our country that the American people don't deserve or aren't able to handle the truth. While in rare instances this might be true for good reason, normally they are just covering up mistakes or crimes that they perpetrated to enrich and empower themselves. There is a great line uttered by Jack Nicholson in *A Few Good Men*: "You can't handle the truth." The real truth is that people in power who serve We the People simply have no right to classify, hide, and manipulate society with propaganda to serve their own interests. This is a nation formed by We the People and they serve us. We get to decide how we handle the truth, not them.

When information is withheld from people, it creates distrust. Most people know when they are being lied to or if something simply doesn't make sense. It also breeds speculation and many divergent assumptions and conclusions being drawn by people in order to try to make sense of things that simply don't add up. Human beings have a natural drive to find reasons and explanations for things they can't explain or don't understand. This creates a societal landscape where nothing seems true, everything is speculation, and we have even created a new lexicon to define "your truth" to add to this total lack of grounding in truth, facts, and reality. Keeping secrets from others, and having them kept from you, can lead to people trying to "construct" a truth. Truth can't be constructed. Truth simply is. Living in a world where there is no truth is a recipe, as we have seen, for disaster.

As many of you may know, one of my favorite writers, Hannah Arendt said, "the ideal subject of totalitarianism is…people for whom the distinction between fact and fiction [and] true and false…no longer exist[s]." Does this sound like where we are now? We are being propagandized to think that genders don't exist. A man can be a woman and a woman a man or a cat or a furry. I could go on and on about the mass messaging and confusion of our populace but hopefully you see that living in a world with no truth, where facts are manipulated and history rewritten is catastrophically bad and has in fact been the primary catalyst to much of the ills of ourselves and our nation. Thank you, mainstream media, fact checkers, Big Tech, and our intelligence agencies. Houston, we have a problem. And the solution is…no more secrets!

Be courageous in the face of fear, understanding the risks and the stakes of your action: We have already noted courage as being one of the four classical virtues. Defining the true essence of courage has been the work of many over time. How best to sum it up? I have had the honor and privilege to speak with many great leaders in our military and what I have learned is that courage is not the absence of fear, it is in fact selfless action in the face of fear. Being courageous is being able to move through fear. Some learn to control fear, some get used to fear, and some simply push through it in the moment, but courage is always an action where risk is involved. It is best to understand the risks you are taking, and the stakes on the table will be the primary motivator, but ultimately you will have to find your own courage.

One thing good decision makers don't do is act out of anger or emotion. Emotions can generate irrational and extreme responses and lead to poor judgment as we are enveloped in the fight or flight mode. Showing courage isn't about acting rashly or impulsively, and it is definitely not about acting out of anger. An act of courage should be as rational a decision as any other important one you might make. You need to assess the situation you are in, and you need to rationally figure out what needs to be done. If the circumstances require you to do something that places yourself at risk, then if you do, at least you know that it will be worth taking that risk because it matters to you.

You are going to need courage to act to save our country and to work, and stay with, this program. Don't let your emotions get the better of you. Stay focused on the mission, remember the stakes on the table and use your tools to overcome challenges. In the end, winners never give up. They may lose battles but they persevere to win the war.

Apply critical thinking, discernment, and skepticism in all your affairs: René Descartes is considered by many to be the founder of using reason as a method. His work is also often credited with bringing to an end the witch trials and persecutions rampant through Europe and in the United States during the seventeenth century and prior. While you might not know much about him, most people do know the phrase he coined when logically proving his own existence: cogito, ergo sum (I think, therefore, I am). Descartes called man a "thinking thing." Using that as a definition, lately in America we have been trying really hard to disprove our own existence.

Critical thinking can be defined as applying objective reason and dispassionate evaluation in order to form a judgment. Judgment also can be thought of as a conclusion or an opinion. A critical thinker starts with an event and works toward an opinion.

Critical thinking is further defined by Michael Scriven and Richard Paul as "the intellectually disciplined process of actively and skillfully conceptualizing, applying, analyzing, synthesizing, and/or evaluating information gathered from, or generated by, observation, experience, reflection, reasoning, or communication, as a guide to belief and action."

Discernment can be defined as the quality of being able to grasp and comprehend what is obscure by Merriam-Webster or the ability to judge people and things well by Cambridge.

Skepticism as explained by the Center for Inquiry comes from the ancient Greek "skepsis," meaning "inquiry." Skepticism is, therefore, not a cynical rejection of new ideas, as the popular stereotype goes, but rather an attitude of both open-mindedness and critical sense. In essence, being a skeptic means you doubt something that is presented as true, factual, or useful and it keeps you on your toes and forces you to be more of a critical thinker with better discernment. My partner Rob is a great skeptic and critical thinker. There is a reason he picked up the name Rob Really?

When you are in a state of addiction you will look very hard for ways to justify destructive addiction thoughts and actions. We must break our bad habits and lose our confirmation biases. As you have interactions throughout your day, you are going to have to force yourself to walk through the deliberate process of applying reason instead of emotion to handle situations as they present themselves. You also need to teach others how to do the same. We the People must use our skills and tools to accomplish our mission of winning hearts and minds to save our country one soul at a time.

Think of all the times we have been misled by those in power telling us things that were not only not true but out-and-out lies. Unfortunately, even a recent list is nearly endless. We have learned that much of what we hear and even see must be thoroughly vetted in order to even consider it as possibly true. It is a sad state of affairs but this is reality in today's information warfare climate. Any blind acceptance and obedience of narratives can have devastating and deadly effects and we must be constantly on guard when consuming any information.

Those of you who follow *The Mel K Show* know that I follow the money. Follow the money and you will see who is behind an agenda or narrative. By following the money you use another critical thinking and discernment tool by asking yourself, "Who benefits?" Think of all the times that a leader, or some organization, announces some sort of new "program" designed to accomplish some greater social good. They always make their program sound so wonderful and appealing. This programming is in fact a linguistic tactic and it's used pervasively by those deceiving you, but if you stop to think about who is really benefiting, and who might actually be hurt by the same thing, you might just discover that there is something more at work than just what you are being told.

In your daily interactions you will undoubtedly come across cynics. Cynical people mainly just discount or disagree with everything, especially if it doesn't fit in their dogmatic thinking.

Somebody who tries to be skeptical without going through a proper thought process of critical thinking and discernment is simply cynical. Cynicism is a character weakness. It is lazy and small-minded and it generally leads to conflict. Skepticism is a method that leads to solutions.

Develop the discipline to think critically and skeptically and you will improve your discernment and reduce your chances of conflict and chaos relapse greatly.

Change how you use social media: People are not going to change their social media behavior, nor do you have control of others' behavior, but you do have control of your behavior. By changing your behavior you can influence others, set an example, or certainly turn down the temperature by not engaging in overly confrontational behavior.

I get attacked all the time on social media. Why? I don't know, but clearly when I speak against the narrative some "people" or bots or paid trolls attack me. My partner Rob has always told me to focus on what I do and not what others say. It is clear that many of these negative comments are placed to elicit engagement, which is in fact the goal of many of these platforms and these platforms have figured out that fighting and stirring up negative emotion is the most engaging behavior. I know that much of the nasty comments are placed to fish for a response and once you respond, well, now you are in a dialogue—a fight maybe, but a dialogue nonetheless. If you have the willpower to not engage with nasty comments then it is likely that the comments will end there. What's that old saying that if a tree falls in the woods and no one is there to hear it does it make a sound?

If you engage then you are in a conversation of sorts that can escalate and expand. Of course there are times to fight and defend yourself, restate your point, or refute nonsense, but often negative comments are just injected to inflame and elicit a response. You should especially notice that many of the attacks lack substance and are directed at the person to demean and degenerate their effectiveness. This is a Marxist, Saul Alinsky tactic. Try not to care what others say about you and just run your own life the best you can. Spread truth and informed opinions and move on. Always try your best to make good choices. Try using the tactic of asking people questions on social media when they use strong or derogatory rhetoric. This falls back on the time-tested Socratic method. Don't ask snarky questions either. Ask real ones. This is a discipline that isn't easy. Your first thought is likely to be, "Why would I bother with this person?" The question is natural to ask, but think about it this way, if we have that attitude toward everyone, we won't be able to change anyone. You can't reach everybody, but you can reach out. Asking questions is one of the very best ways to lower temperature.

Don't let the opinions of others become your own: I was able to build a relatively successful daily podcast where I get to share my research and insights along with extraordinary guests free to share their own on a wide variety of topics and thoughtful, well-researched insights on so many issues affecting humanity. I always make it a point to tell my audience that they need to go out and find things out for themselves, to do their own research. I'm not just saying that, I know from experience that uncovering information or facts and developing informed opinions is far better when you empower yourself with knowledge and come to your own conclusions. I admit that early on in my work there were times that I considered some sources to be trustworthy, but I have learned that you must always research for yourself even if the information comes from those you believe to be trusted sources. When you do the work and trust yourself you become confident, empowered, and able to put forth a well-thought-out and genuine argument.

I try my best to educate my audience with truth and facts, provide sources, and encourage them to do their own research. I also encourage others to evaluate sources and empower and educate themselves to become well-informed, confident, and articulate citizens. My resource page is one of my great gifts to discernment and a treasure to be shared. Many of my listeners have become their own detectives and share information, and many have started their own podcasts or projects once they realized they, too, could be a voice of truth and transparency on this information battlefield.

There is a kind of interesting paradox that many consumers of information can find themselves in. In their personal lives, they are often unwilling to let the opinions of those closest to them influence their behavior, yet they will blindly follow the constant drum of trusted sources on all forms of media. We must break the bonds of the propaganda media, narrative control, and manipulation. Do not give anybody the power to make you think or feel anything. That is your power exclusively. You need to be your own master. Do not surrender yourself to another and don't judge yourself by others. You cannot be controlled, and the only person with whom you are competing to "do better" is you.

Empty your head on paper: This is the oldest tool in the recovery toolbox. Every new incoming recovery soul is encouraged by their sponsor to start journaling. There are several advantages to be gained from this process:

- It serves as a self-directed form of cognitive behavioral therapy. It helps you change your own distorted beliefs, thoughts, and attitudes because by writing things down and then reading them you are confronting yourself on a regular basis.

- It can help you start to measure the distance between who you are and who you want to be by keeping track of what you have done and how you have engaged others versus what you had hoped and intended to do.
- It can help you to set goals.
- It provides an outlet for anger and fear so that you don't act out on either during your daily encounters.

There are other benefits but those alone should convince you that the discipline of sitting down and emptying your head on paper can be therapeutic and even cathartic. It is also a way to look in the mirror and see if you're the person you wanted to be.

Ask for help: In traditional recovery programs, people are encouraged to get a sponsor. A sponsor guides you through the Twelve Steps and is also someone you turn to when you find yourself thinking about using again. Sponsors have been talking sponsees off the using ledge for a century. It is the sober person's version of the buddy system.

You can't be successful working this process alone. There is so much conflict in this country today that you are going to find yourself being drawn into it on a daily basis. Moreover, since you are wanting to help combat it you are going to have to be right in the middle of it. It is going to be difficult to not start "using" again! Turn to others in your community for help. Raise your hand. Tell somebody, "I'm about to lose it." Remember, together we do get better, and a problem shared is a problem cut in half.

There is an expression coined by poet Devon Brough, and built upon by motivational expert Christina Giordano, that says, "Choose your hard." In this context, we know that staying vigilant, avoiding addiction to conflict, and living in the solution isn't going to be easy. This is hard work. But it is also hard to imagine our country surviving under its current condition of hate and intolerance.

Each one of us has to choose our hard. We hope you choose the hard work of staying away from conflict and chaos and towards the mission of saving our country.

Ready to work a Tenth Step? Here are some ideas for you or members of your group to discuss and implement:

1. List three things or situations or subjects that personally tend to trigger you to engage in conflict and chaos.
2. Develop a strategy to deal with each trigger above.
3. Consider and list three strategies as to how you can alter your use of social media, if you are regularly engaged, for a more positive outcome or improved personal mental health.
4. Commit to and start a handwritten Americans Anonymous journal you write in daily if even for a few minutes a day.
5. List a few like-minded buddies to help you through the rough times.
6. Make sure you unplug. List a few things that you can do that take you out of the battles and put you in a calm space, such as exercise, a good movie, or time in nature.

CONTINUE TO STRIVE FOR A MORE PERFECT UNION: OUR FOUNDING DOCUMENTS AND PRINCIPLES WILL LEAD THE WAY

THROUGH PRAYER, POSITIVE ACTION, AND REGULARLY REVISITING OUR FOUNDING PRINCIPLES AND DOCUMENTS WE REMAIN CONSTANTLY FOCUSED ON STRIVING TOWARDS A MORE PERFECT UNION FOR OUR COUNTRY BASED ON THE RIGHTS TO LIFE, LIBERTY, AND THE PURSUIT OF HAPPINESS.

OUR FOUNDING DOCUMENTS AND PRINCIPLES WILL LEAD THE WAY.

Revisiting principles is important no matter what the topic or process is. As you work on your own tools and reach out to more people and get them engaged in a positive way, you need to remember what the key principles are that we want to reinforce. By keeping them in mind always, you will also notice where they are missing in your everyday life and then you can work to try to restore them.

Principles are special things because they can be universally applied and are portable. You can use the principles we describe here in your journey to help America conquer its addiction to conflict and chaos. Here are some key principles to keep in mind as you continue your journey towards moving towards reviving our more perfect Union.

This country was founded by We the People. Take a look at some of these constitutional rights of citizens. We think you will agree they are all very positive:

Citizens are guaranteed by law:

a) freedom of speech;
b) freedom of the press;
c) freedom of assembly, including the holding of mass meetings;
d) freedom of street processions and demonstrations.

These civil rights are ensured by placing at the disposal of the working people and their organizations printing presses, stocks of paper, public buildings, the streets, communications facilities and other material requisites for the exercise of these rights.

There are more…

The inviolability of the homes of citizens and privacy of correspondence are protected by law.

...in order to develop the organizational initiative and political activity of the masses of the people, citizens...are ensured the right to unite in public organizations—trade unions, cooperative associations, youth organizations, sport and defense organizations, cultural, technical and scientific societies...

These all sound like pretty good rights for citizens to have. If you don't recognize them from our Constitution, don't feel bad. They aren't ours, they belong to the Soviet Union Constitution of 1936, right at the height of the Stalin purges and show trials.

Obviously, these rights of the citizens were not honored in the Soviet Union. We can argue that those rights being ignored was immoral, but there is another way of looking at it. The Soviets had every "right" not to honor those rights that were granted because in that system the grantor of rights was the government. Whoever grants the rights has the power to take them away.

In America, it was We the People who granted certain power to the government and with severe limitations being assigned to that power. Our nation was built from the bottom up. The Soviet Union was built from the top down. Stalin had every right to limit the rights he had granted, and We the People have the right to attempt to peacefully reign in the overexercise of power that the government has assumed over what we had originally intended. We own the place.

As James Madison, one of the most influential and prolific writers among our Founding Fathers, wrote, "the people are the only legitimate fountain of power, and it is from them that the constitutional charter, under which the several branches of government hold their power, is derived..."

One principle of business is that absentee owners typically have the employees run roughshod over operations. Inventory disappears, the cash register is short, and there are lights out on the signage. We the People have been absentee owners and our business is starting to look like it is going out of business. The fact that we started as a bottom-up organization is an important principle to remember. Harry Truman was wrong. The buck doesn't stop with the president. The buck stops with us. Let's stop passing the buck and take ownership of our ownership.

We are a nation of limited government: Remember how we have pointed to the English philosopher John Locke as likely being the single most influential intellectual force behind the decisions our Founders made in creating the structure for our new nation. Locke wrote that "government has no other end but the preservation of property" and "every man has a property in his own person: this nobody has a right to but himself." Locke's take on natural rights became our Founders' take. They wanted to create a framework wherein the government could only take the actions necessary to protect life, liberty, and property.

We can all see that the government today, at all levels, has gone far beyond what was sanctioned by Locke and embraced at the Constitutional Convention. Government has become invasive in every element of our lives. We have flipped our foundation on its head and have allowed the formation of a leviathan, a state so large and so powerful that most Americans have long since lost track of the original principle of limited government.

It must be remembered that having large governmental units at every level, with unified bureaucracies of unelected leaders within them, is functionally the same as being ruled by a monarch (something we fought a war to escape). It might actually be worse insofar as with a king or queen, at least there is a single throne at which to point when their rule becomes insufferable. In America today, who is in charge? Where do we point? At whom are we pointing? I have been speaking a lot lately about tyranny by bureaucracy. The systems of control in our society are so large and opaque that there is unlimited control and power with zero accountability by those in power.

The Bill of Rights is more than just the first ten amendments: We shared that the Bill of Rights was proposed essentially contemporaneously with the original Constitution because some of the Founding Fathers were worried that the Constitution itself wasn't specific enough in making clear that the newly formed government could not encroach into certain areas of individual liberty. Turns out they were right, and it turns out that even their Bill of Rights hasn't been enough in some cases.

So important is the Bill of Rights that we present it below and ask that you take the three minutes required to review. As you do, note the similarities between some of these specific limitations of government to the rights granted to citizens by the Soviet Constitution.

THE BILL OF RIGHTS

First Amendment: Congress shall make no law respecting an establishment of religion, or prohibiting the free exercise thereof; or abridging the freedom of speech, or of the press; or the right of the people peaceably to assemble, and to petition the Government for a redress of grievances.

Second Amendment: A well regulated Militia, being necessary to the security of a free State, the right of the people to keep and bear Arms, shall not be infringed.

Third Amendment: No Soldier shall, in time of peace be quartered in any house, without the consent of the Owner, nor in time of war, but in a manner to be prescribed by law.

Fourth Amendment: The right of the people to be secure in their persons, houses, papers, and effects, against unreasonable searches and seizures, shall not be violated, and no Warrants shall issue, but upon probable cause, supported by Oath or affirmation, and particularly describing the place to be searched, and the persons or things to be seized.

Fifth Amendment: No person shall be held to answer for a capital, or otherwise infamous crime, unless on a presentment or indictment of a Grand Jury, except in cases arising in the land or naval forces, or in the Militia, when in actual service in time of War or public danger; nor shall any person be subject for the same offence to be twice put in jeopardy of life or limb; nor shall be compelled in any criminal case to be a witness against himself, nor be deprived of life, liberty, or property, without due process of law; nor shall private property be taken for public use, without just compensation.

Sixth Amendment: In all criminal prosecutions, the accused shall enjoy the right to a speedy and public trial, by an impartial jury of the State and district wherein the crime shall have been committed, which district shall have been previously ascertained by law, and to be informed of the nature and cause of the accusation; to be confronted with the witnesses against him; to have compulsory process for obtaining witnesses in his favor, and to have the Assistance of Counsel for his defence.

Seventh Amendment: In Suits at common law, where the value in controversy shall exceed twenty dollars, the right of trial by jury shall be preserved, and no fact tried by a jury, shall be otherwise re-examined in any Court of the United States, than according to the rules of common law.

Eighth Amendment: Excessive bail shall not be required, nor excessive fines imposed, nor cruel and unusual punishments inflicted.

Ninth Amendment: The enumeration in the Constitution, of certain rights, shall not be construed to deny or disparage others retained by the people.

Tenth Amendment: The powers not delegated to the United States by the Constitution, nor prohibited by it to the States, are reserved to the States respectively, or to the people.

We would like you to consider two things. First, imagine that there was no other part to our Constitution and that these ten amendments, these ten almost secular commandments, were all we had available with which to govern ourselves. If we followed them, imagine just how good life might be. It is their simple, yet comprehensive and universal nature, that makes each of them a principle which we must fight to maintain and to restore when violated.

The second thing to consider is just how badly we have allowed these ten strong limitations to be chipped away at over time. These principal freedoms, the limitations on government authority, thought so important by our Founders, have come to resemble the ruins of ancient Athens or Rome. What have we done? What have we let be done?

We are a nation of opportunity not a nation of entitlement: There has been a shift that has taken place in our country, beginning with the New Deal programs of the 1930s and accelerating with the Great Society programs of the 1960s. These entitlement programs and the concepts behind them have taken us further away from being a self-reliant people focused on having the opportunity to achieve toward a society that is more focused on being entitled to outcomes. This is a radical departure from a key first principle. We could write an entire book on the agendas behind these programs but suffice to say, these social safety net programs are not accidents and the agendas are not benevolent. Remember hard times make strong men.

Our nation was built on the idea that barriers to individual fulfillment ought not to be artificially erected by the government or any other institution. Importantly, reaching fulfillment was up to the individual and their willingness to work hard, pursue their own goals, and chase their own dreams. That doesn't mean that we are not meant to help one another, and it certainly doesn't mean we are to exploit others in following our own pursuits. It simply means we were not to expect others to do our work for us.

We have been corralled to become increasingly dependent upon government through the government's control mechanisms. Through the use of licensing, zoning, rules, regulations, social safety nets, handouts, and an unending array of laws the citizens of America have been pushed to believe that the government makes the rules, enforces the rules, and solves the problems. What problems? Almost any problem. Even at the micro level of cities and municipalities, when the citizens see something wrong they are forced to turn to the city council members to "fix it." This is our country. These are our cities. We need to find ways and mechanisms to fix things ourselves or at minimum ensure that our elected officials who are supposed to represent We the People do so honestly, ethically, and effectively.

We have stated that we have turned this into a binary country where everything has to be a yes-no, black-white type of answer. Too often the debates are "for or against welfare," or "for or against public healthcare." These are not for-against issues, they are problems to be solved by compassionate people lucky enough to live in the most affluent nation ever seen in history. Being compassionate and helping others in need does not require making them dependent. Assistance and dependence are not synonyms.

If you are a collectivist, seek a government-centric world where the people are reliant upon the system of control for the good of the many then that is your choice and we are not condemning you for that view. What we are saying is that is not an American principle. We the People are working to help restore our founding principles and values through civility and conversation. We respect the difference, but it is a very big difference.

We are a nation founded on Judeo-Christian ethics: We are a nation that was founded on the concepts of the Golden Rule and the ten commandments as moral guideposts and we have to remember that these ideas were woven through Western civilization for thousands of years before our founding. One nation under God means something and the Founders knew it.

Recall the passage from the New Testament where we are told to love our neighbor as ourselves. For all the corruption done by man to Christ's teaching over millennia, the teachings themselves lie somewhere within the heart of who we are and how this nation was built. Set the God part aside if you must, but do acknowledge the influence of His teachings and the importance of His moral code on and in the structure of our society.

Likewise, the Ten Commandments (those other Ten Commandments) have played a principal role in forming the American experience. We printed the Bill of Rights, so here are those "other" ten (recognizing scholarly disagreements over translations):

1. You shall have no other Gods but me.
2. You shall not make or worship any idols.
3. You shall not misuse the name of the Lord your God.
4. You shall remember and keep the Sabbath day holy.
5. Respect your father and mother.
6. You must not murder.
7. You must not take someone else's husband or wife.
8. You must not steal.
9. You must not lie.
10. You must not be envious.

Good stuff. Rules about decency. So much of Western law has been built around these basic ideals. While the first four can be set easily aside by the atheist, the remaining six are part of our culture. Note the proscriptions against envy and stealing. Somewhere in there is a message supporting private property and natural rights and another warning against becoming angered over your position vis-à-vis others (envy being at the root of such notions).

Not only is God mentioned in our founding documents, but He is also mentioned only in the singular. This is a clear sign of the influence of the monotheism near-unique to the Judeo-Christian belief system. Don't run from it, excuse it, or try to hide it. Embrace the best of it and know that it is part of who we are.

We are meant to be citizen servants: Who exactly are our elected leaders?

Is anybody really taking a good look at who is running for, and serving in, elected office? We have created something anathema to our Founding Fathers: the career politician.

Everyone should know that George Washington was our first president under our new Constitution. What many people don't know is that Washington accepted the position with a great deal of reluctance. It is a popular view among historians that without Washington's involvement in each step along the way in the nation's formation process, we just might not have made it. That involvement didn't end with the Constitution being ratified. Washington was the clear choice to be the first president of the United States of America, a position which you would think any statesman of that time would have coveted.

Not so, Washington. He accepted the idea with great reluctance. Read below his letter to his Continental Army colleague Henry Knox just twenty-nine days before being sworn in as the first president:

Mount Vernon April 1st. 1789

My dear Sir;

The Mail of the 30th. brought me your favor the 23d. – For which, & the regular information you have had the goodness to transmit of the state of things in New York, I feel myself very much obliged, and thank you accordingly. –

I feel for those Members of the new Congress, who, hitherto, have given an unavailing attendance at the theatre of business: – For myself, the delay may be compared to a reprieve; for in confidence I can assure you – with the world it would obtain little credit – that my movements to the chair of Government will be accompanied with feelings not unlike those of a culprit who is going to the place of his execution: so unwilling am I, in the evening of a life nearly consumed in public cares to quit a peaceful abode for an Ocean of difficulties, without that competency of political skill – abilities [*inserted*: & inclination] which is necessary to manage the helm. – I am sensible, that I am embarking the voice of my Countrymen and a good name of my own, on this voyage, but what returns will be made for them – Heaven alone can foretell. – Integrity & firmness is all I can promise – these, be the voyage long or short, never shall forsake me although I may be deserted by all men. – For of the consolations which are to be derived from these (under any circumstances) the world

cannot deprive me. – With best wishes for Mrs.
Knox, & sincere friendship for yourself – I remain

Your Affectionate

Go: Washington

Such humility is difficult to imagine in today's political leaders who seem to treat their elected position as a form of entitlement. They cling to that entitlement until they decide it is time to step aside, typically with a sort of golden parachute or lucrative "consulting" opportunities and board appointments awaiting them.

Our Founders imagined a government where people would take leave of their daily lives, come to serve, and then return to their prior lives. It was a sort of "voluntary conscription" to find a way to better their country.

Our political people today have become a permanent "inside the Beltway" class of rulers, taking little time to spend among their "subjects." They operate under seemingly different laws and with special elitist privileges. Does this mean they are serving for the wrong reasons? Not necessarily, but most of their actions point to self-interest and not to serving We the People. Of course some are doing their best and for the right reasons but many are not. We really don't know why they are serving. But a better question to ask is why aren't we serving?

We return, again, to Franklin's warning: "A republic, if you can keep it." We must remember that the government belongs to We the People and it is ours to guide through time. We have surrendered the power over ourselves to a class of people intent on ruling and maintaining the status quo by accumulating wealth and power as a career. That is the exact opposite of what was intended in our design.

We have lost our way. Like any addict who is deep into their addiction we have forgotten about the things that should really matter to us. If you understand where we are and you are ready to do better, you must remind yourself of the things of which you have lost track as you were heading toward rock bottom.

———

Ready to work an Eleventh Step? Here are some ideas for you or members of your group to discuss and implement:

1. Read the Declaration of Independence. Write down how this document is or is not still alive and well in America.
2. Read the US Constitution. Write down how this document makes you feel. Did you learn anything new? How can this document help force positive change and return our country to its founding principles? Which are the most important parts to you?
3. Read the Bill of Rights. Memorize these word for word. Print out a copy and keep it somewhere you can be reminded if needed. Research the other amendments.
4. Read the ten commandments and seven deadly sins. Do you feel our culture is leading in a positive or negative direction? Is it because these are being commingled or inverted? Which is the most dangerous deadly sin to you? Why?

STAND UP, SPEAK OUT, AND SHOW UP: DON'T DO NOTHING

WE WILL SHARE THE SPIRIT AND THE POSSIBILITIES OF THIS PROCESS WITH ANYONE WHO HAS THE HONESTY, OPEN-MINDEDNESS, AND WILLINGNESS TO ENGAGE. WE WILL PLACE A SPECIAL EMPHASIS ON SHARING THE PRINCIPLES OF THIS PROCESS WITH OUR CHILDREN AND THE YOUNGER GENERATION WHO MAY NOT BE FAMILIAR WITH OUR HISTORY OR OUR FOUNDING.

HAVING MADE THIS COMMITMENT TO BE A PART OF THE SOLUTION, I WILL SHARE THE MESSAGE AND INVITE OTHERS TO JOIN ME IN SPREADING THE MESSAGE OF INDIVIDUAL PARTICIPATION, PERSONAL RESPONSIBILITY, AND POSITIVE ACTION AT ANY OPPORTUNITY PRESENTED AHEAD.

SPREAD THE WORD AND FOCUS ON THE YOUTH.

Congratulations for working your way through this program designed to help us all beat our national addiction to conflict and chaos that has been making our national lives unmanageable for far too long. As you progress and continue on it is important to "carry the message to the addict who is still suffering." It is also critical to impart this message to young people to help prevent them from a lifetime of suffering. We can't give them the results of our recovery, but we can share our knowledge, tools, and experiences.

In traditional recovery it is said that we keep what we have only by giving it away. In that spirit, if you agree that what is happening in America isn't net positive, then you have a sort of "great commission" being placed before you: the mission to save America as founded. You have a responsibility to be willing to embrace this journey in your daily life, to get out of your comfort zone and be courageous. You are duty bound to share the concepts and tools you have learned here in every possible interaction in a respectful and thoughtful manner. Be engaging and not enraging. Step boldly into the world with a positive attitude and a zealot's enthusiasm. Blessed are the peacemakers.

As you step out into the world, here are a few things that you should promise to yourself. The hardest kind of promise to break is the one we make to ourselves because when we break it, we feel the hurt and shame both from the perspective of the promise-maker and the promise-taker. We double the pain. Let us then make a few promises to ourselves and aim to keep them.

I will use this information to start or join a group and involve others: This program is not meant to be a secret. We are as sick as our secrets. We want the message to be shared, and to do that you are going to have to get other people to participate. To start, you might want to find people who are like you simply because it is easier to convince them to come along. Immediately, however, you need to reach out to a cross section of people so that you get all kinds of different voices in the room. If ever there was a program that is not intended to be an echo chamber, this is it. By definition, it can't be. The goal is to get people talking again, build bridges, find commonly accepted solutions, and start reconciling differences.

I will be authentic: We often talk about different sorts of looks or behaviors that are "attractive." They are things that others find easy on the eye or easy on the mind. Being authentic triggers the active form of that word. When you are authentic, you are attracting others to you. We all know the phrase, "Let's be real." To work this program and share it with others, you are going to have to be real. If you aren't, people will spot phony from a mile away and you will lose your chance to effect change. The more knowledge and conviction you have, the more action you, take the more authentically you will present yourself because it's real.

The best way to share this program with others in an authentic way is to combine three elements that are inside of each of us, but are unique to each of us in their composition. Imagine a triangle, the strongest of all geometric shapes, with each side the same length.

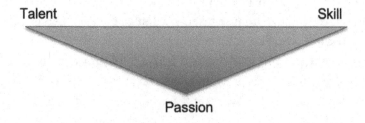

Talent   Skill

Passion

At the base of the triangle, its foundation, lies your passion. These are things that really get you going, things that are core to who you are and get you emotionally excited and driven. Finding a way to make a positive contribution that involves something about which you feel passionate will help keep you motivated.

Talent gets distinguished from skill because it is something that seems to be innate to you. Talent is something that, at least to some degree, you are just born having. If you disagree, try taking off from the free throw line and dunking like Michael Jordan or try writing a piece of music comparable to Beethoven's Ninth while deaf. Some people just have a talent for some things. So do you. Find it.

Skills are the things that we learn, things that don't even necessarily come naturally to us, but through a combination of choice, circumstance, and lots of hard work, we have acquired them.

If you can combine your passion, talent, and skill to come up with a way to share the principles of this program, you will be more effective. That is because you will be authentic. Only you have the exact combination of those three legs of the triangle. Your authenticity will then be attractive to others.

I will build stronger boundaries: A big part of being authentic is having the strength to break free from the ties that bind you and that might be holding you back. For most of us, if we take an honest inventory of who we are, we will have to admit that we have been keeping parts of ourselves locked in a box. Typically, we lock parts of ourselves away because we are experiencing one of the three forms of fear. Those fears, as we have discussed, can be paralyzing.

In today's culture, one of the key causes of fear and one that can trigger any one of fear's three forms is the cancel culture in which we live. We have become obsessed about not being "canceled." Of course, every act of cancelation is an act of aggression, which is exactly what we are fighting against. We can't let ourselves fall to our fears in general, and in fighting back against conflict, we especially can't give in to a fear of being canceled because we will face that threat at every turn. If we lose we will get canceled anyway, so might as well put up a fight.

We did not get to this point in America overnight and we are not going to be able to get out of it anytime soon. We are also not going to be able to get out of it without paying some sort of cost. It's called a sacrifice and nothing worth gaining comes without sacrifice. We might pay that cost in our workplace, in our classroom, even in our living room. We might lose a job or an educational grant, but if we stay true to our mission, what we won't lose is ourselves. In fact, a passionate warrior often finds many unexpected rewards for their bravery and leadership. Fear not, for fear is the mind-killer.

Be willing to let go in the healthiest of ways. Be as smart as you truly are. Be as creative as you know you can be. Be courageous when it is called for. If you are religious, "let go and let God." If you aren't, "let go and let the best of you rise up."

I will intercede in conflict—I'll become a peacemaker: Part of letting go, especially of fear, will dictate that we can't just sit back any longer and watch what is happening. We are going to have to step up and step in. You don't need a tight T-shirt or bulging biceps to do this. What you really need is the ability to properly articulate, "Hey, what's going on?" We know that sounds simple, we also know that it isn't. People in conflict don't usually want to be interrupted. These societal bar fights we are getting into are intense. The fact is, if somebody doesn't step in to try to break them up, a nation is going to get killed.

Everyone knows in recovery that you can't reach the addict who is currently drunk or high. They have to be sober to hear you. In America, we are going to have to be willing to break up some fights to get people ready to listen.

I will find meaningful ways to connect with others: Anyone who has ever traveled overseas to multiple countries on the same trip and tried to plug something in knows that finding the right connection method can be a challenge. Likewise with people, connections are difficult to make and require finding the right "match," sender to receiver.

There are three key ways to connect with people: empathy, compassion, and forgiveness. Some people view these as signs of weakness, a sort of "giving in" to the other person. We see them as strengths when properly viewed. Let us make that point by demonstrating not what each one of them is, but by demonstrating what they are not.

Being empathetic does not mean losing yourself: We can tend to think of showing empathy as a way of surrendering yourself to another's feelings. It isn't. Properly understood, empathy requires you to embrace what is going on inside another person and then processing that within your own internal framework. You don't lose yourself; you simply take them in and make them part of who you already are. Being empathetic means to truly understand from another's perspective what they may be going through.

Showing compassion doesn't mean you are condoning: We made it clear earlier that we want to reach people who feel victimized whether that victimization is real or perceived. We can get far too judgmental with others by thinking, "This person isn't really a victim. Why should I affirm that attitude?" We might not agree with how a person sees themselves in terms of their own condition, but we can feel compassion for them nonetheless. Compassion is understanding and appreciating what someone might be going through whether you agree with how they feel or not.

Forgiving doesn't mean forgetting: We would be fools to forget the things that led us to the point where we needed to forgive someone. It is the remembering that allows us to watch for new occurrences of old behaviors. That said, if we don't forgive them, we literally can't move past whatever has already happened. In traditional recovery, this happens all the time when someone "gets clean" and those around them have a hard time forgiving them for their past behavior, even after they have made amends. What they should do is forgive and then remember those old habits in case that addict in their life starts to show signs of relapse.

Using these tools, and whatever other positive tools you might identify, can help you connect with others in a meaningful way and bring help to the conflict addict who is still suffering.

I will stop labeling others: We have been labeling everyone everywhere without any regard as to what is inside the person. This has created a major problem because as soon as we read the label, we make a decision as to what is inside.

We need to start to think of people as though we are all just out at the old-time county fair. No labels exist there, just a collection of humanity, milling about and enjoying simple pleasures. If we approach somebody in an ice cream line, we do so without preconceived notions, save for that they probably like ice cream.

One trick to avoid labeling is to catch yourself when you are about to label and ask yourself, "What is the opposite of the label I'm about to give?" One label tends to infer the existence of the opposite label. So stop labeling and start asking people what they are actually about.

I will focus on youth: We have let our children down today as in many ways we were let down by an educational system that has been slowly fostering division and driving us away from traditional American principles and values. We mentioned the pernicious and pervasive influence of the Frankfurt School. We have all fallen victim to outside destructive influences and we are paying for that now. But with our newfound understanding and tools, now it is time for us to reach out to young people and end this multigenerational cycle of programming and growing conflict addiction.

Imagine a scenario where you were able to time travel and sit down with yourself at, say, the age of ten, sixteen, or eighteen. What would you tell yourself in order to prevent the mistakes that you made up to your current moment in life? This is a good way to think about the value of reaching young people. Young people are some of our most vulnerable and we have a duty to protect and guide them. Be a leader and make a difference.

It is paradoxical to think that as adults we do all sorts of estate planning to make certain that our children are provided for financially in the inevitable event of our demise, either unexpectedly or in the natural course of things. What we haven't been doing is worrying about providing a safe and stable country for them to live in when our time has passed. What fruits of our labors will they inherit? It is time to check our priorities.

There are those people, and you might be one of them, who get discouraged about trying to reach adults and open their minds because they are just too "set in their ways." If that's the case, then by all means, turn your attention to reaching young people. They are our future. If you are looking for legacy, there is no better, more constructive way to create it.

This program is yours. It will work if you work it. If you have found anything missing in these pages designed to help change the nature of conversation in this country, add it. If you disagree with something, identify why and find a way to replace it constructively or, for that matter, disregard it completely. But don't do nothing. Many people feel they personally can't save the country, but they also know they can do something. This is their something. If this doesn't work for you, and we hope that it will, then ask yourself what is your solution? What will you do? As one of my guests on my show says when I ask him what people should do, he says and I repeat over and over again, "For the sake of yourself, your family, God, and country, just don't do nothing."

———

Ready to work a Twelfth Step? Here are some ideas for you or members of your group to discuss and implement:

1. Consider starting a group or local program that engages parents and children in your neighborhood or community. Make a plan and steps you could take to accomplish that.
2. What are you passionate about? List three.
3. What are your special skills? List three.
4. What are your innate talents? List three.
5. Consider who, where, and how you can engage and educate young people with each of the above.

PART 3

CONCLUSION AND ADDITIONAL CONTEXT

A DISCUSSION ON INDIVIDUAL LIBERTY, PERSONAL RESPONSIBILITY, AND ACCOUNTABILITY FOR ALL

Much of what you were told or programmed to believe about our nation and history in general is false. It has instead been used to manipulate the masses to behave in ways that have led to mass social engineering and general apathy that have allowed nefarious forces to keep people uninformed, distracted, and disengaged by design. Some people describe this as learned helplessness, or the deep-seated false belief that one's individual actions don't make a difference, so why engage at all? Heavy lifting is required at this stage of awakening to accept this reality and to embrace the freedom and liberation that comes from becoming a truly informed, fully realized citizen changemaker.

For far too long we have outsourced our critical thinking, curiosity, and circumstances to the blob of big government, mainstream media, trusted authorities and, more recently, big-tech-controlled social media. The purposeful work and actions needed to regroup to reclaim your individual sovereignty and fully engage your imagination, talent, and ingenuity is the promise of this time. Mark Twain said, "It is easier to fool people than to convince them they've been fooled." To me, realizing I was fooled, as much as I resisted, was the spark that lit a fire for my quest for truth, freedom, and action I never knew existed. If we see this as an adventure or exploration into how to build, cultivate, and realize a better future from the bottom up, it will unlock endless energy and potential within all who pursue that path and the ripple effect will be exponential.

In order to truly change the trajectory for America and beyond, not just for ourselves but for all of humanity who long for the freedom and liberty endowed by our creator, we must each start by looking at our own actions, boundaries, emotions, and bias first. Not in a superficial way, but as an excavation of the most important thing in the main battle, which is the battle for your brain. Admitting first that I, we, and yes, you, are the problem, and at the same time realizing we are also the solution takes raw, hard honesty. It is time to begin the work of unpeeling sometimes decades of deception or purposeful denial, and reject your ego for the humility that is required where lasting change is desired and can truly occur.

Before I lay out some ways to put the lessons of this book into immediate action and help you personalize them into a new mission statement for yourself, I want to say congratulations and thank you for taking this journey thus far with me. You are already way ahead! We have clearly passed the point of no return in what was once America, and we can analyze and investigate what has worked, what hasn't worked, and what could work better going forward. It is your choice to embark on this very exciting, inspirational journey ahead to create what can and will be America's future. The spirit of those who stood up to tyranny and fought for our independence long ago is stirring within each of us once again in such electrifying ways. It is this time, right now, that will be recognized in future history books as the most decisive and important period in America since 1776. In that time, like now, determined patriots from all walks of life throughout this great nation stood together, united for freedom, and defined the destiny of this nation going forward.

By embracing the extraordinary, life-changing opportunity to be part of something so monumental as playing a role in determining the future of this awesome republic, you are actively defining history and redefining yourself at the same time. Ask yourself what you will tell your children and grandchildren you did during this game-changing period when tyranny and totalitarianism came knocking on the doors of our nation. Really think about the answer, take pen to paper, and specifically define it. What do you want your role to be exactly? When you define it you must begin to manifest that reality starting today. I am confident that if you are a good, honest person who truly understands the stakes we face in our country and worldwide, beyond this realm to the good versus evil aspects of the battle, you will understand that you really don't have a choice in your heart except to become a leader. We all have a responsibility to light the spark that sets the brush fires of liberty ablaze and become an unstoppable force for good in the war to save our nation, our children, our future, and our world.

THE LANGUAGE OF LETTING GO

Beside my bed for well over a decade I've had a book that has sustained me through the hardest times of my life called *The Language of Letting Go* by Melody Beattie. It is tattered and falling apart, marked with tears, red wine spillage, and quite a few coffee stains. It is a book about letting go, not to be confused with giving up. I was gifted the book after I experienced sudden, very early success in my career, followed, just as quickly, by an unexpected and devastating failure. That failure led to deep disillusionment and depression, as is par for the course for a very young ambitious screenwriter new to Los Angeles.

My first several years in Hollywood would repeat that pattern of exciting highs and debilitating lows, a rollercoaster of wins and losses in such a whirlwind that I nearly lost myself and almost lost my life in the process. But for the grace of God I had a good friend lead me on my early journey in recovery where I bonded with other people in similar situations looking for a better, healthier, more harmonious path forward. I developed a fellowship of like-minded, equally committed warriors, and that program literally saved my life. It allowed me to redefine my purpose, giving me a far better, more solid foundation from which to grow forward without being constantly whipped around by the volatile nature of my chosen life path. It was during that time that I had to excavate my own history, get brutally honest with myself, look at where I failed and what part I played in that, lay out the nature of my problems, and learn the critically important language of letting go. In searching for what could possibly heal the divide and addiction to conflict and chaos plaguing our nation and so many good Americans right now, it hit me that the same exact path I took to find a better way forward could be the solution on a massive scale for our society.

Beattie's book is 365 pages long with one anecdote or story per day along with a meditation/prayer related to it reinforcing the concept of letting go daily. My days, since starting my personal journey to be better, do better, and live healthier almost two decades ago, have begun with my daily *Language of Letting Go* reading, the Lord's Prayer, and the Serenity Prayer as a means of maintaining perspective. It reminds me to focus on what really matters in life while reminding me of what I can and cannot control. Letting go in the sense of this book is about letting go of that which is toxic, demoralizing, untrue, unproven, or isolating. These negative elements in our lives lead to self-sabotaging ideas and behaviors that harm you, your relationships, and society as a whole.

Many of us are hit with the gushing water hose of nonstop information, conflicting narratives, demoralizing social media, family issues, financial issues, work conflicts, and any number of stressful or distracting things from the minute we wake up until we lay our head on the pillow at night. I have come to learn and truly understand that this is not just life, but that more is at play here. We are in the midst of a very real cognitive warfare operation on a military scale beyond the usual aspects of life that cause normal stress. If you haven't seen the playbooks on cognitive and psychological warfare on my resource page at *The Mel K Show* website, now is a good time to read these documents. What's most scary and telling is that they are from our own intelligence agencies and worldwide military alliances along with powerful quasi-governmental groups. What is being inflicted on the masses both overtly and subconsciously without our consent and for deeply nefarious purposes has to be understood, recognized, and acknowledged in order for us to begin to become immune to it. Knowledge is the best inoculation to propaganda and manipulation. It is my belief that for the past eight or so years we have been coerced into and are experiencing an orchestrated color revolution playbook. The goals and consequences of this operation include national destabilization, societal divisions, and financial stress, generating conflict and chaos all manufactured to divide and conquer our nation.

Once we understand this, then we are well on our way towards defeating its plans and its hold on us and our minds.

With the introduction of smartphones and smart devices coupled with controlled media, complicit corporate messaging, and government pressure, our supply of—and hence our addiction to—conflict and chaos is all-encompassing and pervasive. If we do not develop the self-discipline and conscious understanding that it is our choice to be engaged and participate beyond what is healthy or useful for us, we will not rise above the subtle or not so subtle nudging it strives to achieve. The manufacturers, suppliers, and dealers of conflict and chaos have deceived us into believing these are amazing devices that are convenient, helpful, and absolutely necessary for daily life function. But, as I've contended many times, they are actually being used as tools for monitoring and surveilling you, manipulating your behavior, and invading your privacy. We the People are being lulled daily farther and farther into a system of total external control, a full track-and-trace digital gulag, without stopping to think how our participation is optional and not automatic.

It is important to understand that after the unconstitutional and deceptively named Patriot Act was passed it was quickly weaponized against We the People. This act codified extraordinary governmental powers over We the People in the name of fighting terrorists and keeping us safe. From extrajudicial powers to mass harvesting of our personal data without our knowledge or consent, the government has become a very dangerous and extraordinarily powerful monolithic institution. Couple this with infiltration and subversion across all our institutions of power and you can begin to see how bad it has become, especially in our law enforcement, judicial systems, and the medical-industrial complex. Consider the no bail, no jail, defund-the-police movement, the weaponization of justice through lawfare, the mass censorship of truth, the perversion of our educational systems, and the COVID operation, and you can clearly see the controlled demolition of America for what it is. Whether you actively engage or not, systems, devices, and platforms, often with the promise of safety and convenience, are corralling, tracking, tracing, surveilling, and collecting everything about you and your relationships. With the infrastructure in place and the data streaming in, the powers that be are further enhancing their power using artificial intelligence to determine how best to control you and your behavior every minute of every day. Unfortunately, the people who control these systems have proven time and time again that they do not have our individual nor our country's best interests in mind. So it is critical to know and understand these control systems and to find ways to limit participating in them and their ability to influence you as much as possible. Become more self-sufficient, avoid systems of control, and resist, resist, resist!

As I lay out on *The Mel K Show* website, and what extensive research has shown me, is that we are all being manipulated subconsciously and physiologically into a constant state of confusion, negativity, anxiety, and heightened suggestibility without even realizing it. If we understand this system of manipulation and put in countermeasures to oppose its functionality, we do have a fighting chance of beating it.

If we force ourselves to modify our habitual reliance and unhealthy attachment to our devices, our growing inability to connect in healthy and meaningful ways with other human beings would be greatly improved. As Hannah Arendt said regarding totalitarianism, it is most easily accomplished on a massive scale where isolation and loneliness are heightened in a society, when intimate and authentic human interaction are limited, as they were during the lockdowns, and restrictions are imposed to those ends. We are being groomed into totalitarian rule and it is plain as day if you care to look. It is clear to me that we have been programmed to believe social media has brought us closer together and enhanced our connection to our fellow man, but it is my contention that it has in fact done the exact opposite. It has siloed us and pushed authentic human relations farther apart with its lack of authenticity, the loss of the exchange of in person energy and the exchange of real human emotion, and it's insidious ability to allow people to create anonymous or false personas to attack without consequences and to get lost in complete fantasy outside of their actual reality. The digital world as constructed today, including the world of virtual reality, is not a utopia but an insidious trap.

The human condition needs community, comradery, cooperation, and healthy connection to be positive and life-affirming. The normalization of living a life online, judging your worth or self-esteem by likes or clicks or followers, adds to the push towards *Ready Player One*-type virtual reality experiences and interactions that are soulless and emotionally disconnected. These experiences leave us devoid of that which enhances life and creates a purposeful and meaningful existence. Once we see the matrix we are in and sliding more deeply into, we can begin to free ourselves from it in miraculous and life-enhancing ways.

Letting go is hard, especially when you aren't used to doing it. As humans, we are more inclined to hold on too long rather than to let go when it's time. We are creatures of habit, and change is not always easy. Some would even say letting go is courageous. Letting go of what is holding you back or unhealthy for you is even harder because it requires a reckoning with the most important person in your life, yourself. When you engage in purposeful, intense introspection, looking at your life more closely and honestly than you may have ever done before, it can be uncomfortable and overwhelming. At first you're likely to feel great resistance or face distractions everywhere, but if you push through the obstacles you will come out on the other side clearer, more focused, and inspired.

It takes commitment, courage, practice, daily reminders, mindfulness, patience, and radical acceptance to engage your mind, body, and spirit on this positive purposeful journey ahead. Often we are reacting to people and situations based on our unconscious perceptions or assumptions about others that we can't possibly know are true without engaging them directly. One thing that helps is to ask yourself if what you believe is based on factual information supported by concrete evidence you yourself have seen and can prove. We need to condition ourselves to stop and think before we auto-respond out of emotion or supposition. We must begin to ask ourselves to prove our conclusions and opinions to ourselves first. This is a good way to let go, as it takes you out of an emotional, reactionary state and into a critical-thinking, discerning state.

When you do your own research and are skeptical as you look for answers, you will find that you become more confident and less prone to engaging in unproductive conversations because you have a solid factual foundation that is supported by evidence. When you form your understanding and beliefs over time, continually asking questions until you have answered them for yourself, you will no longer need to be right, to prove your point, or engage in conflict. It is empowering to be confident in your own understanding after doing your own work and coming to your own independent conclusions. When I say to do your own research as I do, it's also because I love putting together the puzzle and digging deep into all the information I can possibly find. I find it immensely satisfying formulating my own conclusions and then sharing them with other people to then do their own research. We are bombarded with fake news, insanely siloed and conflicting content, and emotion-based analysis online. By giving yourself the gift of knowing what is going on around you and being able to articulate that clearly and concisely, you become a positive weapon in the information war. A frontline warrior for truth and transparency. Calmly coming from a position of strength that only the truth can give you, you have a chance to inspire others, align with other like-minded folks, and find the right fellowship and allies going forward.

Few people do the empowering step of investing the time it takes to personally gain the clarity that proof and facts provide. Imagine how many millions of unnecessary energy-robbing conflicts could and would be avoided if more people took the time to prove their own assumptions to themselves first. You also become more discerning as to who is dealing in truth, interested in learning and finding solutions, and who has good intentions. When you don't rely on celebrity influencers, questionable journalists, or what I call Twitter-lebrities, and instead on your own work, it gives you a grounded foundation and peace of mind as you get more involved in your community and invested in your purpose.

Letting go is not giving up or surrendering, it's the opposite. It's about strengthening your self-esteem, self-respect, and your inherent self-worth. There are so many demoralizing and dehumanizing things coming at us constantly these days from all sides that it is difficult not to succumb to the negative programming. But when we do not allow ourselves to be brought down or triggered by the conflict and chaos swirling around us because we have specific knowledge and understanding it gives us an obvious edge. It is about holding yourself, your time, and your priorities in high esteem, and protecting your boundaries and personal space as sacred and not open for unnecessary energy-sapping disruption.

Defining what really matters to you, no matter what happens outside of your personal, protected bubble of family and established personal relationships, and trusting and leaning on that priority before ever engaging in public debate or political action is also key to being a successful positive change agent. Those engaged in the battle to save this nation right now have lost friends, family, jobs, and more because they decided that standing up for freedom, liberty, sovereignty, and the Constitution truly and deeply mattered to them. Losing cherished connections or a job you loved should not be the price one pays for having beliefs and opinions, nor should wanting to be a part of solutions and change have a downside, but for many people it has and continues to be so. This if an information war that yields casualties and requires sacrifices. Remember, we are working to heal the world.

We need to look at why and how today's societal behavior and structure became normalized, and do our part to be the best we can be individually rather than participating in perpetuating the cycles. Letting go of the need to be right, the need to convince or convert, and the need to shame or shut down another person in the name of solving the issues that we all face is instrumental in being a force of and for good in this world. Until we start refusing to allow emotions or self-sabotaging behaviors to control our actions, the necessary group unity that can truly change the course of history for the better will be elusive on the scale we need.

> If we weren't trying to control whether a person liked us or his or her reaction to us, what would we do differently? If we weren't trying to control the course of a relationship, what would we

do differently? If we weren't trying to control another person's behavior, how would we think, feel, speak, and behave differently than we do now? What haven't we been letting ourselves do while hoping that self-denial would influence a particular situation or person? Are there some things we've been doing that we'd stop? How would we treat ourselves differently? Would we let ourselves enjoy life more and feel better right now? Would we stop feeling so bad? Would we treat ourselves better? If we weren't trying to control, what would we do differently? Make a list, then do it.

Melody Beattie,
The Language of Letting Go

INDIVIDUAL LIBERTY

When you say you stand for liberty what does that mean to you?
The definition of liberty according to Oxford Languages is:

1. the state of being free within society from oppressive restrictions imposed by authority on one's way of life, behavior, or political views.
2. the power or scope to act as one pleases.

JUDGE LEARNED HAND, "THE SPIRIT OF LIBERTY," MAY 21, 1944

We have gathered here to affirm a faith, a faith
in a common purpose, a common conviction,
a common devotion. Some of us have chosen

America as the land of our adoption; the rest have come from those who did the same. For this reason we have some right to consider ourselves a picked group, a group of those who had the courage to break from the past and brave the dangers and the loneliness of a strange land. What was the object that nerved us, or those who went before us, to this choice? We sought liberty; freedoms from oppression, freedom from want, freedom to be ourselves. This we then sought; this we now believe that we are by way of winning.

What do we mean when we say that first of all we seek liberty? I often wonder whether we do not rest our hopes too much upon constitutions, upon laws and upon courts. These are false hopes; believe me, these are false hopes. Liberty lies in the hearts of men and women; when it dies there, no constitution, no law, no court can even do much to help it. While it lies there it needs no constitution, no law, no court to save it. And what is this liberty which must lie in the hearts of men and women? It is not the ruthless, the unbridled will; it is not freedom to do as one likes. That is the denial of liberty, and leads straight to its overthrow. A society in which men recognize no check upon their freedom soon becomes a society where freedom is the possession of only a savage few; as we have learned to our sorrow.

What then is the spirit of liberty? I cannot define it; I can only tell you my own faith. The spirit of liberty is the spirit which is not too sure that it is right; the spirit of liberty is the spirit which seeks to understand the mind of other men and women; the spirit of liberty is the spirit which weighs their interests alongside its own without bias; the spirit of liberty remembers that not even a sparrow falls to earth unheeded; the spirit of liberty is the spirit of Him who, near two thousand years ago, taught mankind that lesson it has never learned but never quite forgotten; that there may be a kingdom where the least shall be heard and considered side by side with the greatest.

And now in that spirit, that spirit of an America which has never been, and which may never be; nay, which never will be except as the conscience and courage of Americans create it; yet in the spirit of that America which lies hidden in some form in the aspirations of us all; in the spirit of that America for which our young men are at this moment fighting and dying; in that spirit of liberty and of America I ask you to rise and with me pledge our faith in the glorious destiny of our beloved country.

Like it or not, the current state of this nation and many other places in the still free world is that We the People have ceded our power to governments that have ceded their power to those who control the multinational corporations, global private banking institutions, and the supranational globalist blob known as the global public-private partnership. These self-anointed, elitist-billionaire-backed "stakeholders," and their controlled web of foundations and NGOs they've operated out of for decades, believe themselves to be the rightful rulers of sovereign nations and entire governments. The public in public-private partnership is not us, it is the government they weaponize or task with implementing their will and self-serving agenda upon us. The public side to them, our elected officials and unelected bureaucrats, are our handlers in their goal of nudging us towards their consolidated global control grid.

When we are honest about how much power We the People actually have left, we realize much of what is rightfully ours and only allowed with the consent of the governed, us, has been systematically infringed upon and usurped. Beyond that, with eyes wide open, it becomes increasingly clear that our own elected officials likely have very little if any power themselves, and they too have been systematically marginalized and compromised over the last several decades. The permanent class that remains no matter who is elected along with the generationally wealthy oligarchs and their globally aligned friends know this is the case, and for the first time in possibly a hundred years they now know we know. We are seeing and living in an extraordinary paradigm-shifting reality.

Yes, we can take back power to the people—the honest, the moral, the competent—but that requires both individual and collective action towards the goals and ideals we have described in our book. How we got here should be on the mind of every person reading this and anyone who feels that being a citizen of the United States actually does entitle you to the unalienable rights of life, liberty, and the pursuit of happiness. Every citizen should take their duty as protector and shepherd personally and seriously. There are tens of millions of us, way more than the overlords or their operatives, and we come from all backgrounds, races, and religions. We have to understand that harnessing the full power to force positive change requires us to resolve the festering conflict and chaos in order to unite as a front, for freedom for all above all else. That is where our unity lies. That is also what the puppet masters fear the most.

We understand life is hard, especially while being surrounded by manufactured crises and chaos from all sides. Many people are maxed out on time, energy, and resources just keeping their own houses and lives afloat. Our system ensures that most citizens are on a proverbial hamster wheel of stress and distraction that makes it difficult to step back and think about much else, let alone make time to protect and participate in preserving our nation's freedom and future. This has allowed for people to falsely believe and unconsciously accept that what is happening in their local and state governments and all the way in DC, doesn't really directly affect or concern them, nor that their getting involved will make a difference or have any reward. That is programmed and purposeful and some would call it learned helplessness. Ask anyone doing anything in and for the cause for freedom right now and you will understand that it is the exact opposite. Getting involved and taking action, whether locally or on any level in an area you are interested in or passionate about, has a ripple effect throughout your entire life and adds value beyond what anyone imagines.

THE FALSE PREMISE OF "PROTECTING DEMOCRACY"

The Founders fighting for independence and freedom from tyranny thought democracy as defined could easily become tyranny by mob rule. They viewed democracy to be as dangerous as the monarchy they laid their lives and futures on the line to oppose and gain independence from. We are not a democracy by design. The Founders discussed all forms of government dating back centuries during the many years prior to choosing the constitutional republic model, and purposefully made sure that the federal government was not and would never be based on majority or mob rule. A corrupt or depraved, beat down and exhausted, demoralized or dehumanized majority would not be able to choose the best, most just and righteous path for all. Right now the cognitive domain is fully exploited by mass manipulation of information making it nearly impossible to identify, define, or articulate what the actual American majority even is, let alone universally believes. We have fraudulent polling, purposely skewed census data, overtly compromised elections, a controlled and complicit media, and intel-agency-infused social media narratives leading to clearly erroneous claims of who the supposed majority is or what they support. Thus, again, why a return to the Founders' wisdom of a constitutional republic where states are the proper place for most everything not explicitly defined as being the federal government's purview remains the best way to reclaim a functioning union now and moving forward.

To the Framers of the Constitution, the purpose of the government was to secure the right to life, liberty, and property. The Constitution was crafted to protect the individual's liberty and rights *from* the government, not the other way around. The Constitution as written lays out very clearly enforceable guidelines to protect individual rights, making what the government can lawfully do very specific and limited. It also lays out that economic liberty, which includes the ability to grow and prosper, is protected for the individual from government overreach. When the Constitution was ratified in 1789 it contained very specific language, a fifty-two-word preamble, seven articles, and ten amendments known as the Bill of Rights. That's it!

The American people, by shirking individual responsibility and not taking personally what is happening to our country for whatever reason, have allowed the government blob to become an unaccountable, unelected web of bureaucracies, lobbyists, think tanks, and elitist lawyers serving their clients' and funders' interests almost completely devoid of concern or care for what the people of this nation actually want. We have stood by while the DC establishment and uniparty violate our founding documents time and again, allowing the government and its out-of-control, largely unconstitutional agencies to arrogantly ignore the Constitution and Bill of Rights as written without oversight or consequences. This is on us, and it is in these same documents they ignore that we can find the keys to return power to the people where it belongs.

One thing that makes America so unique and powerful is that We the People united have very special rights and the ability to change our destiny enumerated and laid out clearly in our founding documents. The Constitution is still, right now, the law of the land, but if no one is adhering to it, and we are waiting for them to recognize and self-correct, we will lose our standing for good. This fact, that we have a Constitution and Bill of Rights that are so clear, concise, and powerful, is why much of the world is looking at our nation with shock and dismay as to why we aren't uniting to put an end to the corruption and infiltration with the tools we already have. Many citizens of the world recognize that We the People have not done what is in our power to do, to right the very wrong direction our nation is heading in. While many nations have massive rallies and protests, they look to us in America wondering where our collective fight for our own nation has gone.

AYN RAND, "THE ONLY PATH TO TOMORROW," READER'S DIGEST, JANUARY 1944

> The greatest threat to mankind and civilization is
> the spread of totalitarian philosophy. Its best ally

is not the devotion of its followers but the confusion of its enemies. To fight it, we must understand it.

Totalitarianism is collectivism. Collectivism means the subjugation of the individual to a group—whether to a race, class or state does not matter. Collectivism holds that man must be chained to collective action and collective thought for the sake of what is called "the common good."

Throughout history, no tyrant ever rose to power except on the claim of representing "the common good." Napoleon "served the common good" of France. Hitler was "serving the common good" of Germany. Horrors which no man would dare consider for his own selfish sake are perpetrated with a clear conscience by "altruists" who justify themselves by the common good.

No tyrant has ever lasted long by force of arms alone. Men have been enslaved primarily by psychological and spiritual weapons. And the greatest of these is the collectivist doctrine that the supremacy of the state over the individual constitutes the common good. No dictator could rise if men held as a sacred faith the conviction that they have inalienable rights of which they cannot be deprived for any cause whatsoever, by any man whatsoever, neither by evildoer nor supposed benefactor.

This is the basic tenet of individualism, as opposed to collectivism. Individualism holds that man is an independent entity with an inalienable right to the pursuit of his own happiness in a society where men deal with one another as equals.

The American system is founded on individualism. If it is to survive, we must understand the principles of individualism and hold them as our standard in any public question, in every issue we face. We must have a positive credo, a clear consistent faith.

We must learn to reject as pure evil, the concept that the common good is served by the abolition of individual rights. General happiness cannot be created out of general suffering and self-immolation. The only happy society is one of happy individuals. One cannot have a healthy forest made up of rotten trees.

The power of society must always be limited by the basic, inalienable rights of the individual.

The right of liberty means man's right to individual action, individual choice, individual initiative and individual property. Without the right to private property no independent action is possible.

The right to the pursuit of happiness means man's right to live for himself, to choose what constitutes his own, private, personal happiness and to work for its achievement. Each individual is the sole and final judge in this choice. A man's happiness cannot be prescribed to him by another man or by any number of other men.

These rights are the unconditional, personal, private, individual possession of every man, granted to him by the fact of his birth and requiring no other sanction. Such was the conception of the founders of our country, who placed individual rights above any and all collective claims. Society can only be a traffic policeman in the intercourse of men with one another.

From the beginning of history, two antagonists have stood face to face, two opposite types of men: the Active and the Passive. The Active Man is the producer, the creator, the originator, the individualist. His basic need is independence—in order to think and work. He neither needs nor seeks power over other men—nor can he be made to work under any form of compulsion. Every type of good work—from laying bricks to writing a symphony—is done by the Active Man. Degrees of human ability vary, but the basic principle remains the same: the degree of a man's independence and initiative determines his talent as a worker and his worth as a man.

The Passive Man is found on every level of society, in mansions and in slums, and his identification mark is his dread of independence. He is a parasite who expects to be taken care of by others, who wishes to be given directives, to obey, to submit, to be regulated, to be told. He welcomes collectivism, which eliminates any chance that he might have to think or act on his own initiative.

When a society is based on the needs of the Passive Man it destroys the Active; but when the Active is destroyed, the Passive can no longer be cared for. When a society is based on the needs of the Active Man, he carries the Passive ones along on his energy and raises them as he rises, as the whole society rises. This has been the pattern of all human progress.

Some humanitarians demand a collective state because of their pity for the incompetent or Passive Man. For his sake they wish to harness the Active. But the Active Man cannot function in harness. And once he is destroyed, the destruction of the Passive Man follows automatically. So if pity is the humanitarians' first consideration, then in the name of pity, if nothing else, they should leave the Active Man free to function, in order to help the Passive. There is no other way to help him in the long run.

The history of mankind is the history of the struggle between the Active Man and the Passive, between the individual and the collective. The countries which have produced the happiest men, the highest standards of living and the greatest cultural advances have been the countries where the power of the collective—of the government, of the state—was limited and the individual was given freedom of independent action. As examples: The rise of Rome, with its conception of law based on a citizen's rights, over the collectivist barbarism of its time. The rise of England, with a system of government based on the Magna Carta, over collectivist, totalitarian Spain. The rise of the United States to a degree of achievement unequaled in history—by grace of the individual freedom and independence which our Constitution gave each citizen against the collective.

While men are still pondering upon the causes of the rise and fall of civilizations, every page of history cries to us that there is but one source of progress: Individual Man in independent action. Collectivism is the ancient principle of savagery. A savage's whole existence is ruled by the leaders of his tribe. Civilization is the process of setting man free from men.

We are now facing a choice: to go forward or to go back.

Collectivism is not the "New Order of Tomorrow." It is the order of a very dark yesterday. But there is a New Order of Tomorrow. It belongs to Individual Man—the only creator of any tomorrow's humanity has ever been granted.

So how do we begin? Well, the first thing we can do is proclaim that any bureaucratic agency or enforcement entity that is blatantly unconstitutional must be disbanded or dissolved right off the top. This requires organizing with others who agree to begin the process with our local and state legislatures and judicial branches. Our Constitution is very clear on what the federal government should and should not be. If we held to that, likely 85 percent of the blob in DC could be sent home and would have to return to the private sector where they belong. The monstrosity of the web of overreaching agencies and their regulations and laws, with hundreds of thousands of unnecessary employees working in unconstitutionally sanctioned jobs with unelected or appointed executives and leaders, should be cut loose immediately. Anyone unnecessary as per the Constitution in DC that is paid by the federal government, meaning by our tax dollars, needs to go. They can do what they do somewhere else, hopefully in a productive way instead of wasting endless taxpayer dollars providing nothing to the economy or to the country. We need to fully focus our population, including those unnecessarily wasting skill and talent on our dime, on rebuilding our economy. Get back to producing, creating, manufacturing, inventing, and innovating on all fronts to lift this country back up. We need to refuse to allow any government entity that does not have powers enumerated in the Constitution the ability to continue legislating or passing any bills or regulations that grow the totalitarian framework that the massive federal government matrix is on the brink of becoming.

Next, we need to make lobbying illegal. After all, it is government-sanctioned bribery that the private sector considers illegal. We need to defang the think tanks and NGOs making them ineligible for government grants or subsidies of any kind along with yanking their tax exempt status. Fully vacate DC of as much waste and overreach as possible, and transfer the powers back to the states where it is most able to actually insure the will of the people. In fact, I believe that elected officials in both senate and Congress should have to reside in the jurisdiction they represent, and only go to DC when absolutely necessary. These representatives should have fully transparent schedules, oversight by their constituents, and not be allowed to profit or enter quid pro quo contracts or obligations of any kind. If you work for the people, everything you do should be subject to the light of day and full transparency. Wherever corruption and secret backdoor meetings happen we must demand those doors are shut for good. These entities and work-around institutions are unnecessary and rob the people of their power and consent.

The Bill of Rights is even more clear in its purpose. The Bill of Rights protects the people from the state infringing on our liberty and freedom. Those protections include things that were considered sacred when written and should still be considered so now. The entire purpose of the Bill of Rights was to constrain and limit the government, and all of that was in the name of individual liberty. There is a reason the global elitists and supranational over-lords don't respect our founding documents: they limit their abil-ity to control us from the top and preserve our individual rights. Our rights are not for anyone to take, especially our government or their adjuncts, and that was clearly stated from our founding. Many have died to preserve those rights, and it is up to us to stand up now if we are to reclaim and persevere our God-given, unalien-able rights and all that allows us to exercise unencumbered free-dom and liberty going forward.

JOHN STUART MILL, ON LIBERTY:

The object of this Essay is to assert one very simple principle, as entitled to govern absolutely the dealings of society with the individual in the way of compulsion and control, whether the means used be physical force in the form of legal penalties, or the moral coercion of public opinion. That principle is, that the sole end for which mankind is warranted, individually or collectively in interfering with the liberty of action of any of their number, is self-protection. That the only purpose for which power can be rightfully exercised over any member of a civilized community, against his will, is to prevent harm to others. His own good, either physical or moral, is not a sufficient warrant. He cannot rightfully be compelled to do or forbear because it will be better for him to do so, because it will make him happier, because, in the opinions of others, to do so would be wise, or even right. These are good reasons for remonstrating with him, or reasoning with him, or persuading him, or entreating him, but not for compelling him, or visiting him with any evil, in case he do otherwise. To justify that, the conduct from which it is desired to deter him must be calculated to produce evil to someone else. The only part of the conduct of any one, for which he is amenable to society, is that which concerns others. In the part which merely concerns himself, his independence is, of right, absolute. Over himself, over his own body and mind, the individual is sovereign.

In modern times perhaps no elected official has been more outspoken or adamant about the cause of liberty and its importance than Ron Paul. Over the years he has time and again differentiated himself from the establishment blob by clearly stating the government overreach that, under the guise of protecting us, actually slowly but surely led us towards the current debt slavery model and creeping tyranny we face today. His calls for ending the Fed, tax policy overhaul, and individual responsibility along with limited government may have been ridiculed by those who feared losing power or control, but for those awakening now to how out of control and greedy DC has become, his years of challenging the status quo hold more possibilities and solutions we can unite behind than ever.

RON PAUL ON THE EVE OF HIS RETIREMENT FROM GOVERNMENT

Liberty can only be achieved when government is denied the aggressive use of force. If one seeks liberty, a precise type of government is needed. To achieve it, more than lip service is required.

Two choices are available.

1. A government designed to protect liberty—a natural right—as its sole objective. The people are expected to care for themselves and reject the use of any force for interfering with another person's liberty. Government is given a strictly limited authority to enforce contracts, property

ownership, settle disputes, and defend against foreign aggression.

2. A government that pretends to protect liberty but is granted power to arbitrarily use force over the people and foreign nations. Though the grant of power many times is meant to be small and limited, it inevitably metastasizes into an omnipotent political cancer. This is the problem for which the world has suffered throughout the ages. Though meant to be limited it nevertheless is a 100 percent sacrifice of a principle that would-be tyrants find irresistible. It is used vigorously—though incrementally and insidiously. Granting power to government officials always proves the adage that: "power corrupts."

Once government gets a limited concession for the use of force to mold people habits and plan the economy, it causes a steady move toward tyrannical government. Only a revolutionary spirit can reverse the process and deny to the government this arbitrary use of aggression. There's no in-between. Sacrificing a little liberty for imaginary safety always ends badly. Today's mess is a result of Americans accepting option number two, even though the Founders attempted to give us option number one.

PERSONAL RESPONSIBILITY

Personal responsibility, meaning the action of taking care of one's own business and accepting the consequences of how one goes about doing that, is one of the inherent instincts and traits of man on earth since the beginning of time. We have the Constitution and judicial system to deal with situations when one person's choices or actions infringe upon or harm another person's ability to live and prosper as they choose. Unfortunately, as the government has evolved it expanded all out of proportion in directions it never should have gone, and its defined purpose was lost in a web of overreach and infringement. We have allowed the government to unconstitutionally legislate, regulate, interfere, and impose itself into our private lives and worlds by using coercion or force with little if any push back against the harm this has done to our individual sovereignty and liberty along the way.

For every new rule, piece of legislation, or regulation in the name of protecting individuals or groups of people, land, or animals, we have seen government exerting unwarranted and unconstitutional control over our actions, behavior, and speech. Meanwhile, the groups they cite they are protecting to justify this overreach of unallocated authority rarely if ever get any relief or benefit. What we get is less freedom and liberty for all. It's a scam. Any regulation or law to monitor, limit, or control the freedom of any citizen proves time and again to be just a bigger power grab by the blob in DC to usurp our rights while enriching and empowering themselves.

Somewhere along the way, on both illusionary left and right paradigms of the uniparty, individual responsibility and accountability has been coaxed, pushed, and politicized out of definable reality. Imposing irrational mandates, regulation, and legislation for one side to stop the supposed other side's similar mandates, regulations, and legislation leads to more and more loss of individual freedom and accountability, allowing this problem to fester within our institutions and in society as a whole. Supposed victimization and the protection of perceived victims against perceived oppressors has become the norm, having little if any impact other than leading us all towards less freedom and liberty. What is going on here?

In our country and based on our common values found in our founding documents, the individual should be the sole decision maker in taking risks, making decisions, choosing behaviors, and dealing with the consequences—good or bad—of those individual choices, period. Legislating how people speak, think, behave, or live their private lives is not our government's business and should certainly not be decided by anyone in the power-hungry, compromised, and corrupt halls of our governmental institutions. It is none of the government's or enforcement agencies' business how any individual chooses to exercise their pursuit of happiness in their private lives. It never should have been up for debate to begin with. The pursuit of happiness is unique to every individual and how far they want to go towards achieving their potential and life's purpose. As long as that does not harm or impede any other person it should be off limits to Big Brother and government overreach.

RONALD REAGAN, JANUARY 1967

> Freedom is a fragile thing and it's never more
> than one generation away from extinction. It is
> not ours by way of inheritance; it must be fought
> for and defended constantly by each generation,
> for it comes only once to a people. And those in

world history who have known freedom and then lost it have never known it again.

Knowing this, it's hard to explain those among us who even today would question the people's capacity for self-government. I've often wondered if they will answer, those who subscribe to that philosophy: if no one among us is capable of governing himself, then who among us has the capacity to govern someone else? Using the temporary authority granted by the people, in increasing numbers lately at all levels of government, have sought control even of the means of production as if they could do this without eventually controlling those who produce. And always they explain this as necessary to the people's welfare. "The deterioration of every government begins with the decay of the principle upon which it was founded." This was written in 1748, and it's as true today as it was then.

We are not truly free as long as we have false idols, elevated frauds, and dozens of agencies with compromised appointees mandating or legislating our daily life choices or how we go about our private business. Elevating public servants, from the president to your governor to your city council member above yourself, as if they know better or should be allowed to decide against the will of those they claim to represent, has been an abdication of civic responsibility combined with an orchestrated attack that has led to the untenable situation in which we currently find ourselves. Many of the operatives infringing upon our citizens' rights are people who were chosen, recruited, or groomed to go into politics or influential organizations above the political, they are not anointed or smarter, more deserving or superior to We the People, and we must stop acting like it. It's a job, we pay many of their salaries either directly or through government grants. Many do not even pay taxes nor contribute their huge funding back into our country at all. Anyone getting a government salary or subsidy works for us, and we need to remember that as if we are the employer, because we are. Our government does not make money directly, they need our taxes to fund everything they do. Let's redefine our entire paradigm when it comes to our relationship with our government now. That is in our control. That we can definitely take more personally and be more hawkish about going forward.

I am confident that if we honestly educate our citizens, especially our children, on what is and is not the responsibility of our local, state, and federal governments, not from a partisan side but from a constitutional view as a nation, we would be well on the road to recovery. We must meet in person to assess where we are and where we want to go. We the People need to oversee our elected leaders and devise forums of debate to evaluate policies, agencies, and committees. I am confident that in doing so we would find that most Americans would agree that many of these regulatory bodies and bureaucratic agencies are in violation of the Constitution in the first place, and that our elected officials have violated their oaths in allowing unconstitutional edicts and unelected people who We the People pay for to have undue and unwarranted control over our private lives. Imagine the financial resources and explosion of ingenuity that we could free up and harness if we eliminated overbearing governmental and regulatory waste and fraud in our current system and we went back to every man, woman, and child being responsible and accountable for themselves, their lives, and their destiny without red tape, government intrusion, and arbitrary unwarranted control. Why can't We the People do that?

THEODORE ROOSEVELT, "CITIZENSHIP IN A REPUBLIC," DELIVERED AT THE SORBONNE, IN PARIS, FRANCE, ON APRIL 23, 1910

> ...In the long run, success or failure will be conditioned upon the way in which the average man, the average woman, does his or her duty, first in the ordinary, every-day affairs of life, and next in those great occasional crises which call for the heroic virtues. The average citizen must be a good citizen if our republics are to succeed. The stream will not permanently rise higher than the main source; and the main source of national power and national greatness is found in the average citizenship of the nation. Therefore, it behooves us to do our best to see that the standard of the average citizen is kept high; and the average cannot be kept high unless the standard of the leaders is very much higher.

RESPONSIBILITY AND JUDGMENT

If we demand active participation and personal responsibility for ourselves, we must adhere to the idea that every person who exercises individual liberty and freedom of choice should be held accountable for their actions and behaviors and rewarded or punished for the results of such. This standard of personal responsibility must apply equally to all citizens, but especially to any elected official or government employee whose salary is funded by We the

People's tax dollars. They are literally our employees. We should be acting like that in our community, county, state, and especially toward those we send to the federal government.

This is the key problem I believe we need to address to return America to the people, and to the proud, prosperous land we all long for it to be. You knowing your local and state officials names is far less important than them knowing yours. Show up, speak up, be known as your own individual representative by them and their staff. Even better, create a group and form a citizen oversight team, a community task force, and make sure all these bureaucrats and officials know that as part of your commitment to your country and insuring the will of the people and true consent of the governed, you will be watching and overseeing their work and all the bills and contracts they enter into as your representatives.

If you've heard any of the dozens of speeches I've made in the last few years, I often say our nation is as sick as our secrets. Research proves that throughout history, much has been hidden from We the People to our detriment by those with power in control. My research has shown me that JFK's public execution was likely, in part, a mass-demoralizing trauma event creating a suggestible and easily programmable populace to accept whatever was presented in its aftermath. From that fateful day, it seems quite clear that our nation's intelligence, governmental, judicial, and intelligence communities have been involved at the highest level in one cover-up after another, and that inexplicably continues to this day. I contend that the coup against this nation, the most recent one at least, was committed on November 22, 1963, and everything since then has been purposefully memory holed and hidden by design, allowing for a massive blackmail, bribery, corruption, and coercion operation that has continued to steamroll this country to this day.

We have allowed the evolution of this culture of corruption and lack of accountability or punishment of the worst offenders within our government to become the foundational rot below and above the DC blob. If we are committed to returning power to the people, We the People must demand transparency and disclosure of long-hidden crimes committed by our government and their proxies no matter how ugly, devastating, or psychologically harmful the truth may be at first for the sleeping masses. This will eventually allow for a new, cleaned out, more healthy foundation on which to chart a better course going forward. In order to heal our nation and truly return to a unified country, all things hidden must be brought to light. Many of the original co-conspirators from 1963 are dead, many who replaced them are retired or retiring, but only a full accounting and truth of any wrongdoing by our own government will force an actual catharsis and healing our nation truly needs, regardless of where it leads or if who is exposed is living or deceased. Only by naming the specific names and their individual actions, then demanding that justice be meted out in proportion can We the People actually detox the bowels of DC in order to reestablish trust and have true integrity restored, which will be crucial going forward.

The ingenious idea of calling anything that does not align with the government or intel agency's designated narrative a "conspiracy theory" has worked for far too long to silence dissent and skepticism among the populace. Then came COVID. Seeing the government overplaying their hand during the COVID operation, most people began to realize many of those theories dismissed as such were actually the truth. The term "conspiracy theory" was first widely used by the CIA and their partners to describe anyone or anything that questioned the fraudulent *Warren Commission Report* on the murder of JFK. Label anyone who has honest questions about any number of inconsistencies crazy or paranoid and it ends the discussion. Today, finally, it appears that it was in fact an actual conspiracy, and those theories are now being acknowledged as plausible all these decades later. Most honest people believe this pertinent historical information needs to be shared publicly, debated, and investigated. Unfortunately, these suspicious incidents recur over several years, retraumatizing and leaving the masses yet again highly suggestible and demoralized enough to just accept what they are told by a complicit media and move on again and again.

Still, many people continue to hunt for answers about underlying reasons why were actually in Vietnam, Iraq, Afghanistan, or Libya, as well as behind-the-scenes machinations surrounding any of the various nations where we have been involved in regime change operations or where the dreaded UN Responsibility to Protect principle was activated, violating international law on demand. Many of our agencies, such as the NED or CIA, as well as government and oligarch-funded NGOs and globalist philanthropy groups, have been present and on the ground for years prior to prolonged and deadly color revolutions and occupations of nations in corners of the world most Americans have never even heard of. Many want honest investigations and answers on the murders of MLK, RFK, Malcolm X, and dozens of other assassinations or supposed suicides since JFK. A lot of people do not believe the official story of 9/11, the Las Vegas massacre, or that Jeffrey Epstein killed himself, along with the outrageous denial of him having any complicit clients or evidence of him running a worldwide, government-connected blackmail ring. Time and again we allow honest questions to remain unanswered because the media and their partners in the intel agencies tell us it is over and to move on, while you and I are forbidden to ask any more questions or are threatened to stop investigating for undefined "reasons of national security."

JFK warned us that that secrecy is repugnant to our democratic republic. Secrecy in our government, institutions, and in all manner of power systems has become the norm, not the exception. The practice and term "classified" is so widely abused that the public neither sees nor hears virtually anything that is true. We have come to realize that much of what we are told is false or half-truths, and that often the lack of disclosure is simply a cover-up of crimes or terrible errors. We have learned from brave whistleblowers and journalists that when our government invokes secrecy for reasons of national security, the reason is often that our own government, military-industrial complex, intel agencies, or individuals broke the laws of our nation, committed war crimes, or violated international law, often with the caveat that they were protecting democracy or because our homeland was somehow in unexplained danger.

We have seen evidence that our agencies, particularly the intel agencies and DOJ, regularly overuse the "confidential" stamp or redact way more than they actually should be allowed to on FOIA requests and declassified documents to cover up crimes committed by staff or senior officials within the agencies or bureaus. Crimes you and I would go to prison for are essentially ignored and black-holed as a matter of business as usual inside the beltway. To throw salt on the wounds, it is We the People who pay for the commitment of these crimes, the funding of their investigations, and the cover-ups that put them to bed. And yet, this criminality, corruption, and secrecy perpetuates through our sick system, which does not serve the people, justice, or the Constitution as intended, but the sick power structure system itself. If justice were truly blind, crimes against individuals or humanity would be top priority and pursued vigorously to mete out justice no matter what is exposed in the process holding our government officials and officers of the law to a standard above reproach. It is a consequence of the rich and powerful totally controlling the system from above, often those who are also indirectly or directly involved in many of these incidents—rather than We the People with honestly-elected-by-us, committed representatives truly working on our behalf—that it continues unabated.

It is often because of the fear of persecution, prosecution, or coercion. Anyone who dares demand the truth ends up being silenced, disappeared, assassinated, or in the case of Julian Assange, tortured in a jail cell until they no longer exist. Once people see those who dare to speak the truth regardless of personal consequences erased and publicly destroyed using lawfare or complicit media before their eyes, they often stop their hunt for truth and justice, opting for self-preservation rather than becoming another casualty. Truth truly dies in the dark, and the light must be shone brightly on all that is hidden to fully realize a true mass awakening. Luckily, we are in the beginning phases of such a time, where citizens like you and I are defying the controlled narratives and pointing to uncomfortable truths en masse.

It is important that we seek transparency early in a process and not decades after incidents or crimes are committed like we have the last sixty-something years. Be it through FOIA requests, citizen journalists, citizen juries as the tactical civics folks suggest, or by good old fearless investigations that we help fund and support outside of the cloaked halls of secrecy and corruption within the government and media. We see people like the brave Intelligence Community and IRS whistleblowers, many of whom have had their lives destroyed, who do move the needle, and get just enough truth out that we know there is more. If no one is held accountable when crimes are committed by our elected officials or government bureaucrats, or Wall Street bankers or nefarious oligarchs, then we will never have a real government by the people for the people, only a corrupt, Mafia-like government of made men and women who other people control via blackmail, bribery, or threats, and who will do anything they must to keep themselves or their family members out of jail or harm's way. That is on us. We need to be brave enough and resolute enough, in big numbers, to effect change in the criminal enterprise that is sitting above our country and destroying our nation from within.

CHARLIE REESE, "545 VS. 300,000,000 PEOPLE"

Politicians are the only people in the world who create problems and then campaign against them.

Have you ever wondered, if both the Democrats and the Republicans are against deficits, WHY do we have deficits?

Have you ever wondered, if all the politicians are against inflation and high taxes, WHY do we have inflation and high taxes?

You and I don't propose a federal budget. The President does.

You and I don't have the Constitutional authority to vote on appropriations. The House of Representatives does.

You and I don't write the tax code, Congress does.

You and I don't set fiscal policy, Congress does.

You and I don't control monetary policy, the Federal Reserve Bank does.

One hundred senators, 435 congressmen, one President, and nine Supreme Court justices equates to 545 human beings out of the 300 million are directly, legally, morally, and individually responsible for the domestic problems that plague this country.

I excluded the members of the Federal Reserve Board because that problem was created by Congress. In 1913, Congress delegated its Constitutional duty to provide a sound currency to a federally chartered, but private, central bank.

I excluded all the special interests and lobbyists for a sound reason. They have no legal authority. They have no ability to coerce a senator, a congressman, or a President to do one cotton-picking thing. I don't care if they offer a politician $1 million dollars in cash. The politician has the power to accept or reject it. No matter what the lobbyist promises, it is the legislator's responsibility to determine how he votes.

Those 545 human beings spend much of their energy convincing you that what they did is not their fault. They cooperate in this common con regardless of party.

What separates a politician from a normal human being is an excessive amount of gall. No normal human being would have the gall of a Speaker, who stood up and criticized the President for creating deficits. The President can only propose a budget. He cannot force Congress to accept it.

The Constitution, which is the supreme law of the land, gives sole responsibility to the House of Representatives for originating and approving appropriations and taxes. Who is the speaker of the House now? ... He is the leader of the majority party. He and fellow House members, not the President, can approve any budget they want. If the President vetoes it, they can pass it over his veto if they agree to.

It seems inconceivable to me that a nation of 300 million cannot replace 545 people who stand convicted—by present facts—of incompetence and irresponsibility. I can't think of a single domestic problem that is not traceable directly to those 545 people. When you fully grasp the plain truth that 545 people exercise the power of the federal government, then it must follow that what exists is what they want to exist.

If the tax code is unfair, it's because they want it unfair.

If the budget is in the red, it's because they want it in the red.

If the Army and Marines are in Iraq and Afghanistan it's because they want them in Iraq and Afghanistan.

If they do not receive social security but are on an elite retirement plan not available to the people, it's because they want it that way.

There are no insoluble government problems.

Do not let these 545 people shift the blame to bureaucrats, whom they hire and whose jobs they can abolish; to lobbyists, whose gifts and advice they can reject; to regulators, to whom they give the power to regulate and from whom they can take this power. Above all, do not let them con you into the belief that there exists disembodied mystical forces like "the economy," "inflation," or "politics" that prevent them from doing what they take an oath to do.

Those 545 people and they alone, are responsible.

They, and they alone, have the power.

They, and they alone should, be held accountable by the people who are their bosses.

Provided the voters have the gumption to manage their own employees.

We should vote all of them out of office and clean up their mess.

Another place people are aligning beyond the division is that We the People in general are exasperated by endless committee hearings and investigations of agencies that lead nowhere even when the people testifying lie or clearly committed crimes. It's a Kabuki theater and never leads anywhere close to accountability as it would for any private citizen in such circumstances. It's insulting and disrespectful to all of us equally. We must demand specific actors be named, just and honest prosecutions be held, and crimes be revealed publicly so that we can begin to bring the entire dirty house of cards down.

I would posit that one way to return this country to truly being by the people for the people is to investigate and prosecute the crimes of our leaders who have participated in working against our nation, bringing us to the brink of another world war and pending financial and societal collapse.

Some say let's just go forward—a reconciliation of sorts—and it can be better ahead, but at this point, the level of deceit and the extent to which these corrupt leaders participated in the selling out of our nation and our futures cannot be excused nor forgotten. Maybe that is the best way to detox this nation and cleanse our past in order to start fresh for a better future. I'm not really sure and I will keep an open mind, but my research proves to me that a very small, incestuous, complicit group of self-anointed elitists hiding behind the facade that is the uniparty hold the truth to much that has been purposefully hidden from the people, and to truly get the swamp drained may mean to completely flush it out.

We must disclose the truth and seek equal justice to unite America, unmask the illusion of the two-party system, and recognize we are all on the same side. We must dismantle the blackmail and bribery networks, and put people in prison no matter who they are if they have been complicit in crimes against this nation and its people.

HANNAH ARENDT, *ON REVOLUTION*, 1963:

Well, if young people in Germany, too young to have done anything at all, feel guilty, they are either wrong, confused, or they are playing intellectual games. There is no such thing as collective guilt or collective innocence; guilt and innocence make sense only if applied to individuals. Recently, during the discussion of the Eichmann trial, these comparatively simple matters have been complicated through what I'll call the cog-theory. When we describe a political system—how it works, the relations between the various branches of government, how the huge bureaucratic machineries function of which the channels of command are part, and how the civilian and the military and the police forces are interconnected, to mention only outstanding characteristics—it is inevitable that we speak of all persons used by the system in terms of cogs and wheels that keep the administration running. Each cog, that is, each person, must be expendable without changing the system, an assumption underlying all bureaucracies, all civil services, and all functions properly speaking. This viewpoint is the viewpoint of political science, and if we accuse or rather evaluate in its frame of reference, we speak of good and bad systems and our criteria are the freedom or the happiness or the degree of participation of the citizens, but the question of the personal responsibility of those who run the whole affair is a marginal issue. Here it is indeed true what all the defendants in the postwar trials said to excuse themselves: if I had not done it, somebody else could and would have.

For in any dictatorship, let alone a totalitarian dictatorship, even the comparatively small number of decision makers who can still be named in normal government has shrunk to the figure of One, while all institutions and bodies that initiate control over or ratify executive decisions have been abolished. In the Third Reich, at any rate, there was only one man who did and could make decisions and hence was politically fully responsible. That was Hitler himself who, therefore, not in a fit of megalomania but quite correctly once described himself as the only man in all Germany who was irreplaceable. Everybody else from high to low who had anything to do with public affairs was in fact a cog, whether he knew it or not. Does this mean that nobody else could be held personally responsible?

When I went to Jerusalem to attend the Eichmann trial, I felt that it was the great advantage of courtroom procedure that this whole cog-business makes no sense in its setting, and therefore forces us to look at all these questions from a different point of view. To be sure, that the defense would try to plead that Eichmann was but a small cog was predictable; that the defendant himself would think in these terms was probable, and he did so up to a point; whereas the attempt of the prosecution to make of him the biggest cog ever—worse and more important than Hitler—was an unexpected curiosity. The judges did what was right and proper, they discarded the whole notion, and so, incidentally, did I, all blame and praise to the contrary notwithstanding. For, as the judges took great pains to point out explicitly, in a courtroom there is no system on trial, no History or historical trend, no ism, anti-Semitism for instance, but a person, and if the defendant happens to be a functionary, he stands accused precisely because even a functionary is still a human being, and it is in this capacity that he stands trial. Obviously, in most criminal organizations the small cogs are actually committing the big crimes, and one could even argue that one of the characteristics of the organized criminality of the Third Reich was that it demanded tangible proof of criminal implication of all its servants, and not only of the lower echelons. Hence, the question addressed by the court to the defendant is, Did you, such and such, an individual with a name, a date, and place of birth, identifiable and by that token not expendable, commit the crime you stand accused of, and Why did you do it? If the defendant answers: "It was not I as a person who did it, I had neither the will nor the power to do anything out of my own initiative; I was a mere cog, expendable, everybody in my place would have done it; that I stand before this tribunal is an accident"—this answer will be ruled out as immaterial. If the defendant were permitted to plead either guilty or not guilty as representing a system, he would indeed become a scapegoat. (Eichmann himself wished to become a scapegoat—he proposed to hang himself publicly and to take all "sins" upon himself. The court denied him this last occasion for elating sentiments.) In every bureaucratic system the shifting of responsibilities is a matter of daily routine, and if one wishes to define bureaucracy in terms of political science, that is, as a form of government—the rule of offices, as contrasted to the rule of men, of one man, or of the few, or of the many bureaucracy unhappily is the rule of nobody and for this very reason perhaps the least human and most cruel form of rulership. But in the courtroom, these definitions are of no avail. For to the answer: "Not I but the system did it in which I was a cog," the court immediately raises the next question: "And why, if you please, did you become a cog or continue to be a cog under such circumstances?" If the accused wishes to shift responsibilities, he must again implicate other persons, he must name names, and these persons appear then as possible codefendants, they do not appear as the embodiment of bureaucratic or any other necessity.

AMERICAN'S ANONYMOUS MEETINGS: WE THE PEOPLE UNITE FOR FREEDOM

Of all the things I have gathered and experienced during the past nearly four years on my extended patriot road trip zigzagging across America, the one thing I feel most confident in saying is that the insidious demoralization and dehumanization campaign that escalated during the COVID/Great Reset operation has had profoundly negative consequences on society and the people of this nation as a whole. This recurring mental manipulation and psychological operation tactics have been induced by sporadic public mass trauma events, endless wars, forced mass migration creating division, mainstream and social media programming, our warped and ineffective education system, and the influencers in entertainment and sports that have all combined towards driving mass conflict and perpetual chaos. This has led to a society that is struggling with reality, divided, angry, and unable to discern who the real enemy is or is not, as our nation, communities, and connections continue to fragment more each day.

Authentic human interaction, intimate communication with others, and group gatherings have been all but eliminated or replaced, which was exacerbated by the ill-conceived extended lockdowns of 2020. Community and family have been degraded so much that many forgot that life without either is not a fully lived or truly human experience. We long for human connection, human interaction, friendship, authenticity, companionship, and love beyond all. We the People, it seems, are increasingly having to fight outside forces to keep any semblance of humanity, community, and a healthy social life intact.

As I've shared many times, when I first moved to Hollywood I was way too young and naive, not to mention alone, without the thick skin and crucial support required to compete in that world. It didn't take too long before I found myself in a very deep, recurring depression to the point of frequently feeling broken and suicidal. At that time I lacked the personal understanding, tools, resources, and support structure I needed to process my early experiences and instead kept soldiering on, burying my pain until it inevitably popped up again. Luckily, God had sent me an angel in the form of a somewhat annoying and persistent neighbor who was a musician having a similar experience herself in her field and whom I had watched regain confidence and power, transforming herself over a couple of months. She watched me deteriorating and kept knocking on my door, trying to get me to go to some meeting with her regularly. She never quit trying until I finally decided I had nothing to lose, and if I went once she might stop. I could not deny the fact that she was somehow completely reborn to the point that her life and career followed her personal transformation on a very positive trajectory. So, finally, one Sunday night I joined her at her meeting in an all-purpose room in the bottom of Cedar Sinai Hospital on Beverly Boulevard. It is no exaggeration to say that night saved my life, and I began a journey that transformed who I was and would become forever. But for the literal grace of God go I since!

What I found at that meeting, and the hundreds of them since, was the acceptance, support, hope, and solutions I believe can also be used to start a freedom movement among the citizens of America to save our country and each other going forward right now. In retrospect, I believe it was divine intervention that lead me into a world of authenticity, strength, and fellowship in a room full of strangers that I had not known truly existed prior. Real human compassion, support, and hope permeated the rooms. People shared their stories, their lives, their fears, their experiences, and their solutions openly without fear or judgment. The idea that there existed a world where simply walking through a new door and sitting down in a room full of equally flawed and uniquely individual strangers could be so completely life-changing was a miraculous revelation to me. I was hooked on the possibilities for all of us from day one, and still to this day know that at any time, no matter where I am in America, a meeting just like that first one can be located and attended easily by just picking up the phone and getting an address.

My experience over the last four years driving all over this nation led me to become increasingly confident that the same model used in recovery meetings for any number of addictions can work right now on a massive scale to heal our nation and ourselves one community meeting at a time. Literally taking back power to the people, by the people, for the people on a grand scale. There is a workable model in place that can positively and purposefully unite millions of individuals who no longer see party or politics as the answer for our future. Those seeking to be part of the solutions we all can agree are desperately needed can begin to come together anywhere there is the will from coast to coast in small towns and large cities in a new way that helps move beyond politics and programming in order to find workable solutions to our common problems.

Welcome to my vision for Americans Anonymous. Where We the People come together in a fellowship committed to preserving freedom and liberty, privacy and property, sovereignty and self-determination, as stewards of hope for a better future one neighborhood and community at a time. I am confident that the same simple model, first established for hopeless alcoholics in Twelve-Step meetings back in the thirties by Bill W. and the Doctor, can be implemented all over this nation using the same format for meetings, maintaining the self-sufficient and self-sustaining group model focused on the concept of love and respect for thy neighbor, to improve communication and cooperation and rein-vigorate and restore what it means to be a citizen, one person at a time. This model, and the creation of like-minded, loosely con-nected yet self-sustaining networks aligned with defined purpose across this nation, can and I believe will bring massive positive change and help in healing the division among men and women that is holding so much of our promise and potential back.

Back when I started my journey I sat in awe that I had found a place where everyone in the group, regardless of background, class, race, gender, age, education, status, or disability, was equal and equally sure that something was terribly wrong in their world, and accepted the truth that that something was themselves. What a beautiful and freeing place to be, surrounded by open, honest, eagerly willing, fully aware human beings who knew not only that they were their problem, but that without ego and with humility, turning to God as they understood him while engaging actively in solutions-oriented fellowship, that they could and would make massive progress towards lasting changes for a better future. The faith in oneself, in their fellows, and in God would and could restore sanity, and the same could happen for our nation one gath-ering at a time.

We the People need to understand and accept that we have all been lulled into a place of learned helplessness and apathy by a steady stream of manipulation and programming which has allowed our nation, our communities, our families, and ourselves to lose perspective and our individual power to determine our outcomes. We can and must do our best to come together without ego and in humility and begin to heal, reconnect, and rebuild a better country and a better world for ourselves and our future. It is hard to comprehend that a relatively small, highly parasitic and predatory group of people have consolidated near-total control of all of the financial, political, academic, industrial, corporate, and media levers of power and control over billions of people. These power-hungry sociopaths are now in the last phases of their dystopian plan for We the People while they revel in their twisted vision of a utopian future for themselves. But I am confident that by the grace of God, in the nick of time, humanity is waking up with enough energy and strength of force to say no, no more, we will not partake in this agenda. Not now, not ever.

A worldwide great awakening is definitely upon us. People are realizing that isolation and living through technology while funding the coffers of global elitists with our hard-earned money as we consume their diet of dehumanizing and distracting propaganda is making life unbearable and unmanageable. We must understand that by doing the exact opposite of what we have been doing the last several years we can and will defeat tyranny and evil, charting a brighter, more harmonious path forward. We the People can and must reclaim our Founders' vision for life, liberty, and the pursuit of happiness as our destiny. A simple program and a small commitment could and should be the spark that lights the brush fires of liberty that will sweep across the nation in the aftermath of such a movement.

Will those who seek our compliance and subjugation just give up if we opt out in droves? No. Not right away. That's why we are tasked with building a movement that continues to do outreach and getting more people to unify under the same tent. There is no way out for the Great Resetters and tyrants to win if we don't play along, and at some point their plans and agendas will collapse because they need us more than we need them. In fact, we don't need them at all. So it is up to us to unite in the fight for our freedom and to organize to survive the storm ahead. We will need to reprioritize ourselves, family, neighborhood, and community, and collaborate in a setting that is open, free, apolitical, and focused on common concerns and positive projects where all hands are on deck for the shared cause of liberty. We need to understand and reject their upside-down slogans and manipulation of language and redefine our goals for humanity, breaking barriers that we do not need to accept, dealing in facts and truth that can be proven and built upon, and demanding transparency for ourselves and those who opt to take leadership roles ahead.

This vision for saving our nation draws on many well-worn strategies for unifying and mending our fractured society and country, but it will require a commitment and consistent collaboration. Sometimes you need to fake it until you make it, meaning you may not want to go to the meeting after work on Tuesday at 7 p.m., but you made a commitment to your fellow citizens and yourself to be the change you want to see and take the lead to inspire others. We need to be the ones to lead the charge in our own neighborhood and community, along with reaching out to other like-minded local groups for regular county and statewide gatherings. We should prioritize our needs as individual citizens and community groups, leaving political parties and alliances at the door, and define new methods and apolitical strategies to achieve our shared goals and priorities.

When you set up your meetings I suggest certain elements, such as religion and politics or any other tribal or potentially divisive identities or affiliations, be left outside your discussions, as these meetings are about preserving the vision of our Founders in standing for life, liberty, and the pursuit of happiness for all people equally. This is about America and our founding documents; all who believe in protecting and preserving that and them are welcome. I suggest revolving leaders, including a group leader, a treasurer, and teams that address specific issues together. Several committees or teams can include neighborhood preparedness that works with the local sheriff to solidify and inform the members of emergency procedures and plans in the event of a disaster or attack of some kind. A team can support local businesses and set up a barter program to ensure no matter what happens the community will continue to flourish and function autonomously. A local farming or community garden initiative can be formed, along with food and prepper drives and classes and a contact list of active membership that can be called upon to step up and help out as needed. A regular agenda can be created to go over local contracts with government oversight of both financial and legal agenda items of the local government, a watch on globalist agenda items or surveillance implementation that violates our Constitution or Bill of Rights, and a regular checkup report card on all elected and appointed officials to do citizen oversight on a regular consistent basis. Add to the list what makes sense depending on your community makeup, and add or subtract as time goes on.

A woman who had heard me discussing my idea for Americans Anonymous recently told me her and a friend, not having the money or time to formally rent a space or create professional posters, created flyers with markers saying "You know something is wrong. We know it too. Let's find solutions together. No politics welcome," and, thinking they had nothing to lose, they listed a day and time at a local park, then went about posting the signs all up and down Main Street and on community bulletin boards everywhere they could. The day came and they put together a list of things they figured everyone in town may agree could use some attention. When they showed up they were blown away to find about thirty neighbors eagerly waiting to get started, all interested in being part of the solution. The meeting continues bi-monthly to this day, and has grown even bigger and more productive along the way. These strangers are now friends who have potlucks and go to community board and city council meetings together, who have created freedom networks for themselves and their kids that have tangibly changed their lives and their communities in a relatively short time.

Americans Anonymous, in my ideal vision, would be a place neighbors of all backgrounds bring ideas for improving the community to discuss, not debate, just to present, and where small businesses, entrepreneurs, farmers, and artisans can present their products or share in barter or bring attention to what they are doing and how their contribution can benefit the community and the culture. A good piece of the time should be people acknowledging wins and achievements, inviting people to join projects or initiatives, and hearing from people who do need help or a hand in accomplishing their own visions or upgrades. It should be a forum not to debate but to inform, to encourage others to be vigilant and educated on all government activity large and small that affects the group and the community directly. Educational, informational, and nonconfrontational. Ideally the anonymous aspect, no phones, no press, no social media, no recording, and no infiltration will be the commitment and the code among the creators, which may be the biggest challenge, but it is absolutely doable and achievable as it has been since the 1930s in recovery rooms all over America and around the world.

In history this has been suggested before. That bottom-up government was the only way to truly have a government by the people for the people. As Madison said, "When the people fear the government that is tyranny, but when the government fears the people that is liberty." Let us reverse the cycle, turn this thing upside down, and together decide our destiny once again.

JOHN STUART MILL, *ON LIBERTY*, 1859:

> He who knows only his own side of the case knows little of that. His reasons may be good, and no one may have been able to refute them. But if he is equally unable to refute the reasons on the opposite side, if he does not so much as know what they are, he has no ground for preferring either opinion... Nor is it enough that he should hear the opinions of adversaries from his own teachers, presented as they state them, and accompanied by what they offer as refutations. He must be able to hear them from persons who actually believe them...he must know them in their most plausible and persuasive form.

IN CONCLUSION:

We are in the battle of our lifetime, and possibly an epic battle unlike anything we have seen in the past. With the specter of global totalitarianism looming, not one nation or principality, but the entire world is at stake. As I say all the time, they are not after the United States; they are after conquering and capturing the world, and the United States is in the way. Once they defeat and destroy our nation from within and without, they can easily take the rest of the world. That is why we must stand in our power, remain firm in our commitment to truth, be fearless and brave, refuse to comply, and neither capitulate nor allow one more inch of infringement on our sovereignty or freedom.

There must be a clear and unified message that our inalienable rights as defined by natural law are the permanent rights of all people everywhere on this planet without exception. There is no authority that can give or take away so-called human rights, as all rights are endowed by our Creator. Saying any institution is fighting for or protecting them insinuates they can be bestowed or taken away, and that is a lie we must call out anywhere it is spoken. We must stand in the truth that only laws that are just, fair, and in America's case constitutional, are enforceable. Enforceable not by a government but by the constitutional trial by jury of one's peers only after an actual offense or harm is perpetrated and facts are proven. We must demand and reject any lawfare, political persecution, and any infringement on any constitutional rights by the government that has no authority to do such a thing. When false claims are knowingly brought or indictments handed down with knowledge that they are fraudulent, the person laying claims or perpetrating the fraud on the court and the people should then be tried and held accountable. We should not allow judge shopping or jury selection to manipulate verdicts, it should always be random and selected by means without bias or manipulation.

The totalitarian blob behind the Great Reset and the public-private partnership stakeholders along with their UN/WEF tentacles and the international banking cartel have invested everything in their *Agenda 2030* and 17 Sustainable Development Goals of total power, control, surveillance, and slavery system that will not be defeated without our full commitment to our freedom and future against them. This will be a trying and difficult road ahead for everyone who values what we have and what we are very close to losing if we do not reject the divide-and-conquer program. We must acknowledge and accept truth while actively rebuking the false narrative and lie of a benevolent master class just looking out for our best interest. This was not the case with any totalitarian regime, and definitely is not the case with the current worldwide iteration that has no allegiance to any flag or nation or people or god, only themselves and a top-down *Hunger Games*-like utopia for them and dystopia for those of us they allow to remain. It is that serious, as absurd as it sounds to those who refuse to believe in good versus evil or the existence of this truth.

We have seen through so many decades of proven lies and bloodshed and the coordination of the pandemic and Great Reset across the globe that these self-anointed oligarchs and their minions will do whatever it takes to extinguish freedom, justice, and peace on earth. This is not a time for cowardice or waiting on the sidelines for the next phase. There is no next phase if we do not all equally decide to join together and refuse their plans. Those who decide they don't want to participate and will wait it out or go along to get along will suffer either way.

Those of us who know and see the truth know we have nothing to lose at this precipice and everything to gain right now at this moment in time.

The goal must be to not destroy what they have planned or created for the masses but to ignore what they are imposing upon us and our society. We can ignore them, mock them, or push through them, but we must stand for our sovereignty and the law of this land being the Constitution and the Bill of Rights of the United States, which makes it clear that no global or multinational entity has any authority over We the People or our destiny or future. They do not, and must not, have the consent of the governed as required in this great nation. We the People must resist. When I say often to go read the Declaration of Independence and the twenty-seven grievances and ask you to evaluate where we are, and if in fact we are still honestly fighting for those same things but against a different tyranny, most people admit it does seem so. So that should be enough to light the spirit of liberty and justice within. We must decentralize, build a parallel economy locally where you are, and become the founders of this new struggle to regain independence and that which we believe to be our God-given rights and shared destiny. This will require replacing deeply ingrained habits and decades of subversion locally and countrywide. Locally is where we have the most ability to effect change and install new systems. We will have to start small and in the margins to remain peaceful and methodical to lead to lasting change and maximum impact. Our goal is unity, peace, and true liberty. We will have to navigate the current laws and dictates of the captured uniparty for now, but we can openly and with alternative choices withdraw our consent and challenge its legitimacy by peacefully refusing to participate.

Our purpose, each and every individual's commitment, should be to live as an example of what is possible, strive to show others it can be done, and be mindful in all you do that your actions and outcomes will attract more people to join the cause of restoring true freedom and liberty. Courage is contagious; so is being polite, helpful, kind, generous, and encouraging to others. We reject tyrants and bullies, and we must be the example of the opposite. We will be leaders in this historical turning point. You and I must choose to be better, be braver, and engage more when needed. If we simply commit to showing up and creating fellowships across all people seeking freedom, We the People will change our country from the bottom up. We will succeed, of that I am certain. United we stand, one nation under God, indivisible, with liberty and justice for all.

THE DECLARATION OF INDEPENDENCE

IN CONGRESS, JULY 4, 1776

The unanimous Declaration of the thirteen united States of America, When in the Course of human events, it becomes necessary for one people to dissolve the political bands which have connected them with another, and to assume among the powers of the earth, the separate and equal station to which the Laws of Nature and of Nature's God entitle them, a decent respect to the opinions of mankind requires that they should declare the causes which impel them to the separation.

We hold these truths to be self-evident, that all men are created equal, that they are endowed by their Creator with certain unalienable Rights, that among these are Life, Liberty and the pursuit of Happiness.--That to secure these rights, Governments are instituted among Men, deriving their just powers from the consent of the governed, --That whenever any Form of Government becomes destructive of these ends, it is the Right of the People to alter or to abolish it, and to institute new Government, laying its foundation on such principles and organizing its powers in such form, as to them shall seem most likely to effect their Safety and Happiness. Prudence, indeed, will dictate that Governments long established should not be changed for light and transient causes; and accordingly all experience hath shewn, that mankind are more disposed to suffer, while evils are sufferable, than to right themselves by abolishing the forms to which they are accustomed. But when a long train of abuses and usurpations, pursuing invariably the same Object evinces a design to reduce them under absolute Despotism, it is their right, it is their duty, to throw off such Government, and to provide new Guards for their future security.--Such has been the patient sufferance of these Colonies; and such is now the necessity which constrains them to alter their former Systems of Government. The history of the present King of Great Britain is a history of repeated injuries and usurpations, all having in direct object the establishment of an absolute Tyranny over these States. To prove this, let Facts be submitted to a candid world.

He has refused his Assent to Laws, the most wholesome and necessary for the public good.

He has forbidden his Governors to pass Laws of immediate and pressing importance, unless suspended in their operation till his Assent should be obtained; and when so suspended, he has utterly neglected to attend to them.

He has refused to pass other Laws for the accommodation of large districts of people, unless those people would relinquish the right of Representation in the Legislature, a right inestimable to them and formidable to tyrants only.

He has called together legislative bodies at places unusual, uncomfortable, and distant from the depository of their public Records, for the sole purpose of fatiguing them into compliance with his measures.

He has dissolved Representative Houses repeatedly, for opposing with manly firmness his invasions on the rights of the people.

He has refused for a long time, after such dissolutions, to cause others to be elected; whereby the Legislative powers, incapable of Annihilation, have returned to the People at large for their exercise; the State remaining in the meantime exposed to all the dangers of invasion from without, and convulsions within.

He has endeavored to prevent the population of these States; for that purpose obstructing the Laws for Naturalization of Foreigners; refusing to pass others to encourage their migrations hither, and raising the conditions of new Appropriations of Lands.

He has obstructed the Administration of Justice, by refusing his Assent to Laws for establishing Judiciary powers.

He has made Judges dependent on his Will alone, for the tenure of their offices, and the amount and payment of their salaries.

He has erected a multitude of New Offices, and sent hither swarms of Officers to harass our people, and eat out their substance.

He has kept among us, in times of peace, Standing Armies without the Consent of our legislatures.

He has affected to render the Military independent of and superior to the Civil power.

He has combined with others to subject us to a jurisdiction foreign to our constitution, and unacknowledged by our laws; giving his Assent to their Acts of pretended Legislation:

For Quartering large bodies of armed troops among us:

For protecting them, by a mock Trial, from punishment for any Murders which they should commit on the Inhabitants of these States:

For cutting off our Trade with all parts of the world:

For imposing Taxes on us without our Consent:

For depriving us in many cases, of the benefits of Trial by Jury:

For transporting us beyond Seas to be tried for pretended offences

For abolishing the free System of English Laws in a neighboring Province, establishing therein an Arbitrary government, and enlarging its Boundaries so as to render it at once an example and fit instrument for introducing the same absolute rule into these Colonies:

For taking away our Charters, abolishing our most valuable Laws, and altering fundamentally the Forms of our Governments:

For suspending our own Legislatures, and declaring themselves invested with power to legislate for us in all cases whatsoever.

He has abdicated Government here, by declaring us out of his Protection and waging War against us.

He has plundered our seas, ravaged our Coasts, burnt our towns, and destroyed the lives of our people.

He is at this time transporting large Armies of foreign Mercenaries to complete the works of death, desolation and tyranny, already begun with circumstances of Cruelty & perfidy scarcely paralleled in the most barbarous ages, and totally unworthy the Head of a civilized nation.

He has constrained our fellow Citizens taken Captive on the high Seas to bear Arms against their Country, to become the executioners of their friends and Brethren, or to fall themselves by their Hands.

He has excited domestic insurrections amongst us, and has endeavored to bring on the inhabitants of our frontiers, the merciless Indian Savages, whose known rule of warfare, is an undistinguished destruction of all ages, sexes and conditions.

In every stage of these Oppressions We have Petitioned for Redress in the most humble terms: Our repeated Petitions have been answered only by repeated injury. A Prince whose character is thus marked by every act which may define a Tyrant, is unfit to be the ruler of a free people.

Nor have We been wanting attention to our British brethren. We have warned them from time to time of attempts by their legislature to extend an unwarrantable jurisdiction over us. We have reminded them of the circumstances of our emigration and settlement here. We have appealed to their native justice and magnanimity, and we have conjured them by the ties of our common kindred to disavow these usurpations, which would inevitably interrupt our connections and correspondence. They too have been deaf to the voice of justice and of consanguinity. We must, therefore, acquiesce in the necessity, which denounces our Separation, and hold them, as we hold the rest of mankind, Enemies in War, in Peace Friends.

We, therefore, the Representatives of the united States of America, in General Congress, Assembled, appealing to the Supreme Judge of the world for the rectitude of our intentions, do, in the Name, and by Authority of the good People of these Colonies, solemnly publish and declare, That these United Colonies are, and of Right ought to be Free and Independent States; that they are Absolved from all Allegiance to the British Crown, and that all political connection between them and the State of Great Britain, is and ought to be totally dissolved; and that as Free and Independent States, they have full Power to levy War, conclude

Peace, contract Alliances, establish Commerce, and to do all other Acts and Things which Independent States may of right do. And for the support of this Declaration, with a firm reliance on the protection of divine Providence, we mutually pledge to each other our Lives, our Fortunes and our sacred Honor.

GEORGIA

Button Gwinnett
Lyman Hall
George Walton

NORTH CAROLINA

William Hooper
Joseph Hewes
John Penn

SOUTH CAROLINA

Edward Rutledge
Thomas Heyward, Jr.
Thomas Lynch, Jr.
Arthur Middleton

MASSACHUSETTS

John Hancock

MARYLAND

Samuel Chase
William Paca
Thomas Stone
Charles Carroll of Carrollton

VIRGINIA

George Wythe
Richard Henry Lee
Thomas Jefferson
Benjamin Harrison
Thomas Nelson, Jr.
Francis Lightfoot Lee
Carter Braxton

PENNSYLVANIA

Robert Morris
Benjamin Rush
Benjamin Franklin
John Morton
George Clymer
James Smith
George Taylor
James Wilson
George Ross

DELAWARE

Caesar Rodney
George Read
Thomas McKean

NEW YORK

William Floyd
Philip Livingston
Francis Lewis
Lewis Morris

NEW JERSEY

Richard Stockton
John Witherspoon
Francis Hopkinson
John Hart
Abraham Clark

NEW HAMPSHIRE

Josiah Bartlett
William Whipple

MASSACHUSETTS

Samuel Adams
John Adams
Robert Treat Paine
Elbridge Gerry

RHODE ISLAND

Stephen Hopkins
William Ellery

CONNECTICUT

Roger Sherman
Samuel Huntington
William Williams
Oliver Wolcott

NEW HAMPSHIRE

Matthew Thornton

THE CONSTITUTION OF THE UNITED STATES

We the People of the United States, in Order to form a more perfect Union, establish Justice, insure domestic Tranquility, provide for the common defense, promote the general Welfare, and secure the Blessings of Liberty to ourselves and our Posterity, do ordain and establish this Constitution for the United States of America.

ARTICLE. I.

SECTION. 1.

All legislative Powers herein granted shall be vested in a Congress of the United States, which shall consist of a Senate and House of Representatives.

SECTION. 2.

The House of Representatives shall be composed of Members chosen every second Year by the People of the several States, and the Electors in each State shall have the Qualifications requisite for Electors of the most numerous Branch of the State Legislature.

No Person shall be a Representative who shall not have attained to the Age of twenty five Years, and been seven Years a Citizen of the United States, and who shall not, when elected, be an Inhabitant of that State in which he shall be chosen.

Representatives and direct Taxes shall be apportioned among the several States which may be included within this Union, according to their respective Numbers, which shall be determined by adding to the whole Number of free Persons, including those bound to Service for a Term of Years, and excluding Indians not taxed, three fifths of all other Persons. The actual Enumeration shall be made within three Years after the first Meeting of the Congress of the United States, and within every subsequent Term of ten Years, in such Manner as they shall by Law direct. The Number of Representatives shall not exceed one for every thirty Thousand, but each State shall have at Least one Representative; and until such enumeration shall be made, the State of New Hampshire shall be entitled to choose three, Massachusetts eight, Rhode-Island and Providence Plantations one, Connecticut five, New-York six, New Jersey four, Pennsylvania eight, Delaware one, Maryland six, Virginia ten, North Carolina five, South Carolina five, and Georgia three.

When vacancies happen in the Representation from any State, the Executive Authority thereof shall issue Writs of Election to fill such Vacancies.

The House of Representatives shall chuse their Speaker and other Officers; and shall have the sole Power of Impeachment.

SECTION. 3.

The Senate of the United States shall be composed of two Senators from each State, chosen by the Legislature thereof, for six Years; and each Senator shall have one Vote.

Immediately after they shall be assembled in Consequence of the first Election, they shall be divided as equally as may be into three Classes. The Seats of the Senators of the first Class shall be vacated at the Expiration of the second Year, of the second Class at the Expiration of the fourth Year, and of the third Class at the Expiration of the sixth Year, so that one third may be chosen every second Year; and if Vacancies happen by Resignation, or otherwise, during the Recess of the Legislature of any State, the Executive thereof may make temporary Appointments until the next Meeting of the Legislature, which shall then fill such Vacancies.

No Person shall be a Senator who shall not have attained to the Age of thirty Years, and been nine Years a Citizen of the United States, and who shall not, when elected, be an Inhabitant of that State for which he shall be chosen.

The Vice President of the United States shall be President of the Senate, but shall have no Vote, unless they be equally divided.

The Senate shall chuse their other Officers, and also a President pro tempore, in the Absence of the Vice President, or when he shall exercise the Office of President of the United States.

The Senate shall have the sole Power to try all Impeachments. When sitting for that Purpose, they shall be on Oath or Affirmation. When the President of the United States is tried, the Chief Justice shall preside: And no Person shall be convicted without the Concurrence of two thirds of the Members present.

Judgment in Cases of Impeachment shall not extend further than to removal from Office, and disqualification to hold and enjoy any Office of honor, Trust or Profit under the United States: but the Party convicted shall nevertheless be liable and subject to Indictment, Trial, Judgment and Punishment, according to Law.

SECTION. 4.

The Times, Places and Manner of holding Elections for Senators and Representatives, shall be prescribed in each State by the Legislature thereof; but the Congress may at any time by Law make or alter such Regulations, except as to the Places of choosing Senators.

The Congress shall assemble at least once in every Year, and such Meeting shall be on the first Monday in December, unless they shall by Law appoint a different Day.

SECTION. 5.

Each House shall be the Judge of the Elections, Returns and Qualifications of its own Members, and a Majority of each shall constitute a Quorum to do Business; but a smaller Number may adjourn from day to day, and may be authorized to compel the Attendance of absent Members, in such Manner, and under such Penalties as each House may provide.

Each House may determine the Rules of its Proceedings, punish its Members for disorderly Behavior, and, with the Concurrence of two thirds, expel a Member.

Each House shall keep a Journal of its Proceedings, and from time to time publish the same, excepting such Parts as may in their Judgment require Secrecy; and the Yeas and Nays of the Members of either House on any question shall, at the Desire of one fifth of those Present, be entered on the Journal.

Neither House, during the Session of Congress, shall, without the Consent of the other, adjourn for more than three days, nor to any other Place than that in which the two Houses shall be sitting.

SECTION. 6.

The Senators and Representatives shall receive a Compensation for their Services, to be ascertained by Law, and paid out of the Treasury of the United States. They shall in all Cases, except Treason, Felony and Breach of the Peace, be privileged from Arrest during their Attendance at the Session of their respective Houses, and in going to and returning from the same; and for any Speech or Debate in either House, they shall not be questioned in any other Place.

No Senator or Representative shall, during the Time for which he was elected, be appointed to any civil Office under the Authority of the United States, which shall have been created, or the Emoluments whereof shall have been increased during such time; and no Person holding any Office under the United States, shall be a Member of either House during his Continuance in Office.

SECTION. 7.

All Bills for raising Revenue shall originate in the House of Representatives; but the Senate may propose or concur with Amendments as on other Bills.

Every Bill which shall have passed the House of Representatives and the Senate, shall, before it become a Law, be presented to the President of the United States; If he approve he shall sign it, but if not he shall return it, with his Objections to that House in which it shall have originated, who shall enter the Objections at large on their Journal, and proceed to reconsider it. If after such Reconsideration two thirds of that House shall agree to pass the

Bill, it shall be sent, together with the Objections, to the other House, by which it shall likewise be reconsidered, and if approved by two thirds of that House, it shall become a Law. But in all such Cases the Votes of both Houses shall be determined by yeas and Nays, and the Names of the Persons voting for and against the Bill shall be entered on the Journal of each House respectively. If any Bill shall not be returned by the President within ten Days (Sundays excepted) after it shall have been presented to him, the Same shall be a Law, in like Manner as if he had signed it, unless the Congress by their Adjournment prevent its Return, in which Case it shall not be a Law.

Every Order, Resolution, or Vote to which the Concurrence of the Senate and House of Representatives may be necessary (except on a question of Adjournment) shall be presented to the President of the United States; and before the Same shall take Effect, shall be approved by him, or being disapproved by him, shall be reposed by two thirds of the Senate and House of Representatives, according to the Rules and Limitations prescribed in the Case of a Bill.

SECTION. 8.

The Congress shall have Power To lay and collect Taxes, Duties, Imposts and Excises, to pay the Debts and provide for the common Defense and general Welfare of the United States; but all Duties, Imposts and Excises shall be uniform throughout the United States;

To borrow Money on the credit of the United States;

To regulate Commerce with foreign Nations, and among the several States, and with the Indian Tribes;

To establish an uniform Rule of Naturalization, and uniform Laws on the subject of Bankruptcies throughout the United States;

To coin Money, regulate the Value thereof, and of foreign Coin, and fix the Standard of Weights and Measures;

To provide for the Punishment of counterfeiting the Securities and current Coin of the United States;

To establish Post Offices and post Roads;

To promote the Progress of Science and useful Arts, by securing for limited Times to Authors and Inventors the exclusive Right to their respective Writings and Discoveries;

To constitute Tribunals inferior to the supreme Court;

To define and punish Piracies and Felonies committed on the high Seas, and Offences against the Law of Nations;

To declare War, grant Letters of Marque and Reprisal, and make Rules concerning Captures on Land and Water;

To raise and support Armies, but no Appropriation of Money to that Use shall be for a longer Term than two Years;

To provide and maintain a Navy;

To make Rules for the Government and Regulation of the land and naval Forces;

To provide for calling forth the Militia to execute the Laws of the Union, suppress Insurrections and repel Invasions;

To provide for organizing, arming, and disciplining, the Militia, and for governing such Part of them as may be employed in the Service of the United States, reserving to the States respectively, the Appointment of the Officers, and the Authority of training the Militia according to the discipline prescribed by Congress;

To exercise exclusive Legislation in all Cases whatsoever, over such District (not exceeding ten Miles square) as may, by Cession of particular States, and the Acceptance of Congress, become the Seat of the Government of the United States, and to exercise like Authority over all Places purchased by the Consent of the Legislature of the State in which the Same shall be, for the Erection of Forts, Magazines, Arsenals, dock-Yards, and other needful Buildings;—And

To make all Laws which shall be necessary and proper for carrying into Execution the foregoing Powers, and all other Powers vested by this Constitution in the Government of the United States, or in any Department or Officer thereof.

SECTION. 9.

The Migration or Importation of such Persons as any of the States now existing shall think proper to admit, shall not be prohibited by the Congress prior to the Year one thousand eight hundred and eight, but a Tax or duty may be imposed on such Importation, not exceeding ten dollars for each Person.

The Privilege of the Writ of Habeas Corpus shall not be suspended, unless when in Cases of Rebellion or Invasion the public Safety may require it.

No Bill of Attainder or ex post facto Law shall be passed.

No Capitation, or other direct, Tax shall be laid, unless in Proportion to the Census or enumeration herein before directed to be taken.

No Tax or Duty shall be laid on Articles exported from any State.

No Preference shall be given by any Regulation of Commerce or Revenue to the Ports of one State over those of another: nor shall Vessels bound to, or from, one State, be obliged to enter, clear, or pay Duties in another.

No Money shall be drawn from the Treasury, but in Consequence of Appropriations made by Law; and a regular Statement and Account of the Receipts and Expenditures of all public Money shall be published from time to time.

No Title of Nobility shall be granted by the United States: And no Person holding any Office of Profit or Trust under them, shall, without the Consent of the Congress, accept of any present, Emolument, Office, or Title, of any kind whatever, from any King, Prince, or foreign State.

SECTION. 10.

No State shall enter into any Treaty, Alliance, or Confederation; grant Letters of Marque and Reprisal; coin Money; emit Bills of Credit; make any Thing but gold and silver Coin a Tender in Payment of Debts; pass any Bill of Attainder, ex post facto Law, or Law impairing the Obligation of Contracts, or grant any Title of Nobility.

No State shall, without the Consent of the Congress, lay any Imposts or Duties on Imports or Exports, except what may be absolutely necessary for executing it's inspection Laws: and the net Produce of all Duties and Imposts, laid by any State on Imports or Exports, shall be for the Use of the Treasury of the United States; and all such Laws shall be subject to the Revision and Control of the Congress.

No State shall, without the Consent of Congress, lay any Duty of Tonnage, keep Troops, or Ships of War in time of Peace, enter into any Agreement or Compact with another State, or with a foreign Power, or engage in War, unless actually invaded, or in such imminent Danger as will not admit of delay.

ARTICLE. II.

SECTION. 1.

The executive Power shall be vested in a President of the United States of America. He shall hold his Office during the Term of four Years, and, together with the Vice President, chosen for the same Term, be elected, as follows

Each State shall appoint, in such Manner as the Legislature thereof may direct, a Number of Electors, equal to the whole Number of Senators and Representatives to which the State may be entitled in the Congress: but no Senator or Representative, or Person holding an Office of Trust or Profit under the United States, shall be appointed an Elector.

The Electors shall meet in their respective States, and vote by Ballot for two Persons, of whom one at least shall not be an Inhabitant of the same State with themselves. And they shall make a List of all the Persons voted for, and of the Number of Votes for each; which List they shall sign and certify, and transmit sealed to the Seat of the Government of the United States, directed to the President of the Senate. The President of the Senate shall, in the Presence of the Senate and House of Representatives, open all the Certificates, and the Votes shall then be counted. The Person having the greatest Number of Votes shall be the President, if such Number be a Majority of the whole Number of Electors appointed; and if there be more than one who have such Majority, and have an equal Number of Votes, then the House of Representatives shall immediately choose by Ballot one of them for President; and if no Person have a Majority, then from the five highest on the List the said House shall in like Manner choose the

President. But in choosing the President, the Votes shall be taken by States, the Representation from each State having one Vote; A quorum for this Purpose shall consist of a Member or Members from two thirds of the States, and a Majority of all the States shall be necessary to a Choice. In every Case, after the Choice of the President, the Person having the greatest Number of Votes of the Electors shall be the Vice President. But if there should remain two or more who have equal Votes, the Senate shall choose from them by Ballot the Vice President.

The Congress may determine the Time of chusing the Electors, and the Day on which they shall give their Votes; which Day shall be the same throughout the United States.

No Person except a natural born Citizen, or a Citizen of the United States, at the time of the Adoption of this Constitution, shall be eligible to the Office of President; neither shall any Person be eligible to that Office who shall not have attained to the Age of thirty five Years, and been fourteen Years a Resident within the United States.

In Case of the Removal of the President from Office, or of his Death, Resignation, or Inability to discharge the Powers and Duties of the said Office, the Same shall devolve on the Vice President, and the Congress may by Law provide for the Case of Removal, Death, Resignation or Inability, both of the President and Vice President, declaring what Officer shall then act as President, and such Officer shall act accordingly, until the Disability be removed, or a President shall be elected.

The President shall, at stated Times, receive for his Services, a Compensation, which shall neither be increased nor diminished during the Period for which he shall have been elected, and he shall not receive within that Period any other Emolument from the United States, or any of them.

Before he enter on the Execution of his Office, he shall take the following Oath or Affirmation:—"I do solemnly swear (or affirm) that I will faithfully execute the Office of President of the United States, and will to the best of my Ability, preserve, protect and defend the Constitution of the United States."

SECTION. 2.

The President shall be Commander in Chief of the Army and Navy of the United States, and of the Militia of the several States, when called into the actual Service of the United States; he may require the Opinion, in writing, of the principal Officer in each of the executive Departments, upon any Subject relating to the Duties of their respective Offices, and he shall have Power to grant Reprieves and Pardons for Offences against the United States, except in Cases of Impeachment.

He shall have Power, by and with the Advice and Consent of the Senate, to make Treaties, provided two thirds of the Senators present concur; and he shall nominate, and by and with the Advice and Consent of the Senate, shall appoint Ambassadors, other public Ministers and Consuls, Judges of the supreme Court, and all other Officers of the United States, whose Appointments are not herein otherwise provided for, and which shall be established by Law: but the Congress may by Law vest the Appointment of such inferior Officers, as they think proper, in the President alone, in the Courts of Law, or in the Heads of Departments.

The President shall have Power to fill up all Vacancies that may happen during the Recess of the Senate, by granting Commissions which shall expire at the End of their next Session.

SECTION. 3.

He shall from time to time give to the Congress Information of the State of the Union, and recommend to their Consideration such Measures as he shall judge necessary and expedient; he may, on extraordinary Occasions, convene both Houses, or either of them, and in Case of Disagreement between them, with Respect to the Time of Adjournment, he may adjourn them to such Time as he shall think proper; he shall receive Ambassadors and other public Ministers; he shall take Care that the Laws be faithfully executed, and shall Commission all the Officers of the United States.

SECTION. 4.

The President, Vice President and all civil Officers of the United States, shall be removed from Office on Impeachment for, and Conviction of, Treason, Bribery, or other high Crimes and Misdemeanors.

ARTICLE. III.

SECTION. 1.

The judicial Power of the United States, shall be vested in one supreme Court, and in such inferior Courts as the Congress may from time to time ordain and establish. The Judges, both of the supreme and inferior Courts, shall hold their Offices during good Behavior, and shall, at stated Times, receive for their Services, a Compensation, which shall not be diminished during their Continuance in Office.

SECTION. 2.

The judicial Power shall extend to all Cases, in Law and Equity, arising under this Constitution, the Laws of the United States, and Treaties made, or which shall be made, under their Authority;—to all Cases affecting Ambassadors, other public Ministers and Consuls;—to all Cases of admiralty and maritime Jurisdiction;—to Controversies to which the United States shall be a Party;—to Controversies between two or more States;— between a State and Citizens of another State,—between Citizens of different States,—between Citizens of the same State claiming Lands under Grants of different States, and between a State, or the Citizens thereof, and foreign States, Citizens or Subjects.

In all Cases affecting Ambassadors, other public Ministers and Consuls, and those in which a State shall be Party, the supreme Court shall have original Jurisdiction. In all the other Cases before mentioned, the supreme Court shall have appellate Jurisdiction, both as to Law and Fact, with such Exceptions, and under such Regulations as the Congress shall make.

The Trial of all Crimes, except in Cases of Impeachment, shall be by Jury; and such Trial shall be held in the State where the said Crimes shall have been committed; but when not committed within any State, the Trial shall be at such Place or Places as the Congress may by Law have directed.

SECTION. 3.

Treason against the United States, shall consist only in levying War against them, or in adhering to their Enemies, giving them Aid and Comfort. No Person shall be convicted of Treason unless on the Testimony of two Witnesses to the same overt Act, or on Confession in open Court.

The Congress shall have Power to declare the Punishment of Treason, but no Attainder of Treason shall work Corruption of Blood, or Forfeiture except during the Life of the Person attainted.

ARTICLE. IV.

SECTION. 1.

Full Faith and Credit shall be given in each State to the public Acts, Records, and judicial Proceedings of every other State. And the Congress may by general Laws prescribe the Manner in which such Acts, Records and Proceedings shall be proved, and the Effect thereof.

SECTION. 2.

The Citizens of each State shall be entitled to all Privileges and Immunities of Citizens in the several States.

A Person charged in any State with Treason, Felony, or other Crime, who shall flee from Justice, and be found in another State, shall on Demand of the executive Authority of the State from which he fled, be delivered up, to be removed to the State having Jurisdiction of the Crime.

No Person held to Service or Labour in one State, under the Laws thereof, escaping into another, shall, in Consequence of any Law or Regulation therein, be discharged from such Service or Labour, but shall be delivered up on Claim of the Party to whom such Service or Labour may be due.

SECTION. 3.

New States may be admitted by the Congress into this Union; but no new State shall be formed or erected within the Jurisdiction of any other State; nor any State be formed by the Junction of two or more States, or Parts of States, without the Consent of the Legislatures of the States concerned as well as of the Congress.

The Congress shall have Power to dispose of and make all needful Rules and Regulations respecting the Territory or other Property belonging to the United States; and nothing in this Constitution shall be so construed as to Prejudice any Claims of the United States, or of any particular State.

SECTION. 4.

The United States shall guarantee to every State in this Union a Republican Form of Government, and shall protect each of them against Invasion; and on Application of the Legislature, or of the Executive (when the Legislature cannot be convened) against domestic Violence.

ARTICLE. V.

The Congress, whenever two thirds of both Houses shall deem it necessary, shall propose Amendments to this Constitution, or, on the Application of the Legislatures of two thirds of the several States, shall call a Convention for proposing Amendments, which, in either Case, shall be valid to all Intents and Purposes, as Part of this Constitution, when ratified by the Legislatures of three fourths of the several States, or by Conventions in three fourths thereof, as the one or the other Mode of Ratification may be proposed by the Congress; Provided that no Amendment which may be made prior to the Year One thousand eight hundred and eight shall in any Manner affect the first and fourth Clauses in the Ninth Section of the first Article; and that no State, without its Consent, shall be deprived of its equal Suffrage in the Senate.

ARTICLE. VI.

All Debts contracted and Engagements entered into, before the Adoption of this Constitution, shall be as valid against the United States under this Constitution, as under the Confederation.

This Constitution, and the Laws of the United States which shall be made in Pursuance thereof; and all Treaties made, or which shall be made, under the Authority of the United States, shall be the supreme Law of the Land; and the Judges in every State shall be bound thereby, any Thing in the Constitution or Laws of any State to the Contrary notwithstanding.

The Senators and Representatives before mentioned, and the Members of the several State Legislatures, and all executive and judicial Officers, both of the United States and of the several States, shall be bound by Oath or Affirmation, to support this Constitution; but no religious Test shall ever be required as a Qualification to any Office or public Trust under the United States.

ARTICLE. VII.

The Ratification of the Conventions of nine States, shall be sufficient for the Establishment of this Constitution between the States so ratifying the Same.

The Word, "the," being interlined between the seventh and eighth Lines of the first Page, The Word "Thirty" being partly written on an Erazure in the fifteenth Line of the first Page, The Words "is tried" being interlined between the thirty second and thirty third Lines of the first Page and the Word "the" being interlined between the forty third and forty fourth Lines of the second Page.

Attest William Jackson Secretary

done in Convention by the Unanimous Consent of the States present the Seventeenth Day of September in the Year of our Lord one thousand seven hundred and Eighty seven and of the Independence of the United States of America the Twelfth In witness whereof We have hereunto subscribed our Names,

G°. Washington
Presidt.
And deputy from Virginia

DELAWARE
Geo: Read
Gunning Bedford jun
John Dickinson
Richard Bassett
Jaco: Broom

MARYLAND
James McHenry
Dan of St Thos. Jenifer
Danl. Carroll

VIRGINIA
John Blair
James Madison Jr.

NEW HAMPSHIRE
John Langdon
Nicholas Gilman

MASSACHUSETTS
Nathaniel Gorham
Rufus King

CONNECTICUT
Wm. Saml. Johnson
Roger Sherman

NEW YORK
Alexander Hamilton

NORTH CAROLINA

Wm. Blount
Richd. Dobbs Spaight
Hu Williamson

SOUTH CAROLINA

J. Rutledge
Charles Cotesworth Pinckney
Charles Pinckney
Pierce Butler

GEORGIA

William Few
Abr Baldwin

NEW JERSEY

Wil: Livingston
David Brearley
Wm. Paterson
Jona: Dayton

PENNSYLVANIA

B Franklin
Thomas Mifflin
Robt. Morris
Geo. Clymer
Thos. FitzSimons
Jared Ingersoll
James Wilson
Gouv Morris

THE BILL OF RIGHTS

Note: The following text is a transcription of the first ten amendments to the Constitution in their original form. These amendments were ratified December 15, 1791, and form what is known as the "Bill of Rights."

AMENDMENT I

Congress shall make no law respecting an establishment of religion, or prohibiting the free exercise thereof; or abridging the freedom of speech, or of the press; or the right of the people peaceably to assemble, and to petition the Government for a redress of grievances.

AMENDMENT II

A well regulated Militia, being necessary to the security of a free State, the right of the people to keep and bear Arms, shall not be infringed.

AMENDMENT III

No Soldier shall, in time of peace be quartered in any house, without the consent of the Owner, nor in time of war, but in a manner to be prescribed by law.

AMENDMENT IV

The right of the people to be secure in their persons, houses, papers, and effects, against unreasonable searches and seizures, shall not be violated, and no Warrants shall issue, but upon probable cause, supported by Oath or affirmation, and particularly describing the place to be searched, and the persons or things to be seized.

AMENDMENT V

No person shall be held to answer for a capital, or otherwise infamous crime, unless on a presentment or indictment of a Grand Jury, except in cases arising in the land or naval forces, or in the Militia, when in actual service in time of War or public danger; nor shall any person be subject for the same offense to be twice put in jeopardy of life or limb; nor shall be compelled in any criminal case to be a witness against himself, nor be deprived of life, liberty, or property, without due process of law; nor shall private property be taken for public use, without just compensation.

AMENDMENT VI

In all criminal prosecutions, the accused shall enjoy the right to a speedy and public trial, by an impartial jury of the State and district wherein the crime shall have been committed, which district shall have been previously ascertained by law, and to be informed of the nature and cause of the accusation; to be confronted with the witnesses against him; to have compulsory process for obtaining witnesses in his favor, and to have the Assistance of Counsel for his defence.

AMENDMENT VII

In Suits at common law, where the value in controversy shall exceed twenty dollars, the right of trial by jury shall be preserved, and no fact tried by a jury, shall be otherwise re-examined in any Court of the United States, than according to the rules of the common law.

AMENDMENT VIII

Excessive bail shall not be required, nor excessive fines imposed, nor cruel and unusual punishments inflicted.

AMENDMENT IX

The enumeration in the Constitution, of certain rights, shall not be construed to deny or disparage others retained by the people.

AMENDMENT X

The powers not delegated to the United States by the Constitution, nor prohibited by it to the States, are reserved to the States respectively, or to the people.

ACKNOWLEDGMENTS

This book would not have been possible without the encouragement, insight, and wisdom graciously afforded to me in its writing by my friend and author Brent Hamachek of Human Events. I would also like to thank my amazing audience and regular guests for contributing regularly to my ongoing education, and for helping me continually learn and grow through dialogue and research. Without the love and endless support over decades of wins and losses of my parents, Nancy and Robert, I would never have found the courage, determination, or ability to follow my own path and stand up for what I believe in now or along the way. My dad instilled a deep resilience in me from a very young age, best expressed in the words of Rocky Balboa, "You, me, or nobody is gonna hit as hard as life. But it ain't about how hard you hit. It's about how hard you can get hit and keep moving forward. How much you can take and keep moving forward." We may have been hit, but we all have the strength of spirit and gifts from God inside us to get up and keep moving forward. We can and we will! Thank you.

ABOUT THE AUTHOR

Mel K is a conservative journalist, filmmaker, and podcaster known for her well-researched, thought-provoking work. With a background in journalism and film from NYU, she has spent over two decades in Hollywood crafting meticulously researched historical dramas for film and television. Driven by a curiosity to uncover hidden truths and explore complex global issues, Mel K encourages critical thinking and delves into the connections between powerful organizations, highlighting potential corruption and its impact on nations and individuals.

Mel K gained notable attention when she investigated the disappearance of $800 million in taxpayer funds intended for vulnerable populations. This led to the launch of *The Mel K Show* in March 2020, which has become a platform for intellectually rigorous discussions and analysis of pressing issues. With a diverse following of over 500k subscribers, the show fosters a community of critical thinkers from various political backgrounds, providing a forum for open dialogue and the pursuit of truth and understanding.

Central to Mel K's work is a commitment to intellectual honesty, personal empowerment, and the principles of a free and transparent society. She believes in fostering a more informed and engaged citizenry through knowledge and critical thinking. Based in West Palm Beach, Florida, Mel K remains dedicated to shedding light on consequential issues, fostering thoughtful debate, and empowering individuals to draw well-informed conclusions, contributing to a more enlightened public discourse focused on empowering people to empower themselves.